GANGLAND CLEVELAND STYLE

THEIR RISE AND DEMISE

FRANK MONASTRA

Inside the Federal courtroom of the Kefauver

Crime Commission Hearings

Cleveland, Ohio January 1951

The concerned faces of

Front Row, unknown, Jerry Milano, Frank Brancato and

Harry Brook

Second Row, unknown, Chuck Polizzi, unknown,

unknown, Alex "Shondor" Birns

(Courtesy of the Cleveland Police Museum)

TABLE OF CONTENTS

Second Addition

PREFACE

The following information is amazingly factual and shows how the men who controlled the many different strings in the Cleveland underworld, as well throughout Ohio and the Midwest. These people operated successfully with one another and without interference from local and federal law enforcement officials for many years, as they accumulated a vast amount of authority and respect. However, their primary goals for their family organization stayed focused on several key factors. To make money, to take control of other business opportunities, and to expand their territory, whether it be by legal or illegal means and to control politicians. Their admirable focus was to secure a future for their families, their organization, just as any executive would do for his corporation.

It was on December 4, 1892, when an article appeared in the *Cleveland News*, regarding a few murders in and around the city of Cleveland.

Italian residents in the city have the same rights before the law, like all the other citizens no more. They will all receive equal justice when they obey the law, but those of them who interfere with the law by attacking witnesses to a crime are not only injuring the cause they advocate but are creating prejudice in the minds of the general public. There are very many intelligent, trustworthy, and valuable Italian citizens living in Cleveland, and they should bring their influence to bear on their fellow countrymen to prevent any more revenge attacks on witnesses of a crime who have come forward to testify against the guilty parties. The so-called Mafia methods of threats and intimidation will not be tolerated in Cleveland, whether the Mafia exists here or not.

On February 7, 1905, a Cleveland newspaper published an article. A prominent Italian resident in our city took a proud and defiant stand and says the Mafia and Black Hand do not exist.

The incredible tales of chilling stories and the dreaded Mafia or Black Hand have perplexed the police force in several cities, for many years. Such strong allegations and suggestions are what dreams are made up, according to Feruando Melarango, the editor of the Italian newspaper in our fair city. "There is no organization known as the Mafia; there is no such thing as the Black Hand; it is all fiction." A bad Italian who does terrible things will use this title to scare and threaten his victims into submission. Just as there are evil men in other countries, there are awful evil people of Italian descent.

The word Mafia is a corruption of "Mafioso, a Sicilian word meaning "bad boy or an evil man." A large number of terrible Italians have come to America for a new adventure, a new and better life. However, most of them have stayed in New York. We have no terrible Italians in Cleveland; I swear to you.

The headlines read on April 20, 1910, *Cleveland Plain Dealer* announced. **The Black Hand threatens several prominent Clevelanders**.

Cleveland Mayor Baehr was one of over twelve men who received a chilling heart-stopping letter at their home. The mysterious messages reported to be from a local "Mafia Society." The letter was straightforward and demanded payment from $5,000 to $10,000. At first, the men who received this, firmly believed the message was a joke of one kind or another until Police Chief Kohler investigated, and read most of the letters, which were written in Italian. All the letters demanded that their payment is made to them by Sunday Morning, and if they did not comply, they would be dead within forty-eight hours. This is the first time the extortion letters of any kind were sent to English speaking residents and people of authority and power in Cleveland, and not to wealthy Italians.

Two days later, a rebuttal note was printed in the newspaper for the city to read.

"The Mafia is peeved at the Newspaper Story" The Black Hand. It is getting critical of the way the paper has attacked them. The real Italians of our city have continued to be placed all together in one basket with the wicked men who have committed several crimes in our town. For some unknown reason, many peaceful Cleveland Italians have been all lumped together as being a "Mafia or Black Hand" member, and we stand united to demand justice. These criminals continue to rob the city with their arrogant attitude of being better than us. I ask you, is his honesty? Of course not."

1

At one in the afternoon, his once warm body, which was a constant 98.6 degrees, was now cold, almost icy, his face was a pale, whitish color than what it had been just four hours earlier.

Lying face up in the cold basement of St Vincent Charity Hospital, the city's corner has just finished the cumbersome examination of his body and rinsed out the bullet holes which remained. The sixty-year-old grey-haired coroner closed his patient's small brown eyes with his two large fingers. In respect of the dead, he ceremonially said a silent prayer, as he always has done to the newly departed, then covered it with a white cloth.

The Cleveland police did not have to go to the dead man's home and ask his neighbors or his wife of ten years to come down and identify the bullet-ridden body. The police knew very well who he was, after all, he spent many evenings inside one of their jail cells and in front of a local judge.

His wife had seen her loving husband alive earlier in the morning at the hospital and had to leave by 9:30 to attend to their two young children who patiently waited for their father to come home from work. He was frequently home when they woke up in the morning after a good night's sleep, but not today or any other day moving forward.

Detective Cody left the hospital room by 11 pm the night before when the blood-soaked man was breathing shallowly, yet struggling to stay alive. As a matter of fact, he could actually remember the man who shot him. Consequently, Cody needed to visit the dead man's wife to tell her, her husband had died early this morning.

When Cody arrived at the small brick home, he could tell there were people inside. He waited at the front door and heard women praying in Italian as children were outside playing, not knowing what their mothers were doing. Cody soon greeted the wife in a black dress with sad reddened eyes, whom he met last night. She knew instantly what had happened, she could see it on the man's face as she started to cry louder than Cody had heard anyone before. The other woman with her tried to comfort their dear friend, her heart full of grief, Mrs. Frank Alessi.

Her husband had died as a part of the ongoing prohibition Sugar Wars feud, which will continue on.

According to the *Cleveland Press*, Frank Alessi was the brother-in-law to Black Sam Todaro, and a high-ranking Porrello associate, who was killed in cold blood on the streets of Cleveland. This "Vendetta" or revenge killing of Todaro took place on June 11, 1929, by young Angelo Lonardo.

Frank Alessi, in his own right, was a known racketeer in the Cleveland area. Alessi was an alleged gunman and a suspected member of the Lonardo clan at one time before he switched sides and became a Porrello enforcer. Other Cleveland gangsters credited Alessi as having been the man who pointed out Frank Lonardo in the card game inside a local cigar shop where he was killed last October. Earlier, Alessi, along with Dan DiFillipo and Peter Mersurio, were arrested for taking part in the murder plot on October 20, 1929.

It was not unusual to see men sitting in their car any time during the day or night and wasting away a beautiful summer evening. Tonight was just one of these peaceful nights that turned into waiting until the early hours of the start of a new day. A single car pulled up along a quiet street corner where an after-hours pool hall operated. Every night the joint had between ten to fifteen men or more inside relaxing, drinking, smoking, and playing pool or cards. It was their time to relax, have some fun, or just pass the summer evenings in peace, with their countrymen.

It was on Tuesday, August 19, 1930, as the thirty-seven-year-old Alessi was playing cards as he often did at the Novario Bowling Alley with six other men inside an Eastside gambling room located on East Ninth Street. After a long night of drinking and playing cards, which usually started at 9 PM, the game finally broke up at 3 a.m. as three men staggered out of the bowling alley and left for home.

It was a cold, damp morning, about 50 degrees as Alessi was wearing his hat and his suit coat with the collar up to shield his neck from the cold night air. Dizzy and light headed from excessive drinking, Alessi walked toward his Ford Coupe. Parked in the dark Scoville Avenue district (known as the heart of Cleveland's organized crime region.) For some unknown reason, he quickly stopped near his car. To his surprise, he noticed two men, calmly smoking cigarettes, talking in Italian and waiting inside a Studebaker with their windows open, and parked next to his vehicle. Alessi did not recognize them at first until he walked closer to the car. The men slowly exited the vehicle as he noticed their hands inside their suit coat pocket.

Within an instant, both of the men pulled out their small revolvers, ran towards him and opened fire, hitting Alessi with four shots, which likely came from a .32 caliber handgun. Alessi was bleeding badly, and in great pain, then struggled as he tried to stagger to his car, with the slim chance of driving away. Both shooters ran away in different directions as Alessi's card-playing friends, who had heard the shooting, came running out and over to see what had happened. One of his friends ran over to his side, went down on his knees to help him in some way. Seeing that Alessi was severely bleeding and nothing he could do to help the dying man, he picked him up and placed him inside his car and drove him to St. Vincent Charity Hospital in downtown Cleveland to get medical attention as quickly as possible.

Within ten minutes of receiving an emergency call from a citizen, police Detective Sergeant Alex Nagorski of the Cleveland police department arrived at the crime scene. After speaking with several of the men who were now outside the bowling alley trying to get a clear understanding of the dangerous situation and looking at the crime scene and getting a detailed inspection of the area. Nagorski patiently looked at his notes and organized them with constant thoughtfulness. Within an hour, the police ran a check of the two license plates of the cars parked next to Alessi. While inspecting the area of the crime scene, lying on the ground between the two vehicles, the police found a Smith and Wesson .32-caliber revolver. Later they would tie the weapon in with a Youngstown gun dealer named Albert Antonelli. The police found one vehicle owned by a known criminal, Frank Brancato.

Several police officers quickly rushed to Brancato's red brick home on East Thirty-Ninth Street. Not caring what they did to wake him up, they knocked as loudly as possible and almost kicked the wooden door down. The excessive noise quickly got him and his wife, Virginia, and one of their four children out of bed.

"Why did you shoot him, Frank?" one of the officers exclaimed when Brancato came to the door.

Looking confused as if he was sleeping and just woke up with his white t-shirt, baggy pants, and in his strong broken English, he only replied with a puzzled look, "Shoota, who?"

"Frank," was the taller officer's full and angry response. "Frank Alessi?" once again, the shorter officer yelled.

Brancato responded with a bewildered look on his face as he shrugged his shoulders up and acting as if he knew nothing about the earlier shooting.

The officers enthusiastically turned Brancato around and handcuffed him as they took him from his peaceful home directly to Charity Hospital. With both police officers forcibly holding each of his arms, they walked him straight into Alessi's room for a face-to-face confrontation with the dying man. On the way to the police guarded room, the two officers quickly grabbed three other people standing nearby in the hallway. The by standards just happened to be news reporters trying to get a lead story about the shooting for their morning paper.

One officer gently placed his hand on Alessi's shoulder to get his attention; he bent down and softly spoke into his ear to let him know they were in the room. Looking directly into the dull eyes of Alessi, one officer asked, "Frank, look closely at these men, do you know which one of them shot you tonight?"

Alessi was breathing deep and hard and was in great pain while suffering from a significant loss of blood. He was coming in and out of consonous and looked confused at first, then looked into the officer's eyes and replied instantly but softly in his own broken English. With a terrified yet stern look in his eyes, looking for revenge of one type or another. With a tainted blood-soaked wrap around his head, "He shoota me," looking and pointing right at Frank Brancato.

Alessi knew very well that he had just broken the secret and unique code of Omertà that he pledged to, years before. Brancato, with his thin, muscular, stern face, looked profoundly and aggressively into Alessi's glazed eyes. Almost as if he was looking into his dark soul, and said as he vigorously shook his head, "No, no; that man is crazy; I never shot him, and I can prove it."

Brancato was still in handcuffs locked behind his back. The officers grabbed Brancato's shoulders and pulled him out into the hallway as he claimed he had been in a pool room nearby, playing cards with friends. When asked about his car, Brancato announced he had left his car in that parking lot because it would not start, so he got a ride home from a friend. In his broken English, Brancato continued to insist that he was innocent, and he did not shoot the crazed man. Before the three reached the hospital room door, Brancato stopped and turned as he looked right at Alessi once again and stared deep into his cold-dying eyes for several unspoken minutes.

The next day a doctor telephoned the police headquarters to say that Frank Alessi was not doing well and was not going to make it much longer. Inspector Cody acted quickly then sent Sgt. Charles Cavolo, one of the few Italian speaking officers to the hospital to get a sworn, signed statement from Alessi. Cody and Cavolo wanted Brancato arrested and off of their city streets, and there was no better way than to have him convicted of shooting a rival gang member.

When Cavolo arrived at the hospital, he found a weak, somber pain-ridden and distressed Frank Alessi. He seemed tired, scared and reserved as he now refused to make a statement or talk to the police, much less sign a formal declaration, stating Frank Brancato was, in fact, the man who shot him in cold blood.

The police were confused at first, then upset that they did not have a guard on Alessi throughout the evening. They were now thoroughly convinced that after they had left the hospital room, someone must have visited Alessi and reminded him of his code of honor, of Omertà, or silence and that he should not speak of it to anyone, not even the police.

FRANK ALESSI DIED THE NEXT MORNING AS NO ONE PAID FOR HIS MURDER

FRANK BRANCATO

2

PART I

THE CITY OF CLEVELAND, OHIO

The first annual report for the City of Cleveland was filed back in 1858 and recorded one note. There are only a few Italians admitted into the city's hospitals during the last calendar year. This would become an exciting statistic years later. Before 1860, the Federal Census Bureau makes no mention of Italians whatsoever living within the city limits of Cleveland. Unlike many of the northern ports of call, in Cleveland, the Italians were latecomers to our country compared to other European nationalities.

In 1890, while there were still only 864 Italians listed as living in the city limits, twelve of them owned saloons. By 1919, there were eighteen bars along the short two-mile stretch of Mayfield Road alone! The necessary business effort of these proud and hard-working Italian workers was concentrated in the produce markets along Broadway and Woodland Avenues. Included in the area where eight fruit and vegetable sellers, four of whom were Italian, including the Catalano brothers. By 1900, thirteen of the twenty-five produce vendors were Italians, again including the familiar names of Frank and Michael Catalano, LoPresti, Gillombardo, and the Rini Brothers, later they became well-known grocers in Cleveland.

In 1900, some of the twenty-six saloons; and restaurants were owned by Italian immigrants with names such as Cipra, DiFranco, Schiappacase, Mangino, Trivisonno, and Zecarelle. These men and their families established the substantial economic base for a new thriving Cleveland Italian community and provide leadership, direction, and much-needed employment for the thousands who would follow them to Cleveland in the next twenty-five years.

By 1910, Cleveland's population was estimated to be 560,000 with only 950 police officers. Then by 1920, it was determined to have 796,000 residents and just 1450 police officers. In 1930, the Cleveland population soared to 900,000 residents and became the sixth-largest city in the United States.

Another significant Italian settlement in Cleveland, known as "Little Italy," was located from East 119th to East 125th Streets on Murray Hill and Mayfield Roads. In 1911, it was estimated that 96% of the population of this small neighborhood was born in Italy, and another 2% were of Italian parents. Many of these Italians were Neapolitan and were engaged in skilled lacework, the embroidery trades, along with experienced bakers, barbers, and garment making.

Cleveland's Italian community is one of the most exciting and vital aspects of the city's sixty major ethnic groups. Although one of the most recent groups to immigrate to Cleveland. Before Prohibition in 1919, Cleveland enjoyed 1,919 saloons, and by the end of Prohibition, the number grew to over 2,500. Cleveland Italians loved and embarrassed their rich heritage, their delightful ethnic food like so many other nationalities do to this day. For the Italians, they worshiped the "Day of the Assumption" and enjoyed celebrating Columbus Day and proud that an Italian found America.

The Feast of the Assumption, or the **Assumption of Mary** into Heaven, often was shortened to be known as the "Assumption." This festival is about her holy body taking up as the Virgin Mary raises into Heaven at the end of her earthly life. In Catholic churches, the Assumption is a vital festival day and celebrated on August 15. In many countries, the feast is also marked as a Holy Day of Obligation in the Roman Catholic Church. Cleveland, like so many other proud Italian communities across America, celebrates this holy day in the center of the Italian Community at the corner of Murry Hill Road and Mayfield Road. Holy Rosary Church, which becomes the focal point of the grand parade and gala festivities. Holy Rosary started servicing the

Catholic and Italian communities in 1892. Today, literally, hundreds of thousands of visitors of all nationalities flock to this delightful annual three-day event in August. People come from the East and the West side of Cleveland to the small two-mile area of town to enjoy a spectacular festival. Many of the smaller art and ethnic shops opened to show their amazing Italian treasures to everyone. Finding your favorite restaurant and eating is a significant attraction up and down Mayfield Road. Corbo's, Presti's, Mama Santa's, Nino Italia are just a sample of the many family-owned shops. People enjoy the ethnic food they grew up loving, pasta, Lasagna, Cannoli, and Pitzelli, to name only a few. Visitors from the surrounding suburbs come to revive their proud family traditions, heritage and celebrate their Catholic faith.

If you are a person who enjoys gambling, they offer a wide array of table games. Poker, Blackjack, and of course, craps. Generally, the games are set up in the basement of the church to ensure the fun does not get rained out. This may have been seen to be abnormal by some. However, it gave the church one of the most substantial influx of money it candidly needed to serve in the community to sustain the Church over the upcoming year.

The next proud day for Cleveland Italians to celebrate their grateful heritage is the annual Columbus Day Parade. This is said to be a national holiday in many dynamic Italian cities in America, which officially marks the anniversary of Christopher Columbus's arrival to the new world on October 12, 1492. Most states celebrate Columbus Day as an official state holiday, though many marks it as a "Day of Observance" or "Recognition." Most cities celebrate Columbus Day. Sadly, in 2017, there where many cities looking to change the precious "Columbus Day" to "Indigenous Peoples Day."

3

CLEVELAND'S CRIME HISTORY

The beginning story for Cleveland is much like that of many other major cities across the vast, beautiful nation of ours. As we all know at this time in the lives of every community, women stayed at home and took care of the household leaving the men to support them the best way they could. The primary and driving factor was to feed, clothe, and shelter them, and to keep them safe and out of harm's way. Of course, some drove themselves to gain significant personal "Power." When this is blended into harmony with one another, the money starts to roll in, day after day, night after night. It silently went into their pockets, or a desk drawer or possibly a mattress ready to be used later to buy more influence, political power, or a police officer to turn his head at the appropriate time and to take control over whatever they wanted.

By May 1919, with Prohibition, fifty saloons out of the known 1,028 kept serving alcohol. One Cleveland police officer said, "Hell, I am not going to arrest anybody for doing what I enjoy doing." Soon every other saloon, speakeasy, and blind pig in the city were selling tainted or diluted alcohol to their excited guests. It was estimated that over 30,000 Clevelanders were engaged in the sale of some type of liquor in 1923. Throughout the country, ten thousand stills were known to be brewing the enjoyable hard alcohol, and over 100,000 of the fine citizens of Cleveland were enjoying the wanted beverage weekly. In comparison, nationwide between the years of 1923 and 1926, only 112 arrests were made for breaking the new Prohibition laws.

The Cleveland era of organized crime history dates back to before the 1920s, if not earlier and into the present day, in one way or another. Bank robberies at the time were the most comfortable and fastest way for criminals to make some quick cash. Throughout the Prohibition era, Cleveland became very popular because of the vast North Coast sitting on the massive, plentiful Lake Erie as it gave unauthorized and easy access to import whiskey from Windsor, Canada, and other neighboring cities.

Rum-runners ran often and ferociously wild on the Lake Erie shoreline as the illegal booze business made fortunes for many of the men brave enough to navigate the treacherous Northeast winds and dangerous waters of Lake Erie. Some of the impressive boats carried as many as 1,000 cases or more at a time filled with whiskey and beer. Some of the large ships even had machine guns turrets and metal-plated hulls for protection from a strong police force and, of course, greedy robbers.

The criminal community focused on the Cleveland area, later they controlled most if not all of Ohio and enjoyed working alliances in parts of Michigan, as well as parts of Southern Florida, California, and Kansas City.

(Courtesy of the Authors Collection)

In many ways, criminal historians believed that prohibition created the incredible Mobsters mentality that we know of today. It leads them to the necessity to feed the thirst of thousands, if not millions of men and women across the nation. It soon led the brave men into other rackets, including illegal gambling, loan sharking, and much more. Remember, power and respect were what was most important to men of power, so a knife or handgun soon led to machine guns, or shotguns, which in turn resulted in homemade bombings years later.

Some of the criminal activities and opportunities for the new era of crime included stealing automobiles, gangland-style killing, highjacking trucks filled with anything from food, furniture, furs, or anything of value. Of course, we need to include payroll robberies, racketeering, getting into business with the labor unions, gambling, drug operations, and smuggling. We cannot leave out the kidnapping, murder, prostitution, fraud, extortion, loan sharking, bookmaking, bootlegging, and money laundering. The criminals knew that police corruption and political influence would only help them expand their lucrative business before they would look into ligament opportunities for increased their wealth and power.

By the early 1920s, Cleveland had six Italian communities. First, came "Big Italy," located on Woodland Avenue. Then Little Italy on Murray Hill and Mayfield Road. Others included Blue Rock and the Collinwood area on the east side. On the west side of town, there was the area of Clark and Fulton Roads and West 65th Street area. By 1929, the seventh Italian community came to be East 110th and Woodland, which became known as "The Bloody Corner."

In the 1930s, some of Cleveland's largest bank and payroll robberies were led by a man named "Smiling Joe" Flipowski. A laughing criminal who always enjoyed keeping one step ahead of the law. Flipowski was known as a master of escape since he escaped the grips of the police five times over his career. He led a group of men, referred to as the "Flats Gang or the Phantom of the South." Smiling Joe, he enjoyed pulling pistols out of hidden places inside his coat, then to take guns away from unexpected police officers. The comical criminal once held up a shoe repair shop, and held a police officer at gunpoint, after he disarmed him.

Flipowski then had him disrobe, and then he handcuffed him and placed a wastebasket over his head, just to have some fun, and to shame the police officer. In 1939, Flipowski made a significant mistake, he murdered one of his robberies victims. When captured, a brave judge soon sentenced him to thirty years in the state pen.

Next was George "Jiggs" Losteiner, the one-time leader of a group of criminals. Losteiner was considered a bank robber and murderer, who was once called; "The most wanted criminal in America." Back in 1918, Losteiner robbed a bank with several other men on Christmas Day, where he shot and killed an East Cleveland Police officer, which led them to do whatever they could to catch him. Losteiner had the local police after him for close to twenty years before his final arrest. He was captured in Columbus, Ohio, at the same time as Flipowski. Losteiner was soon labeled "the most dangerous man in the state pen."

Now we will review the history and profound look into the Cleveland style of the Italian gangsters who developed a strong tie with one another as they helped Cleveland to become one of the top cities in organized crime during the hay days of the old secretive brotherhood. Over time, many of the gangs across the country were dissolved with bloody feuds, brutal murders, and unprecedented take-overs, just like any other large corporation in America or in the world.

After the Lonardo and the Porrello families were gone, some of the top bootleggers in Cleveland were Morris Kleinman, Lou Rothkopf, Moe Dalitz, Sam Tucker, and Maxis Diamond.

To lend a measured approach to take down the criminal element in Cleveland, one of the country's top crime fighters accepted a move from the Prohibition Bureau, as Eliott Ness brought his polished no-nonsense crime-fighting skills to Cleveland.

DELIVERING HOMEMADE LIQUOR

Ness was born in 1902. Ness was promoted to Chief Investigator of the Prohibition Bureau for Chicago and in 1934 for the Ohio region. Following the end of Prohibition in 1933, Ness was assigned as an alcohol tax agent in the "Moonshine Mountains" of southern Ohio, Kentucky, and Tennessee. In December 1935, Cleveland Mayor Harold Burton hired him as the city's Safety Director.

Ness headed an active campaign to clean out excessive police corruption and to modernize the deteriorating fire departments across the city.

In 1938, Ness' personal life rapidly fell apart while his career began to have frequent failures, troubles, and turmoil. In trying to rebuild his crime-fighting career, he declared war on the Cleveland mob, and his primary targets included, "Big" Angelo Lonardo, "Little" Angelo Sciria, Moe Dalitz, John Angersola, George Angersola, and Charles Polizzi.

Eliot Ness is remembered by many who read the grand stories about his extraordinary career in Chicago, and the television show that glamorized his short and sweet crime-fighting career and sad personal life at the same time. Ness died in Pennsylvania and cremated in a beautiful memorial headstone, which reminds the citizens of his time in Cleveland in the quiet Lake View Cemetery at the top of the Little Italy community on Mayfield Road.

(Courtesy of the Eliot Ness Wikipedia site)

Today, for the adults born after 1985 or so, when Eliot Ness is talked about inside bars and taverns in the Cleveland area, they only think of a highly traditional Amber Lager, a favorite local beer brewed by *The Great Lakes Brewing Company* in Cleveland.

Instead of an essential part of the crime-fighting community and American history that made a high mark for justice during the

Prohibition Era. Ness won a few battles and lost much more to the various demons in his life. His life and career ended with a massive heart attack, which may have been brought on by his love of alcohol, which he could not control as he died at the early age of 54 in 1957

(COURTESY OF THE GREAT LAKES BREWING COMPANY)

4

DOMINIC BENIGNO

(Courtesy of Dennis Sutcliffe)

Cleveland, Ohio, just like the other leading cities across the country where focusing on building their industries and growing stronger every year. However, by the 1920s, Cleveland was rated as the fifth-largest city in the country with an estimated population of 800,000 residences, surpassing the great cities of New York, Chicago, Detroit, and Philadelphia. Cleveland was known as an excellent Steel and shipping town due to the beautiful Lake Erie, which connected with the Great Lakes and soon became a leader in modern-day manufacturing. At this time, eighty percent of the people under the age of thirty were foreign-born, as gang activities and crime were not known to be organized in any fashion at this time.

During the Prohibition era from January 16, 1920, until the repeal on December 5, 1933, Cleveland went through an irregular period with an over-abundance of gangland violence, slayings, highjackings, bootlegging and racket wars. The cities newspapers spoke of rival gangs who fought competitively for supremacy and would often high-jacked each other's profitable liquor loads. Gunfire and murder became a standard tool of their thirst for dominance.

In 1924, most of the organized crime in Cleveland was referred to as the "Black Hand Society." This group of men, where extortion was considered to be "King" was referred to by the American Press as "The Backbone of the Mafia."

At this time, crime in Cleveland currently dealt with bank and payroll robberies since there were no armored trucks to deliver the needed weekly cash, and it was unheard of for companies to use payroll checks to pay their employees. No, it was good old cash that the workers of America wanted to have in their hands every week. One major robbery in the city took place near the Walker Manufacturing Company in 1918. This payroll robbery in Cleveland received an estimated $22,800 (in today's money worth $381,651). Additional criminal activities for the gang known as the Mayfield Road Mob included stealing cars, which would often bring them a quick $500 cash for each one.

In the book *"The Sly-Fanner Murders,"* written by Allan R. May, it was in 1919 as Prohibition took hold, and the need and desire for alcohol grew stronger and more profitable. Criminal, Dominic Benigno played his cards right and started up a group of men, including Biaggio DePalma and Frank Motto. The trio would often work together and branch into the business of highjacking several delivery trucks and seize their essential cargo. Regularly beating up their drivers, or only just leaving them behind while they take the vehicles to a secluded central warehouse where they would unload their treasure and then hide the truck in another location.

The W.W. Sly Manufacturing Company was located at 4700 Train Avenue on Cleveland's fashionable west side. This group of criminals had their sites on this company for a significant robbery, which turned into a violent double murder. This intense action brought the city to a height of pain, frustration, and an overwhelming cry for justice, which the town has not heard of until now.

It was on December 31, 1920, as Wilfred Sly and his partner George Fanner left their company armed with pistols in their pockets for protection as they always did to get their holiday payroll for the seventy or so dedicated employees. The men decisively took different routes to and from the First National Bank, where they picked up the salary of $4,200. On this New Year's Eve day, the two peaceful owners decided to take the path across an old wooden railroad bridge to the bank. After leaving the bank, they arrived in the middle of the bridge as another vehicle came from a different direction, then slammed on their breaks and slid in front of their car and almost pushed them over the small bridge railing and onto the railroad tracks fifteen feet below. Within minutes, the chaos began, while many people witnessed the horrible accident. Sly quickly jumped out of his car and started running towards the other car to see if anyone was injured. When asking what the man was doing and asking for his name and address, the man in the car instantly shot him right in the face. As Sly fell onto the wooden bridge, another man got out from the same side and shot him once again in the head.

While still sitting in their car, George Fanner was stunned and could not move as he watched in horror at the commotion outside. Quietly another man opened up a car door as he reached into the rear door and calmly lifted the briefcase full of money. The robber stood only a few feet away and coldly looked at Fanner without saying a word and fired his weapon into his heart. Fanner died instantly, just as his partner and friend had.

This double murder scared and sent shockwaves and chills throughout the city, and into the hearts of all Clevelanders. The grief-stricken citizens watched in amazement as some of Cleveland's finest police officers, along with the American

Automobile Club, worked diligently together to solve this terrible assignation on the usually happy New Year's Eve.

Several of the eyewitnesses came to the help of the murdered men and their families by giving police investigators their best descriptions of the team in the two-vehicle that attacked Sly and Fanner. Unfortunately, for the prosecutors, their stories did not always match-up and brought a wall of confusion for the police, on which men were actually involved. The police continued their careful investigation, and soon the people participating in the murder would all be identified.

Finally, five of the robbers were located and quickly arrested for their involvement in what would be labeled as the crime of the year! Later, this would bring the lead investigators in the lengthy search to California and even Mexico City. The arrested men included Ignatius "Sam" Purpura, Charles Russo, Frank Motto (aka Frank Amata), Louis Komer, and Dominic Benigno. Other men sought for questioning and interviewed by Detective Charles Cavolo included, Dominic Lonardo who was found using the name Joseph Piazza in San Francisco while another man, Angelo Amato, fled to Italy to avoid prosecution. Amato was eventually captured.

Subsequently, by January 25, 1935, Angelo Amato was jailed on charges of complicity in murder, and waiting for trial in Agrigento, Italy. The Italian government requested that the city of Cleveland send three police investigators. Cleveland was only able to send Detectives Charles Cavolo and Clarence Banks to Agrigento as eyewitnesses against the charges facing Amato.

The Cleveland police force never gave up as the prosecutors as officers search the country for the missing robbers. Their unparalleled investigation led them to arrest a thief in Los Angeles, Mexico City, San Francisco, and finally, in Sicily.

Staying focused on their acclaimed case, it took them fifteen years to make sure justice was finally served for the brokenhearted families of Wilfred Sly and George Fanner.

DETECTIVE CHARLES CAVOLO

(Courtesy of The Cleveland Police Museum)

5

JOSEPH "BIG JOE" LONARDO

Joseph "Big Joe" Lonardo was born Giuseppe in Licata, Sicily, in 1884 and died on October 13, 1927. Joe came to America on February 4, 1901, where he stepped off the vessel "Adelina Corvae" in the harbor of New York, just like so many other immigrants that year.

Moreover, Joe was just looking to build a better life for himself, and a chance to make a peaceful living, like so many other immigrants, wanted. Joe soon made enough money that he sent for his brothers, Frank, John, Dominic, and his sister Angela to come to the land of opportunity. A story is told how "Big Joe" even sent money home for several of his childhood friends, the Porrello brothers. In short, Lonardo wasted no time and asked them to join him in a safe environment and free from the unruly landowners that tortured their homeland.

It is unsure when Joe actually came to Cleveland, but he chose to become a fruit peddler on the city streets. He soon found himself in the wholesale sugar business, which just happened to be the primary ingredient for making alcohol.

Big Joe, became the first confirmed "Crime Boss" in Cleveland in 1925. Joe was first arrested in 1909 at the age of 25 for a robbery and then at 31 for stabbing a man to death and served three years in jail.

Joe's common-law wife was Concetta. They proudly had four sons. The family lived on a beautiful quiet street filled with trees on Larchmere Blvd., in Shaker Heights. A few years later, he became uninterested in Concetta, and the life he was living and left her and married a younger woman, Fannie Lanzonne in Sandusky in 1925. The newlyweds moved in with his brother on Warrington Road in Shaker Heights. The next year, Joe went back to his hometown of Licata, Sicily, where he met another young beauty. The story goes that when Joe returned to America, his new lover's husband left her and traveled to America to find a good job to earn enough money to send for her to join him. A rumor claimed that her husband was gunned down on the streets of Brooklyn. No one had ever been arrested for this murder. Soon after the man was dead, Joe sent for the young beauty. Fascinated by a new life in America, the young woman joined Joe, as he secretly kept her in a comfortable home in Cleveland Heights for many years.

Trying to do the best he could for his boys, Joe sent his son Angelo 15 and his younger brother Frank to an excellent boarding school in southern New York. Several months later, the boys hated it there and soon became homesick. In fact, the boys ran away and took a train back home to Cleveland, and to Joe's side. Joe was viewed by many as a respected "Don" in Cleveland. He often had a bodyguard with him as he wore silk shirts and plenty of Diamond rings to make a glamorous woman jealous.

At the start of Prohibition, Lonardo ruled the city with a firm, steady hand, and a rational mind. He was considered to be a shrewd businessman who knew how to operate a successful business. Lonardos power grew stronger with help from his old friends from Sicily. Joseph Porrello, who soon became his top lieutenant, along with the six of Porrello's brothers, who helped Lonardo's criminal empire grow over the next few years. Lonardo enjoyed an elegant, social, and cultured connection in the New York criminal world.

The Cleveland crime family originated with the four Lonardo brothers (Joe, Frank, John & Dominic) The Lonardo and Porrello brothers first established themselves as legitimate businessmen before Prohibition became law in the country. Before prohibition, the two groups of men dabbled in various criminal activities to make additional money and a small fortune, with crimes such as robbery and extortion. With the advent of Prohibition, Cleveland, like all of the other big cities, experienced a wave of popular lively speakeasies, bootleg-related whiskey robberies, and mysterious murders. The deaths of Louis Rosen, Salvatore Vella, August Rini, and several others produced the same suspects by the local police officers, but no indictments would ever develop. However, like so many times before, no clear evidence or charges could be established or ever seem to come from the local law enforcement officers. These men often were suspected to be members of the Lonardo's brave and often ruthless gang. Several of the murders occurred at the corner of E. 25th and Woodland Ave; this intersection became known by many in the city as the "Bloody Corner." Many of Lonardo's gang members had previous street battle experience.

Soon the "Circulation Wars" started, as a former professional boxer, who would become a significant criminal and wealthy gambler, in his own right, Tommy McGinty was hired as muscle for *The Plain Dealers* circulation department. By 1913, he headed a ruff looking gang of tough labor sluggers using baseball bats or steel bars to intimidate their competing rivals against the other popular newspaper. *The Cleveland News* sluggers were led by the "Mayfield Road Mob" under the watchful eye of Arthur McBride. Cleveland, like the other major cities of New York and Chicago, had a battle brewing over which newspaper would become the strongest and most popular among the daily community readers. The "Circulation Wars" term was used to describe the dangerously tense and terrible altercations of bloodshed.

In 1926, Lonardo was at the height of his superior power and the empire he controlled in Cleveland. It had been said that by this time in his life, Lonardo had saved close to 1 million dollars. That year he decided to travel back to his native home in Sicily to visit his mother and the remainder of his family. During his minor six-month vacation and absence, he lost much of his estimated $5,000 to $8,000 a week in profits to the up and coming power-hungry Porrello brothers who took advantage of his absence, and his weak-minded brothers. John lacked strong business skills, along with the assistance of a large group of men who were disgruntled with the way "Big Joe" Lonardo ran his organization. Several employees helped to loosen the firm hold Lonardo once enjoyed over the city.

When "Big Joe" Lonardo came back from his vacation, the hot-tempered man wanted, no insisted on a meeting with the Porrello brothers to get his weekly reimbursement. Earlier in the year, Lonardo purchased a home for $75,000 on a swank street named Larchmere Road in Shaker Heights, (Today this would be equal to over $1,071,000)

It was on October 13, 1927, "The biggest, bloodiest gangland feud in Cleveland history." Joseph Lonardo, who some estimated weighed nearly three-hundred pounds, and his younger brother John entered a barbershop to merely play a few hands of cards with his former friend and business partner Angelo Porrello. The meeting was set-up to discuss the multitude of problems that have developed between the two families. The Lonardo Brothers quickly walked in and looked forward to a quiet game of cards, and to settle their disputes.

Within minutes of the men sitting down, two unknown gunmen came out of nowhere in front of Lonardo and fired several shots filling the small room with blackish gray smoke. The bullets were aimed at Joseph and John. "Big Joe" was quickly shot three times in the chest. However, brother John was hit only once in the chest by one of the gunmen. John then somehow managed to draw his own gun out from under his topcoat, but before he could return fire, he was shot in the head. Salvatore Todaro, an old friend, an employee of the Lonardo family, was thought to be one of the gunmen who acted in the violent and bloody shooting. Cleveland Police later released that the Lonardo clan offered up a $10,000 reward on the city streets for reliable information for the name of the men who murdered their brothers.

In retribution and retaliation for both killings, police received information that led them to a man who had pointed out Lonardo in the shop. He was a local fruit peddler, Frank Alessi. Alessi was a known gambler and racketeer in Cleveland and related to Sam Todaro through marriage. Soon, Frank Alessi was found shot and critically wounded on a side street after leaving a card game.

Many people believe that revenge is sweet, no matter how long it takes to get it. Angelo Lonardo wanted to avenge his father's death, and how his untimely death was tormenting his dear sweet mother, who was now destitute, dead broke and begging on the streets for money. As Lonardo and his mother pulled up to the warehouse, he summoned someone close by to go and get Todaro, saying his fragile mother wished to speak with him and could not walk to the building. It was later in June 1929 as revenge, and "Vendetta" was anything but sweet for the "Big Joe" Lonardo family.

Salvatore "Black Sam" Todaro, was shot five times and killed by Joseph Lonardo's eighteen-year-old son, Angelo. The Police soon found it was tough to find anyone who actually witnessed the assassination. It was mentioned that at the time of the attack, Todaro was speaking with Angelo "Little Ange" Sciria, a nephew of Big Joe, along with a friend Tony Volpe when he slowly approached the waiting vehicle and his death. Police soon arrested Concetta Lonardo for being a significant part of the murder plot. Angelo and his cousin Dominic Suspirato had already fled the city for safety.

For a short time after Big Joe Lonardo's death, a new man came onto the crime scene in Cleveland. Lawrence Lupo, who was born in Brooklyn, New York. Known as a big-time "Fight Promotor and Beer Baron," he enjoyed wheeling and dealing for a piece of Lonardo's lucrative and profitable liquor business. Lupo was in the slot machine business and a member of Lonardo's crime family for a short time and seemed to enjoy getting other men upset with him. Lupo intestinally lowered the core price of a barrel of beer, just to agonize his enemies, and win over new customers who wanted a lower price. One of Lupo's alleged crimes was when he shot and killed a "slot machine rival" back on August 12, 1927. Lupo admitted that he did kill Deputy Sheriff Ralph Meyer, only in self-defense. According to Lupo's testimony, Sheriff Meyer shot at him first, and he was just defending himself. Lupo was eventually acquitted of the crime against him.

On September 10, 1927, Lupo was attacked by a passing car, while firing rounds of gunshot aimed at him, and a friend of his, Chuck Polizzi (the adopted brother of Big Al Polizzi) while they tried to enter Lupo's automobile. Lupo was slightly wounded while Polizzi received a non-series shot in his neck. Lupo was accompanied by his wife and daughter Laura while Polizzi was with his wife. The women were terrified, and luckily untouched during the violent shooting spree.

About one year after the attempt on his life, Lupo was finally gunned down after a tan Roadster passed by and quickly stopped as Lupo got into the car near a busy speakeasy about 4 PM on May 31, 1928. It has been alleged that Charles Colletti and Charles Polizzi were in the car with a driver at the time. Ten minutes later, Lupo's limp body was tossed out of the car, with five bullet holes in his head.

AN ILLUSTRATION OF THE ASSASSINATION

SCENE OF SAM TODARO

(Courtesy of Dennis Sutcliffe)

The Cleveland Police estimated that over one thousand mourners attended "Big Joe and John's" wake, while he laid in state in a silver coffin as over 700 cars in the procession to Calvary Cemetery, while a band played a mixture of Italian love songs.

1927 FUNERAL FOR BIG JOE AND JOHN LONARDO

(Courtesy of the Cleveland Plain Dealer)

CONCETTA LONARDO WITH HER ATTORNEY AFTER HER

ARREST BEING QUESTIONED BY THE POLICE

(Courtesy of the Cleveland Police Museum)

6

John Lonardo; was a younger brother by fourteen years and born in 1897. John was a self-proclaimed gambler and was arrested on suspicious person charges right after the famous Sly-Fanner murder in 1920. Other members of the Mayfield Road Mob detained in the crime consisted of John Angersola, Dominic Benigno, and Charles Colletto. On January 5, while bail was set at an unusually high amount of $40,000 (equal in today's money at $505,484) given to all the men. Because of their substantial wealth, only John Lonardo was able to make bail for the charges pending against him, Lonardo was out on the streets within two hours. However, there was never any proof that the 23-year-old John Lonardo actually took part in this killing and robbery. John Lonardo died alongside his brother Joe at East 110th Street and Woodland Avenue.

Frank Lonardo, one of the four brothers, and was born in 1891. After his brother, Joe, and John were killed in 1927, Frank work alongside a trusted family friend, Lawrence Lupo, and gain a small fortune of his own through the lucrative beer business. Frank enjoyed to gamble just like his brother John, and would often attend high-stakes poker games throughout the city. Usually, he would join in with Frank Alessi, a known Porrello man, and his brother-in-law to "Black Sam" Todaro. Soon their relationship ended, and Alessi would not be seen playing cards with Lonardo ever again.

It was Sunday, October 19, 1929, when the thirty-eight-year-old Frank was shot and killed, just two short years after his brother Joe and John. Frank, who always carried a gun, became yet another victim of the infamous "Sugar Wars." Frank was shot at least three times, once in the right eye, and twice in the body. The lifeless body was found face down on top of a table in a pile of playing cards inside a card-room behind a local barbershop. Another account of the crime scene claimed there were two gunmen and at least nine shots were fired in the small smoke-filled room. The shop was located at 1735 Chester Avenue and 18th Street. Frank was found without a single shot being fired from his .38-caliber revolver. The owner of the shop told police that there were five men in the back room playing cards while he was in the front with a customer when he heard shots fired. When the barber entered the backroom, the criminals were running out of the rear door. He claims he did not see or know who the men were.

The police picked up thirteen people, including Frank Alessi, on being a suspicious person involved in Frank Lonardo's murder. Two days later, nine of the thirteen men were released by order of Police Inspector Cornelius Cody. Cody mentioned he believes the shooting was not planned ahead of time and that a few out-of-town people may have come in to make the killing, and it is more than likely he was stalked by the men for months before the hit occurred.

(Courtesy of Dennis Sutcliffe)

Dominic Lonardo; was the youngest of the four brothers, and found himself in the middle of significant Cleveland robbery, and assignation. It was the murder of Wilford Sly and George Fanner on New Year's Eve 1920, where police believe that at least seven men participated in the defiant, hateful crime. One of the men involved in the robbery was Louis Komer, who turned informant and told police that Lonardo and Angelo Amato performed the actual killing of the two successful businessmen.

Immediately after that, the massive confusion in the case, it soon escalated. In late April 1921, Prosecutor Edward Stanton and Chief of Police Frank Smith were discussing the situation and felt strongly that Dominic Benigno and Dominic Lonardo fled to Italy or possibly Sicily. It was confirmed several weeks later that it was actually Angelo Amato who was living in Italy. By the end of May or early June, Dominic Benigno and Charles Colletto were the prime suspects of the hideous crime. They had been spotted and held in Mexico City jail for possible deportation to Cleveland. The confusion was plentiful during the gripping investigation as Chief Smith was now cautiously optimistic that Inspector George Matowitz might find Amato and Lonardo hiding out in Mexico City as well. Later Cleveland's Inspector Cody received information that Lonardo could be residing in San Francisco, California. After arriving in California, Lonardo took up a new life and a new secret identity as Joseph Piazza.

It was now early October 1928 when Lonardo-Piazza was found and arrested in San Francisco by a neighborhood homicide detective. The police raided his home in Monterey Boulevard, where he was living with his young wife and two small children. Lonardo-Piazza was quickly arrested along with his neighbor, Dominic DeMarco, who police believed was a nephew of Big Joe Lonardo. Dominic Lonardo declared to the police that he moved to Los Angeles from Cleveland around the end of 1919 and moved to San Francisco sometime in 1924. By the end of November, Lonardo dropped the vague front of being Piazza and claimed he was, in fact, Dominic Lonardo.

Cleveland Prosecutor Edward Stanton worked diligently alongside Detective Cody to formulate a plan to return Lonardo back to Cleveland. Stanton related, Dominic Lonardo has been living a lie and a life as Joseph Piazza. Cleveland's Detective Cody tried in vain to transfer him back to Cleveland, charging him with partaking in the Sly-Fanner murder in 1920. However, several vital witnesses placed Lonardo-Piazza in Los Angeles on the day of the robbery and murder.

On January 8, 1930, in San Francisco Dominic's wife of four years, Constantina reported to the police that her husband Dominic is missing, and expressing intense fear he was "taken for a ride." She went to tell the dispatcher her husband left their quite home back on December 14, and she has not seen or heard from him since. She claimed he was carrying a large roll of cash with one of his large diamond rings she has ever seen.

Local police mentioned Dominic gained his fortune in the produce business while living in California and was merely slain by a local gang member for his money. The arrest warrant for Dominic Lonardo stayed open in Cleveland, just in case he ever showed up alive, or anywhere else in the country or did return to Cleveland.

No records could be found on what did actually happened to Dominic Lonardo since he was never seen in public after his disappearance.

7

JOSEPH "BIG JOE" PORRELLO

Born in Licata, Sicily, and childhood friends with the Lonardo family, the Porrello brothers (Rosario, Vincenzo, Angelo, Joseph, John, Ottavio, and Raymond) broke away from the Lonardo family creating their own Cleveland crime faction in 1926. Joe and his six brothers arrived in Cleveland in the early 1900s as they pooled their physical strengths, strong will, and determination to eventually become successful corn sugar dealers in their own right. Joe was viewed as a brazen "opportunist" and established they're headquartered in the upper Woodland Avenue area around E. 110th Street, known as the first Italian neighborhood.

By 1925, Angelo Porrello operated a traditional Italian grocery store on the corner of Woodland and East 30th Street. Just a few blocks down on East 25th and Woodland, which became known as "The Bloody Corner" of Prohibition. Brother Ottavio operated a barbershop on Woodland and E 130th Street. The peaceful citizens of Cleveland knew very well that the Porrello family focused on distilling liquor from corn sugar and freely selling it on the streets to friends and neighbors.

In 1927 the "Bootleg Kings" gave the Cleveland citizen yet another example of how they will protect their city from outsiders. Unaware of the strength of the Italians, two out of town guests came into Cleveland, thinking they could harass and extort protection money from weaker mob gangs. The men were Ernest Yorkell and Jack Brownstein. Both were from the Philadelphia area and considered to be small-time hustlers looking to make a big score on the north coast. The unlikely pair started by visiting small groups of bootleggers around the city to make their name known, offering "Protection" and to initiate a threat of violence against them. They told the men they wanted their first payment on Friday, October 7. Acting like "big-shots" the two tried to pick up two attractive young waitresses in an eastside restaurant bragging that they would be wealthy and getting $2,000 from a bootlegger on Hough Avenue. The two men never kept their date with the lovely waitresses. The bloody bodies of both men were found in Ambler Park near East Boulevard. Both heads had been blown off, and their bodies shredded with pellet holes from several shotgun blasts. The message was clear to the city, and any other would-be extortionist, Cleveland, was off-limits and not a place to threaten or to lock horns with. Several of Joe Porrello's men were arrested as the principal suspect in the double murder.

Friction and business difficulties continued to escalate between both families. The Lonardo and Porrello families were coming to a heated point in their once peaceful acquaintance. When Lonardo returned to the United States from his vacation, frustration overwhelmed him as he ordered a sit-down to be scheduled between the Lonardo's and the Porrellos to solve their business disagreements over a loss of excessive profits. Not realizing he and his brother were walking into a trap. This brutal and insightful killing of the Lonardo brothers allowed Joseph Porrello to take over as "Boss" of the Cleveland crime family.

Porrello desperately needed and wanted the support from the top Mafia bosses in New York and of various other leading Mafia territories across the United States. His ultimate goal was to completely control the Cleveland area and expand his very profitable business ventures of liquor and gambling across Ohio. It was freezing day on December 5, 1928, as some 27 wealthy-looking businessmen from across the country gathered at the beautiful and elaborate Statler Hotel located on East 12th and Euclid Avenue in downtown Cleveland. At this time, Joe Porrello feared only one man. Frank Milano, who was gaining strength, so he had asked other family members to come and meet with him, leaving Milano out of the crucial meeting. He needed to have his power endorsed by these top Italian mob members from across the mid-west and to be recognized as the official "Boss" of Cleveland.

PICTURE OF THE MEN ARRESTED IN THE STATLER HOTEL ON DECEMBER 5, 1928

Mafia Boss Joe Profaci is seated in the wheelchair.

(Courtesy of Cleveland State University)

Fourteen Sicilian mobsters were stopped at the national meeting of the Mafia held in Cleveland. This event was labeled as the first known, "Mafia Grand Council Meeting" and attended by men from Chicago, Brooklyn, and Tampa, Florida

The story goes, a young and intelligent foot Patrolman Frank Osowski who started his beat at 11 PM and thinking only about going home to his young wife and daughter. He soon noticed many professional-looking men arriving at the hotel in the early morning hours. All the people looked wealthy. After watching the men and then sign into the hotel as guests, and go up to their rooms, he quickly copied the names of the people down. Osowski then handed the names over to his commanders, Police Lieutenant Kurt Gloeckner and Detective Captain Emmet Potts. By 8 AM, seventy-four armed detectives and police officers arrived at the hotel to help Captain Potts raid the upscale hotel. Twenty-one men in all were taken out of the prestigious hotel and down to the Central Police station, then booked on charges of being a suspicious person.

Surprisingly only thirteen revolvers were confiscated when they were searched. Some of the prominent men arrested were Joe Profaci, one of New York's top leaders, and a member of the first Commission. Joe Magliocco, brother-in-law to Profaci and considered to be a high-ranking member of his organization. Vincent Mangano, another member of the first Commission who founded what is now the Gambino family. Pasquale Lolordo, and Joseph Giunta, both men represented Al Capone from Chicago. Capone was not allowed to attend this secret meeting since he was not of Sicilian birth. John Mirabella, originally from Detroit and later settled in Youngstown and Salvatore Lombardio from Newark, New Jersey. Lombardino was the only man arrested and held since he was wanted in New Jersey for murder. Cleveland's, Joe Porrello, and Sam Tilocco were not detained since they did not arrive at the hotel yet for their breakfast meeting set for that morning. Embarrassed beyond belief, both men and Rosario Porrello worked diligently to obtain the necessary bail money for Joe Profaci and some of the other men.

Police investigators learned that in all, over fifty mob bosses were to have come to Cleveland. Porrello managed to come up with a $20,000 bond for each of his arrested friends. Porrello went to the police station with thirty of his friends and claims he gathered the funds from these close friends in the community and his family. Even after this, near fiasco and professional disaster, Joe Porrello's power and wealth grew stronger and was declared the "Boss" and recognized nationwide.

By the end of 1929, Joseph Porrello had made enough money that he was able to move his family to the Upper Eastside suburb of Cleveland Heights on Berkshire Rd. Like Porrello, Sam Tilocco and his new-found fortune moved his family to Norwood Rd in Shaker Heights.

SAM TILOCCO

(Courtesy of the Cleveland Police Museum)

8

THE PORRELLO BROTHERS

Through the year of 1927, and much of 1928, the remaining of the Lonardo faction loyalists, which included a young aggressive and influential, up and coming Mafia group known as the *Mayfield Road Mob.* This rival faction was led by Frank Milano, and his brother Anthony. The Italian group continued to attack the Porrello family and the leadership within the Cleveland underworld. They battled on the city streets for control of the most lucrative criminal rackets outside of the corn sugar business, mainly gambling, and prostitution, which were the most prominent earners for the American Mafia crime families next to bootlegging up to this time.

Angelo Porrello was quoted saying, "The wealth of sugar barons is exaggerated by all. Business in sugar; is not all it is cracked up to be. I may be wrong, but there seems to be a high flow of whiskey coming in from Canada."

It was on June 11, 1929, "Black Sam" Todaro was considered to be the #2 man or underboss in the Porrello, crime family. It became no surprise when he was shot and killed while approaching a parked car to speak to a dear old friend.

ANGELO PORRELLO

SALVATORE "BLACK SAM" TODARO

(Both Pictures Courtesy of Cleveland State University)

The smart businessperson that he was, Joe Porrello, purchased twenty-four revolvers from a man in Youngstown. He planned to use them for protection if and when he needed them. Upset of the latest reaction from his customers, he quickly cut off their credit to many of the homemade stills that were falling behind in the liquor production, and his ultimate profits. Porrello then told his enforcers to speak, beat and convince the people too pay up what they owe. Porrello later became increasingly angered as the group of rum-runners, who continually brought in whiskey from Canada, which cut massively into his profit margins.

On July 5, 1930, at 1 PM, Joseph Porrello and Sam Tilocco were sitting in a quiet café on Woodland and East 110th Street enjoying a brief cup of coffee or expresso when Police Detective Sargent Charles Cavola walked in to take a break. The men exchanged niceties for a few minutes when Porrello and Tilocco suddenly got up and left. It seems they were running late for an invitation to meet with Frank Milano at his *Venetian Restaurant* at 12601 Mayfield Road and Murray Hill Roads in Little Italy. After a few hands of cards and a short meeting, which included several heated words exchanged on both sides. Frustration and anger grew as gunfire soon erupted, and dark smoke filled the room. The old boss, Joseph Porrello, who had just lit a cigarette, was shot three times on the right side of his head and killed instantly. Sam Tilocco was shot twice in the head and three times in his torso. He slowly and successfully crawled, while in great pain to the front door, and somehow made his way out onto the sunlit sidewalk where he soon died. Both men were dead by 2:27 in the afternoon.

Frank Milano and several of his restaurant employees were quickly arrested for taking part in the double murder, including Al and Charles Polizzi, John Angersola, and Charles Colletti. The men were brought in for questioning, but they were only charged with being a suspicious person in the assignation. The police were surprised to learn Milano had a second home next to the restaurant and often stayed there and that they had no substantial evidence of who was at the restaurant or who the actual gunmen were.

Succeeding his brother Joseph in the role of the "Boss," was Vincenzo, "James" Porrello. James viciously spoke about a vendetta and wiping out everyone responsible for his brother's murder. It was only three short weeks after his brother's death when Vincenzo was inside his grocery store on East 110th Street and Woodland Avenue, considered a Porrello stronghold.

On Saturday, July 26, when a Ford touring car with its curtains tightly drawn was spotted by several witnesses as it cruised slowly past the storefront of windows. Soon a couple of shotguns poked out from the car windows, and two loud blasts of buckshot were fired, one through the front window of the storefront and one through the front screen door. A foolish and fearless amateur gunman driving a 1929 Ford somehow got lucky. Two pellets were found logged in the back of Porrello's head as he turned to avoid the loud shotgun blast, which entered directly into his brain. Vincenzo (James) Porrello was quickly rushed to Saint Luke's Hospital. However, he died a few hours later from massive blood loss. Two local petty criminals who the police believed worked with the Lonardo's were soon arrested, and charged with the gangland murder. The men indicted were Louis Cangelosi, as the driver, and Charles Ciuni, the gunmen who used a shotgun. Cangelosi was quickly discharged by a directed verdict; the other man Ciuni was acquitted at his murder trial. A third man Charles Cassaro was held on a $10,000 bond. Like almost all of Cleveland's bootleg related murders, the killers never saw justice inside a courtroom.

THE FUNERAL PROCESSION OF "BIG JOE" PORRELLO

ON JULY 10, 1930

(Courtesy of Cleveland State University Cleveland Press Collection)

Well documented in "*The Rise and Fall of the Cleveland Mafia, by* Rick Porrello. After yet another assignation of his brothers, Raymond Porrello declared revenge once again on August 15, 1930. Although at this time, it was rumored the remaining Porrello brothers were earmarked for extermination by other men who wanted to control their criminal empire. The surviving brothers soon went into hiding for a short time to regroup and to re-aline others to help in their fight to prevail as the decisive leader in Cleveland. Raymond, the dapper younger brother, was known for his cocky, strong-minded attitude and an extremely hot and often brutal temper. He often spoke to his brother James of seeking revenge for the murders his family had to endure. Raymond was streetwise and smarter than his brother had been. He quickly took active measures to protect himself by adding a bodyguard to keep him safe from his would-be attackers. Three weeks after James Porrello's murder, Raymond Porrello's house was destroyed in a violent bomb explosion, hoping to catch him at home and killing him. Luckily, for him and his family, they were not home at the time. The bombing was the gravest of warning to the Porrello's from the Mayfield Road Mob. Soon, the out-gunned Porrello's were closing down their sugar operation across the city and playing it safe, for the time being, looking to the future for a new opportunity to re-take control of the town.

The thirst for revenge had not been very satisfying for the members of the Lonardo family. However, it was also believed that the remaining Porrello brothers, Raymond, along with the eldest brother Rosario still posed the greatest threat of all.

It was apparent that another attack would be made by one family or the other. The final blow was struck on Feb. 25, 1932. Raymond Porrello and his brother Rosario along with their bodyguard Dominic Gulino and a close friend Joe Damanti were relaxing the day away and playing cards in a cigar store at 11103 Woodland Ave. Near E. 110th and Woodland Avenue. Soon in a surprise and a coordinated move, the front door burst open while several men ran inside, in a hail of bullets, which flew around the small and crowded room. The Porrello brothers, their bodyguard, and a bystander Joe Todaro who was already seated in the room went down in the storm of bullets as thick black smoke filled the small room. The Porrello brothers died at the scene. Gulino died a couple of hours later in the hospital after running out of the building. The bystander eventually recovered from his wounds. This shooting was declared as; "Cleveland's deadliest mob hit ever."

ROSARIO PORRELLO   RAYMOND PORRELLO

(Courtesy of the Authors collection)

Later that evening, an old friend and associate of "Big Joe" Lonardo, Frank Brancato, found his way to a hospital with a substantial gunshot wound to his stomach. He declared he was on the west side of town when he was shot. Nevertheless, the police actively believed he received the shot while inside the deadly cigar shop. Only Brancato would be apprehended and placed on trial for the horrific triple assassination.

THE INCREDIBLY LARGE FUNERAL OF THE PORRELLO
BROTHERS IN 1932

(Courtesy of the Archive Division at Cleveland State
University)

9

PART II

JERRY MILANO

The Milano brothers were born in Reggio Calabria in Southern Italy to Pietro and Grazia Milano (née Mazza). Francesco and Anthony eventually immigrated to the United States and made their way to Cleveland, Ohio, by 1913.

Myths and legends have embraced the beauty of Reggio Calabria for centuries. Located in the southern portion of Italy as it sits across from the calm, clean blue sea full and a variety of fish. The unique and magnificent climate. The province is, without a doubt, the heart and soul of the gorgeous Mediterranean.

One of the Milano brothers who had only a slight interaction, in the organized crime business was brother Jerry. Jerry was born in 1903 and maintained a quiet and low profile helping and assisting his colleagues as a slot and pinball machine vendor for many years. It was not until February 1945 when Jerry hit the lime-lite in the Cleveland newspapers where he was listed as a possible suspect in a murder. Police where interest in speaking with him, for the killing of sixty-year-old Nate Weisenberg, who had the title of "Slot Baron" in Ohio.

In was in October of 1948, when Milano was arrested by Sheriff Joseph Sweeney. After his trial, Jerry was only convicted in Common Pleas Court by Judge Frank Merrick of having an illegal "Victor Derby" pinball machine that he placed at a service station in Brooklyn Village. He found himself being fined $500 and served ninety days in the county workhouse.

JERRY MILANO

(Courtesy of Cleveland State University Archives Division)

It was found that by March 1949, Jerry has only paid his $500 fine and as of yet not set one foot inside the Warrensville workhouse located on the corner of Warrensville and Richmond Roads. Jerry Milano's face turned up once again in the pages of Spinning Reels, a magazine for the "Bell-O-Matic Corporation of Chicago, Illinois. Bell-O-Matic was the primary manufacturer of pinball and slot machines at the time and entertained almost one thousand guests and operators at the new Hotel Morrison on January 17 to 19.

The company makes a wide selection of coin-operated machines, which we often referred to as slot machines. The popular brands at the time were Duple Consoles, Token, Blue Bells, and Black Beauties. Milano enjoyed and was accompanied by four beautiful women who Jerry claimed where his lady friends from Ohio.

10

MR. FRANK MILANO

Born Francesco; meaning

"The free one and incredibly generous."

Milano; "One who came from or lived close to Milano, Italy."

The other community named Little Italy of Cleveland was established around 1885 when the master stone and marble cutters arrived from Italy and found employment making the headstones and monuments for the beautiful Lake View Cemetery, located on top of a small hill along what is now known as Mayfield Road.

It was in 1912 when Frank and his brother Anthony found themselves in trouble with the law for the first time in Cleveland. The brothers were arrested on counterfeiting charges. Frank was released without any jail time. Anthony was not as lucky and received a six-year prison sentence. However, he only served fifty-four months for his crime.

By the early 1920s, the two brothers started a social club to help entertain their substantial Italian friends in the community. The club became known as the "Italian-American Brotherhood Club" or referred to as the IABC today. This new club also held the Milano Brotherhood Loan Company. A legitimate business venture that provided loans to the lesser wealthy Italian community which other local banks may not have approved because of their immigration, nationality, or financial status. Some reports tell how the Milano's increased rates to their "Pisano's" while others say they were reasonable and helpful friends of the community. However, you viewed the loan company, it was a way to help their fellow compatriots grow and prosper in America. This simple act gave the community a sense of unity and strength that was desperately needed at this time. The community seemed to work together as they all lived a hard life and struggled to make ends meet. They all prayed at their church, Holy Rosary every Sunday for God's blessing to raise their families in peace and harmony as so many other nationalities of immigrants have done across the nation for decades.

Frank, along with his brother Anthony also started an Italian grocery store on Mayfield Road with their friend and associate Al Polizzi, which became known as Mayfield Imports. Which closed down many years ago. The store specialized in importing hundreds of items from their homeland. By doing this, they helped the Italians in their community once again to be able to enjoy the food that they had grown up with, cherished, and appreciated. Surprisingly to some readers, pasta was not sold at the store since most, if not all of the women all made their own pasta for their precious families' dinners.

The Milano brothers were smart and quick learners, and by this time, they found themselves rising in popularity inside the Italian community and would become the future leaders of the "*Mayfield Road Gang.*"

Around 1924, the Woodland Avenue district of Cleveland was known as "Big Italy." It had come into existence in the 1890s. Astonishingly, the illegal occupation of the Milano brothers taught Frank to do his best to stay as low profile as possible and to keep out of the interest of the local police and, more importantly, out of the daily newspapers.

THE 1960S IN LITTLE ITALY

(Courtesy of Cleveland State Memory Project)

Unlike the Lonardo's and the Porrello's, Frank was admired in his community; Milano made numerous charitable contributions and helped his fellow Italians using the money he made from their illegal activities. The two brothers were viewed by many to be the saviors, nevertheless not all in the neighborhoods felt the same way.

By the year 1925 arrived, Frank was rising up the ranks in organized crime as a highly valued disciple of the Lonardo clan.

Most of the men united on Milano's side with Al Polizzi, his top lieutenant and his stepbrother Chuck, (who was of Jewish descent, and his birth name was Leo Berkowitz), John Angersola along with his brothers Fred and George, Charles Colletti, Frank Brancato, John DeMarco, and several others active and willing enforcers.

The Murray Hill area was quickly becoming the focal point for all Italian-Americans in Cleveland. In the summer months, street vendors would set up daily, selling their homemade delicious fresh fruit, and pastries. Grocery stores like Mayfield Imports would sell Italian meats, such as freshly made Italian pork sausage (either hot or sweet), Pepperoni, Capicola (an Italian spiced ham) with aged Provolone, fresh garlic along with fresh mozzarella balls, Romano and Parmesan cheeses. There would be a grand selection of Italian cheeses, along with excellent wines from Italy and Sicily, and a vast assortment of imported olives and olive oil. The olives would sit peacefully in fifty-five-gallon wooden barrels laid open for the patrons to taste and enjoy. Fish vendors would include the Fulton Fish Market, where fresh fish was abundant for the community to purchase who all grew up on a seafood diet for most of their lives.

The city streets would have a pleasant aroma of fresh Italian bread baking in open-hearth ovens from Presti's, LaPuma, or Corbo's bakeries. The intoxicating fragrance of fresh Italian pastries, second to none, infested the streets of Little Italy, calling everyone into their shops to come and buy their favorite treat.

Many of the older Italians would first go to Holy Rosary Church daily for early morning mass. Then they would leisurely walk up and down the hill, seeing and speaking with friends and relatives and relaxing the day away. They felt like they were home in Italy once again, even if it was for only an hour or so.

Many of the men would enter into the IAB Club to relax and enjoy the morning. During the summer months, many would play the Italian sport of Boccie, a traditional lawn bowling game. They would visit with their friends for hours at a time, playing pinochle or canasta and talking about their current life and the grand old days of being a child in Italy.

Frank Milano would soon open up *The Venetian Restaurant* located on Mayfield Road. The restaurant had a fantastic reputation for homemade Italian foods. For many years, it was a favorite dining spot for the citizens of Cleveland.

By the year 1928, Milano, had gained a stronghold on political influence in the Cleveland area and often used his friends in high places when it aligned with his needs. Milano was inside the power group named "The East-End Bi-Partisan Political League," which included Councilman A.L. DeMaloribus, who had been a past member of the board of directors. Milano; was often attacked by rival political figures for helping his friends into elected offices with expanding their campaign funds, reaching into the thousands of dollars. By the end of the year, Frank found himself in prison for six months on a bootlegging charge and a $1,000 fine.

At this same time, Milano was then alleged to be working alongside Joe Porrello to organize the city, and one of Milano's men was to have partaken in the murder of Larry Lupo, a known Lonardo member. Lupo's death in May helped to ensure Porrello's control of the vast Woodland and downtown Cleveland area.

Allegedly, it was at this time, and with the support of Chuck Polizzi with his Jewish heritage allowed Milano to meet and join forces with Jewish Mobster Moe Dalitz. Dalitz came to Ohio from the Detroit and the Toledo area after starting his adventurous and long career. He left his old name Moe Davis behind. Dalitz was also known as a Salt Lake City Top Hoodlum.

CHUCK POLIZZI ON THE LEFT WITH

FRANK CAMMARATTA THE BROTHER-IN-LAW

OF PETE LICAVOLI.

FRANK WORKED IN THE YOUNGSTOWN AREA

(Courtesy of the Cleveland Police Museum)

11

Milano optimistically started to take his hold of the hugely profitable "Slot Machine" business. He was accused of being the man who ordered the bombing of the "Slot" Czar, Nate Weisenberg's home. It was believed, to take Weisenberg over two years to convince his business associate Frank Joiner; that it would not be in their best interest or for their continued good health to resist any longer, and they soon joined the Milano family.

In 1929, with the growing friendship, Milano had with the "Cleveland Syndicate" known to be made-up of Jewish men named Moe Dalitz and Louis Rothkoph, who were allegedly tied together with the powerful Syndicate boss Meyer Lansky. A Milano associate Chuck Polizzi supposedly accompanied Louis Rothkoph to the famous "Atlantic Conference" in Atlantic City, New Jersey, the home of the Eastcoast Boardwalk Gangster, "Nucky" Johnson.

Early in 1930, Milano's well-respect strength and control were growing at a rapid pace. Even his top competitor Joe Porrello was concerned with the power Milano was gaining. The two men met after Milano expressed the need to speak with one another. Porrello agreed and met Milano's at his *Venetian Restaurant* on Mayfield Road to discuss their mutual business opportunities. Meeting with Milano was his lieutenant Al Polizzi, and Porrello brought with him Sam Tilocco.

Disappointed and concerned that Milano controlled most of the political influence and power in Cleveland. Porrello wanted Milano's, profound political impact as a compelling argument assumed between the two escalated. Nervously Porrello quickly left the restaurant with Tilocco at his side.

By April 1930, Joe Porrello was asked by Al Polizzi to meet with Frank Milano for the second time at the *Venetian Restaurant* to play cards, relax, and have a drink or two, and talk business. Joe's brother Raymond and his friend Sam Tilocco did not like the idea and tried to convince him of going into Milano's "home turf," but Joe was sure he would be "OK" and would not be harmed.

Porrello and Tilocco arrived in the early afternoon and were kindly greeted by Milano. Just as their last meeting went and soon after the game of cards started, the men seemed to begin arguing about their business dealing, as insults and accusations flew at one another. That is when the gunshots rang out.

Later under a possible murder indictment against him, Joiner would tell the Cleveland Police that he noticed Frank Milano inside the restaurant when Porrello was killed; however, he stated he did not see anyone else in the room at the time.

After the incredibly large funeral for Porrello and Tilocco, the Cleveland Police Department finally located Frank Milano in his Lyndhurst home. Milano was quickly taken into custody and charged with the murder of both men. Milano was being held on a $25,000 cash bond, which he could not or would not post. Hoping the judge would believe that he was not as wealthy as everyone in the city alleged him to be.

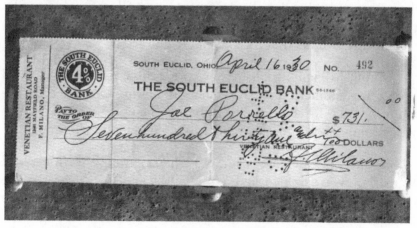

FRANK MILANO GAVE THIS CHECK TO JOE PORRELLO THE DAY HE DIED.

(Courtesy of Cleveland State University)

After months of an in-depth investigation into the double murders by Police Inspector Cornelius W. Cody. Cody was not able to find a single witness or enough substantial evidence to tie in, Milano, Al Polizzi, Colletto, Angersola to these murders.

After a heated and prolonged court battle, Eddie Stanton, who was Milano's attorney at this time, fought an uphill battle for his client as justice prevailed. Stanton successfully won over Judge Mary Grossman. Adding strength to Stantons argument was helped by Inspector Cody of the Cleveland Police Department, who testified his men, in fact, did not have a search warrant at the time when they searched and seized a rifle, gun, and personal records and personal checks from Milano's private office. Stanton viciously and convincingly argued in court that his client, Frank Milano, was facing and charged with being a suspicious person, and though he could not be charged directly with the murder of Porrello and Tilocco. By law, the improper seizure of his personal records and documents were quickly found to be inadmissible in court.

Frustrated over the situation, Judge Grossman had no alternative and ruled that the documents were illegally obtained by the police, and must be returned to Milano at once and could not become a part of his trial for the double murder.

During Milano's trial, the city prosecutor made one comical error after another. It was evident to all in attendance in the courtroom that Milano was the only man being single out and the police's only choice for the murder of the two top rival criminals.

As the only defense witness, Milano proudly testified; and denied he ever gambled and admitted, he did own the rifles the police found in his home, then illegally confiscated after the killings. However, he stated they were for rabbit hunting only. Milano said he was also a well-known grocer and respected citizen in town, and that is how he made his peaceful living. The reasonable doubt approach by his attorney Eddie Stanton played heavy on the minds of the jury members. After their deliberation, they had no recourse except to acquit Frank Milano of being a suspicious person on the scene of the double murder.

It is believed by 1931, Frank Milano joined the National Crime Syndicate with many powerful criminals around the country. With men like Charlie Luciano and Meyer Lansky. Milano was now regarded as the official "Boss" of Cleveland's crime family.

By 1932, Milano had become one of the top American Mafia bosses in the country and a charter member of the new powerful National Commission.

Over the next few years, Milano enjoyed a firm control, and hold over the policy and numbers rackets in Ohio and was collecting up to forty percent of their profits from the men for protection against others and the law. During this time, he made friends with other Jewish gangsters in town, Morris Kleinman, as his friendship with Moe Dalitz grew stronger.

1934

After long deliberation, Milano realized he needed to get out of America and into a safer environment to live in. It is unknown how or why he selected his new home, but he quickly packed up his family and left the United States for Vera Cruz, Mexico, leaving his trusted brother Anthony as the "Underboss." Before he left the city, Frank Milano appointed Al Polizzi to be the "Boss" of the Cleveland family.

According to Rick Porrello's "*To Kill the Irishman*," Milano lived on his spacious ranch in Jesus Carranza, where he had developed interests in the profitable ligament businesses of coffee, lumber, and crude oil operations. It has been firmly believing that both Moe Dalitz and Al Polizzi kept in contact over the years with Frank and would often go to Mexico and visited with him. Frank would often come back to Cleveland to visit his family and to ensure he maintained his citizenship as he flew into Akron, avoiding the watchful eyes of the police and IRS agents. In Cleveland, he would visit with friends and do business as he continued to enlarge his comfortable undercover empire.

In 1936, according to the book *The Rise and Fall of the Cleveland Mafia,* by Rick Porrello, Dr. Romano, the surgeon who had saved Frank Brancato's life back in 1932, after he was shot in the cigar shot that killed two of the Porrello brothers.

Romano became an unwanted and disturbing problem for the Cleveland family, namely Tony Milano and Angelo Lonardo. Romano lived on the east side of town in the city of Willoughby. One or possibly both of these men felt Romano was becoming too powerful and was a threat against the "Mayfield Road Gang," while others felt there were other concerns or questions about why Romano needed to have his life come to an end.

It was on June 11, 1936, as a county worker found Dr. Romano's bloody body in a car along Chagrin River Road in Moreland Hills near his home. Dr. Romano's body was discovered in the back seat of his vehicle. One arm had been broken, and he had sustained a crushing blow to his head. He was shot twice in the head and then shot four more times in the groin. A sure sign for his many encounters and distasteful lifestyle of lust. During this period, only a few men were brought in by the local police for questioning. However, several of the usual suspects were brought in for a quick examination, and no one was arrested or placed on trial or convicted of the murder of Dr. Romano. It would not be until years later when the FBI would find out from a reliable informant the name of the man who actually committed the crime.

Hence, it was learned that John DeMarco, along with his cousin Angelo Lonardo had first requested permission from Frank Milano to avenge the death of Angelo's Uncle Dominic Lonardo, by the hands of Dr. Joseph Romano. Allegedly, Romano put the contract out on Dominic Lonardo. Dominic went missing in California; his body could not be found. Milano realized the importance of the act, and did not hesitate and gave his permission for the brutal hit.

Romano's killing caused exceptional grief for the men in Cleveland organization and went as high as to reach the ears of Lucky Luciano as well as the other top Commission members who were outraged at Milano's impulsive action for allowing the hit to take place without the permission of the "Commission." The Commission members were furious at John DeMarco since he was already a made man and knew the rules of La Cosa Nostra.

However, as far as Lonardo was concerned, he was not at the time a made-man, so he was off the hook for now.

It has been speculated that Al Polizzi needed to react quickly to save DeMarco's life, so he promptly stepped in. The meeting was set up to be in Miami, Florida. Polizzi arrived speaking for Frank Milano and the Cleveland Organization as he took up the great and courageous challenge and the defense of one of their own, John DeMarco. Polizzi calmly discussed the reason why Milano authorized the hit on Romano. After the polished and professional Polizzi had related the critical ideas, they did not know of and had explained the reason for the run on Romano. The Commission decided to accept the strong defense given to them. John DeMarco's life was saved from a condemned death sentence with Milano's help from Mexico and the fantastic display of courage and support by Polizzi.

12

1937

Major racketeer Moe Dalitz teamed up with Frank and Tony Milano and became engaged in the gambling. At first, they began opening up gambling houses and then started muscling their way into some of the best places in Ohio. It is believed that with the help of associates from the Milano family, these men took over a share of the profits without putting up any money. The clubs included the famous *Jungle Inn* in Youngstown, *The Thomas Club, The Harvard Club, The Arrow Club* on Pettibone Road, which would later reopen as *The Pettibone Club* in 1946. Another site near and dear to their hearts was their own *Ohio Villa Club*, owned by the Milano brothers. It was later renamed The Richmond Country Club. This was on the property that Milano's owned in Richmond Heights. Like the other clubs, they fought long and hard with city officials and the Cuyahoga County Sheriff's Department and remained open for many years. For a short while, this site would become the home of the Italian-American Brotherhood Club, which featured the famous Italian singers like Perry Como. The club would later burn to the ground in a massive fire, luckily no one died in the accident.

The trio of men ventured into the southern portion of Ohio, and took over the *Coney Island Race Track* in Cincinnati and helped to rename it "River Downs." Their next step was going to the city of Chesapeake, where they operated a large casino named the *Continental Supper Club*.

By 1939, with Frank being self-exiled to Mexico, he still held power as he was known as the president of the Lubeck Beer Distribution Company, which began operating in 1933, and in 1943, he was referred to as a significant partner in the Tip Top Brewing Company.

Then in 1945, Frank had collaborated with Fred Garmone. Both men were found guilty of operating a wholesaling enter without first obtaining a liquor permit. An article in the famous "LOOK" magazine named Frank Milano as a director of the National Crime Rackets.

It was in early January 1947 when the Los Angeles office of the FBI was advised that their local kingpin, Mickey Cohen was attempting to open up an impressive gambling joint in the heart of Los Angeles, and had imported five men from the Cleveland Syndicate to help him. Cohen had been in contact with singer Frank Sinatra on some sort of deal and introduced Sinatra to Frank Minnitis. Cleveland FBI office then advised that Minnitis was Vice-President of the Standard Excavating Company of Cleveland, and was a close friend of both Frank and Anthony Milano.

Within the same period, the Miami, Florida FBI office advised the Cleveland office that a reliable informant had mentioned how a prominent and influential Chicago underworld figure named Joe Fischetti was now operating in Cleveland. They claimed Fischetti has discrete ties with the Cleveland syndicate through Frank Brancato, and both the Milano brothers. In Florida, last winter Fischetti was seen with Frank Sinatra. It is noted; that Al Polizzi, the old boss in Cleveland, now lives in Florida and that Fischetti had been rumored to be the possible owner of Sinatra's lucrative music contract.

A *Cleveland News* article was written on October 13, 1950, by Drew Pearson. The headline read, **"Mafia uses its Friends and Protectors in High Places."**

Mentioned in the article was Frank Milano from Akron, Ohio. Milano is known as a top force of the Ohio Mafia leaders, and intimately connected to Mafia leaders in Chicago, and in Michigan. He was also the boss of the old Mayfield Road Gang. Milano has connections with West Coast Mafia Boss Jack Dragan and his brother Anthony, who now lives in Hollywood, California.

Mentioned next in the article was "Big Al" Polizzi of Coral Gables, Florida, and considered second to Frank Milano in the Ohio Mafia. It has been told that Al has his fingers into many legitimate enterprises, including importing olive oil and food, along with being an owner of a beer distribution center and a real estate developer in Coral Gables.

Many of the upcoming Kefauver Committee's hearings were being aimed at proving that an Italian–Sicilian organization based on developing strong family ties, and centrally controlled a vast empire of an organized crime conspiracy in the United States.

When the Desert Inn opened in 1950, Frank Milano was said to have been at the gala Grand Opening. It has been strongly alleged that Milano and his Cleveland Syndicate invested $500,000 into the Desert Inn.

By 1950, Sam Haas was considered a wealthy man in many circles. His estimated net worth was claimed to be over $2.5 million, as he successfully invested in over forty companies. Some listed to be Detroit Steel, Warner Brother's Corp., and Morgan Steel.

SAMUEL HASS

(Courtesy of the Cleveland Police Museum)

1953

After a fatal heart attack in January while in Mexico, Frank Milano returned to his home to Akron, Ohio. The reason was to recover and seek better medical attention. It was now June as the sixty-two-year-old Frank Milano, found two agents from the INS waiting for him at his home when he arrived. The officers wished to interview and question him at great length about his recent activities across the border. The agents held no arrest warrant, although they requested him to come to the federal building in downtown Cleveland for an extensive interview. Milano, listen to his attorney's caution and was very careful, not to violate any of the Federal Immigration laws concerning his personal residence outside America. The request to meet with the INS was denied by Milano physician, who claimed Milano's heart was too frail and terribly weak, and this undue pressure and stress could cause a possible second heart attack.

Milano's only comment to the INS investigators was he could not understand why they wish to speak to him. It was a complete mystery. However, he did insist he was covered under a particular section of the naturalization laws and was viewed as the reason for their visit.

Wanting to deport as many gangsters as possible, after the Kefauver Hearings, the government looked for any and all possibilities to get rid of these so-called criminals. An exceptional yet combative condition in the INS laws states, (That a person could lose his citizenship if he lives outside the United States for more than two years at one time.) Milano has been in Vera Cruz, Mexico, since 1934 when he left in fear of a lengthy prison term, as he tried to avoid income tax evasion charges.

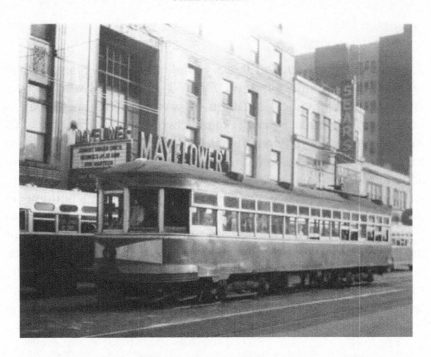

THE MAYFLOWER HOTEL ON MAIN STREET IN AKRON.

(Courtesy of Cleveland State University Memory Project)

One week before the Feds came hunting for Milano, he was in Ohio for the wedding of his daughter Grace, who was married at St. Sebastian's Church. The gala reception was held at the magnificent Mayflower Hotel, where Milano reserved two full floors of luxurious suites for his close friends and out of town guests. Milano states he has not missed a Christmas in Ohio with his family since he went to Mexico, and he has not been in any other violation of any INS regulation. This first and enthusiastic testimony was for the Feds benefit to ensure he does not lose his cherished citizenship.

J. Russell Bramlett, the chief INS agent in Cleveland, stated, "This is not the first time we have sought to interview Mr. Frank Milano. Milano has only one-convection is his lengthy police record, and that was back in 1926 for the possession of beer and wine and fined $300. Milano was considered the prime suspect in the gangland slaying of Joe Porrello and Sam Tilocco back in 1930. Milano was reluctantly released when no evidence could be found connecting him to the double murder. Milano was generally known as; "The King of Mayfield."

In 1958, while Frank was winding down his courageous and influential career, he relaxed and lived part-time in the Hotel Commodore in Los Angles, and the rest of his time between Akron, Ohio and Vera Cruise Mexico, before he passed away with his wife Marie and his children by his side.

13

ALFRED POLIZZI

(Courtesy of Cleveland State University Archives)

Alfred "The Owl" Polizzi, was born on March 15, 1900, and became known as a top Cleveland mobster who helped establish the powerful criminal syndicate operations throughout Northern, Ohio. Alfred was born in Siculiana, a Provence of Agrigento, Sicily. Polizzi immigrated to the United States with his family within the same year.

During the early 1930s, Polizzi worked alongside his older brother Joseph Polizzi, Frank, and Anthony Milano and allied with the powerful Jewish gangster Moe Dalitz. Alfred would marry Philomena Valentino, the sister of Anthony Milano's wife Josephine, the couple was blessed with three children.

In Rick Porrello's *"The Rise and Fall of the Cleveland Mafia"* In 1924, Al was working his way up the criminal ladder with great success and trying to make some extra money, as he found himself involved in the hot, hard-hitting and feverish Circulation Wars.

These wars started in Cleveland when Thomas McGinty, enjoyed a strong reputation as an aggressive organizer as he hired desperate young mean-looking men who chased away Arthur McBride's younger newspaper hustlers from the best locations and corners in the downtown area. McBride quickly retaliated and hired the toughest hoodlums he could find from around the city. The thugs now used lead pipes to break arms and to intimidate and regain control of the most essential selling sites, which returned the highly profitable territories for selling newspapers. Several of the more desperate young thugs went on to join two of the most potent Prohibition forces in Cleveland.

In the Italian community on the Eastside of Cleveland, Frank Milano's gang was active, young, and aggressive as the Angersola brothers Fred, George, and John, alongside Al Polizzi, were known as Frank's right arm or "Lieutenant." Frank Brancato, Charlie Colletti, and several others were seen as low-level "muscle men" at this time. Polizzi was the tallest of the Sicilian men as he stood five feet ten inches tall, and later garnered the nickname "Big Al."

At first, Charles Polizzi was believed by many to be Al's actual brother. The reality was, they were not related at all. Charles found himself an orphan at a very young age when he arrived in Cleveland. Alfred's mother and father adopted him into their loving Sicilian family. Charles Polizzi Jewish heritage had already developed a secure connection with the local Jewish mob.

It was in 1926 when Alfred Polizzi, was first arrested on charges of violating the Prohibition Act and was fined $1,000 and served six months in jail.

1930

From *"The Rise and Fall of the Cleveland Mafia"* by Rick Porrello, 1930 proved to be a significant point in the prohibition era for the Milano Brothers.

Frank Milano told his Lieutenant Al Polizzi to set up a meeting with the boss of the Porrello's gang, Joe Porrello and invited him to join Frank in an Italian card game known as "Ziganette" at his Murray Hill Restaurant called "The Venetian," the meeting was set for a Saturday afternoon. Joe believed it could be useful for business and patch up their differences. Joe thought only about peace between the two rivals, and to hopefully gain control of Milano's slot machine business.

It was August 23, as the city of Cleveland seems to be at its wits end with all the criminal activity when Chief of Police George Matowitz promised to stage his own war on the gangsters and racketeers who continue to threaten their beautiful and peaceful city. It quickly materialized and became a reality when ten men were immediately arrested, and held at the Central Police Station as suspected gangsters. The people picked up on the streets, and among the list of sixty-four known criminals. The alleged criminal watch list was made-up by acting Detective Director Emmett Potts.

Some of the first ten men arrested in the Third Precinct where William Perice, Frank Russo, James Badalammenti, and John Cerni. Others on this so-called police, "hit list," consisted of John Angersola, who was arrested by federal investigators of liquor violation charges and questioned in the connection of the murder of Joe Porrello and Sam Tilocco. Others included were Charles Colette, Solly Hart, and Al Polizzi believed to be a leader of Milano's Mayfield Road Mob, along with Charles Polizzi.

1932

It was now March, and Alfred Polizzi was a partner in Milano and Polizzi Italian Imports, where he was arrested with eleven other men inside of their Italian Imports store. Charles Coletti, Charles and John Angersola, who were known, bootleggers and rumrunners. Also arrested was Frank Milazzo, who owns a local nightclub along with Frank and Angelo Cullura. Angelo has only been out of jail for a mere 2-hours after being accused of participating in the murdering of a rival gangster, Fred Capillo, last Wednesday. Others indicted were Charles Coletti, Mike Arizone, Joe Fratico, Joe Marinelo, and Phil Sidario. These men had been charged with planning to kill Willie Richardson, a well-known black policy-operator.

The twelve-men arrested last month finally came to court in April as Milano, with Polizzi sitting next to their attorney Martin McCormack, seemed to hide from the cameras as the photographers tried in vain to get a good picture of the two colorful gangsters for the front page. McCormack fought hard for his client's rights as he informed Judge Oscar Bell, how the so-called City Ordinance, dealing with being a "suspicious person," needed to be squashed. It was against the current Ohio and United States Constitution. "The arrest of a person must actually be about a particular situation and not how the defendants were seen as a suspicious person in a crime. He appropriately explained, the police cannot go around and just stop anyone they wish on the streets, under this clumsy category."

Assistant Prosecutor Dennis Lyons requested from Judge Bell, a two-week grace period to investigate these controversial comments and accusation and to give the court the proper response. The twelve men proudly stood; walk slowly and confidently out of the courtroom to their freedom. In the hallway where plenty of newspapermen and photographers bothered them once again about taking their picture and asking them silly questions about their arrest and criminal lifestyle.

Over the next several months, the Cleveland detectives continuously brought several of the top known racket men in for questioning. This included Al and Chuck Polizzi.

Over the years, another exciting venture became a reality as the Molaska Distillery operated out of several secure locations across the country. However, the Ohio plant was considered to be one of the largest and located at 5301 Sweeny Avenue. When arriving at the dilapidated property, you would first think the building was vacant and condemned and had been closed down for several years. Unknown to the public was that nearby, at Truscon and Fifty-Fifth Street, sat the massive holding tanks. The property was registered in the name of Molaska Products Company. With incredible yet brilliant planning, by the gangsters, and engineers as they hide the complex, and the plant operation from the local police, and noisy interfering neighbors. The planners brilliantly placed and tied the necessary exhaust vents into the building next door at 5221 Sweeny Avenue, the home of Sweeny Metal Company. The sharp criminal minds added a new six-inch water line into the building, which was routed underground from the primary city water system and was virtually undetected. This allowed the distillery to obtain fresh free water whenever they needed it. Electricity was not a problem as well, as they illegally tapped into a neighbor's building and used their power from the Oxford Machine Company.

Lew Wasserman began his show business career as publicity director at the Mayfair Casino, which opened in Cleveland in 1935. The Mayfair was actually owned by a group of investors, Moe "The Chinaman" Dalitz, his nickname came from his many connections with laundry and dry cleaning business. Louis "Rody" Rothkopf, Morris "The Banker" Kleinman, Sam Tucker, Sam Haas, John Angersola, "Big Al" Polizzi, Chuck Polizzi became the public front for some of their illegal operation. The Angersola's and Polizzi's were now the leaders of the Mayfield Road Mob. Moe Dalitz, Louis Rothkopf, Morris Kleinman, Sam Tucker were known as the Jewish "Big Four" of the Cleveland underworld and was commonly known as "The Cleveland Syndicate."

THE DOROTHY BYTON GIRLS PERFORMING

AT THE MAYFAIR CASINO AND THEATER IN

THE OHIO THEATER DISTRICT OF

DOWNTOWN CLEVELAND IN 1936

(Courtesy of the Cleveland State Memory Project)

14

MOLASKA DISTILLERY

(Courtesy of Mr. Mob and the National Archives)

By the end of the year, The Molaska Corporation, which started out as a small processing plant for dehydrated molasses and grew to become a significant whiskey bottling company, now had filed for bankruptcy and was quickly dissolved. The partners in the Buckeye Enterprises included Dalitz, Tucker, Rothkoph, John Angersola. Chuck and Al Polizzi and several others who claimed to have lost $16,661 on their personal income that year. (In today's money, this is equal to $307,018.) In reality, the mobsters probably profited five times as much or more from their original investment. One estimate placed the total bill to build the plant to be over $250,000.

A few years later, the gangsters closed another plant in Zanesville only after the plant was discovered and raided by ATF agents in January 1935. In their prime, both plants reportedly made

5,000 barrels of 90-proof alcohol per week and shipped it across the country in railroad cars. At one time, the plant was said to have over 48,600 pounds of corn sugar and over 15,000 pounds of molasses stored and ready to be made into beer. The facility also produced over 36,500 barrels of beer, which was shipped out in the same fashion. Whether it is dumb luck, bribery, smart business decisions, or spiritual intervention from above, none of the gangsters were ever convicted of operating this incredible distillery where they all enjoyed great wealth.

On the contrary, Louis Rothkoph was soon arrested after the closing of the plants and was sentenced for illegal liquor production. The so-called information of his involvement in the plant came from a secret government wiretap. The judge condemned him to 4-years in jail, it was no surprise that he served only eight months. His attorney got him out when he showed the feds used an illegal wiretap to catch him.

THE MOLASKA DISTILLERY LOCATED ZANESVILLE, OHIO

(Courtesy of Mr. Mob and the National Archives)

1936

Meanwhile, Al Polizzi was the "Boss" in the Cleveland Mayfield Road Gang; however, he had a secret partnership with the Jewish mob and Moe Dalitz. The men enjoyed a close, respectful, and profitable relationship. Polizzi remained quiet as he became wealthy well into the late 1940s when he moved to Florida.

A memo was found in the *Cleveland State University Special Addition* Center dated July 1938. Alfred "Big Al" Polizzi was telling a newspaper writer that he is no longer a gangster, and now lives in the quiet community of Cleveland Heights. I'm no longer connected with the criminal rackets in any way, nor am I in the slot business, bootlegging, or the policy rackets. I do admit, being a bootlegger many years ago, and connected with the Milano's and the Lonardo brothers. Polizzi did not reply or deny if he was at one-time connected with Frank Joiner and the Slot Machine business when Joiner was murdered. Polizzi states he now controls and operates Lubeck Beer Distributors, which is not a racket owned brewery, and a legitimate company that sells beer they produce to *Thistledown Racetrack*, and *The Ohio Villa Casino* in Richmond Heights only because my friends operate them. No one has ever been forced or under duress to buy from my company. My only connection with *The Ohio Villa* is that I am one of the founders and a proud member of the Italian American Brotherhood Club, which in fact, owns the property.

Nevertheless, I am not a partner or an officer of the club. Charles Polizzi is as close to me as a cousin and called Chuck by his friends, which he enjoys. Polizzi continued and stated that he does not know if Chuck or his brother Raymond was in any of the past criminal rackets, although we all knew he was running the *City Vending Machine Company*, the most prominent licensed company under the old City Slot Ordinance.

Al Polizzi claims he has even gone as far as to warn some of the younger Italians to quit treating shopkeepers with broken windows if they do not pay up a fee for their safety. Polizzi claims the *Lubeck Company* is a significant business operation, and neither his Attorney Eddie Stanton nor Mickey McBride has invested in it with him."

1938

By September, Al Polizzi, the President of *Lubeck Distributing Company,* was withdrawn as a person of interest named in a lawsuit against the notorious *Thomas Club* in Maple Heights. Later this year, *Lubeck Distribution*; would be cited by the Federal Government for selling illegal liquor and lost its license to operate and sell beer.

1939

By mid-June, Al Polizzi and Charles Coletti found themselves in front of Judge Mary Grossman and being accused of three bombing attempts, which have taken place on the Westside of Cleveland in a fight to control the profitable whiskey business. The first bombing occurred at the homes of two men; John Schiemer and Paul Hackett, who operated the *Clean Rite Company*. Both men are also listed as a suspicious person in bombing the house of Nate Weisenberg. The case was scheduled to be heard in October as both men were given a $1,000 bond.

This time, Al Polizzi (aka Alfonso) found himself indicted for testifying falsely in requesting and obtaining his citizenship and naturalization papers, which he received in June 1928. The men are now in jeopardy of losing their citizenship by Federal District Attorney Emerich Freed. The charges alleged Polizzi, Angelo Sciria, and Frank Milazzo, which have all been accused of being in the policy rackets and connected to the illegal gambling club named, The *Paddock Club*. All apparently lied to a naturalization inspector when they falsified information on their application, that they had never been arrested as a suspicious person. Polizzi and his attorney now adamantly protested against the Federal Court ruling; to set aside his current citizenship papers and deny him any privileges as an immigrant status for all time.

By November in an unexpected move: US. District Attorney Emerich Freed was taken by surprise when he received a directive from the INS in Washington to drop the naturalization charges and the prosecution against Alfred Polizzi. Rumors around Cleveland at this time speculating how Polizzi was starting to buy some real-estate in and around the Gold Coast area in Florida. This was seven years before he moved down to Coral Gables and become a permanent and well-respected resident. Polizzi friends the Angersola Brothers, and Mickey McBride was also looking at Florida for a safe, peaceful haven of their own.

IN FLORIDA, LEAVING CHURCH ON SUNDAY.

Al Polizzi in the center in white #1 along with Mickey McBride #3 speaking with a friend.
(Courtesy of Mr. Mob and the National Archives)

15

1943

Closing in on five days before Christmas, Polizzi found himself receiving an unwanted and unexpected surprise. He, along with a business partner Attorney Fred Garmone and Sonny Vogt from Chicago, noticed they have been accused by the federal government of operating and conspiracy of running a "Black Market" sale of illegal whiskey. Garmone is a former assistant police prosecutor in Cleveland, and Al is still the President of the *Tip Top Brewing Company*. The men were arraigned by the now U.S. District Judge, Emmich Freed on twenty-eight charges of a conspiracy, and operating in the black liquor market. The charges consisted of failing to keep accurate records of all purchases and sales as required by federal law, then selling their whiskey at a higher rate than the $21 allowed by the OPA.

It seems the lawsuit was brought to the attention of the Federal Government; Charles Bodek, Abraham Miller, and Joseph Hecht all formerly held controlling shares and stock in *The Tip Top Company*. The brewery was estimated to produce one million barrels of beer a year, which consisted of their popular *Carlings Red Cap Ale and Black Label Beer*. At this time, *Tip Top* was viewed as one of the largest breweries in the country with estimated sales of 25 Million dollars per year.

The three men are alleged to have brought in illegal whiskey into Ohio from Chicago early in February and September this year and selling it at prices above the going rate set by the Office of Price Administration (OPA) ceiling.

ATTORNEY FRED GARMONE IN 1954

(Courtesy of the Cleveland State University Memory Project)

Polizzi, Garmone, and Joseph Deutsch were all being charged with having operated the wholesale liquor distribution dealership without applying for a federal permit or receiving a license that is required by law. One charge against the two- men, states Garmone purchased 801 cases of Old Still Rum and 350 cases {cost of only $10.24 a case} of Stuart Lloyd Whiskey and illegally transported it across the state lines of Illinois into Ohio. Polizzi issued a personal check of $35,856 as a down payment for the liquor purchase, where each case was sold for over $21 a case.

On Christmas Eve, the three men filed not guilty pleas in front of Judge Freed on the charges against them of operating a "Black Market" liquor sale business.

1944

Four of Cleveland's top labor leaders were now being investigated and found to have owned shares in Al Polizzi *Tip Top Brewing and Distribution Companies,* which were both being investigated for partaking in illegal Black-market liquor sales. The stockholders listed were William Finegan, the President of the Cleveland Federation of Labor and business agents of the International Alliance of Theatrical Stage Employees Local #27. Thomas Finegan, Secretary of the Cleveland Federation of Labor. Edward Murphy, the President of the Teamsters Joint Council. John Fitzgerald, the President of the International Alliance of Theatrical Stage Employees and Legislation agent for the Cleveland Federation of Labor. During the intense Federal investigation, it was proven that these men all joined as shareholders in 1941 when Polizzi took over the reins as President of Tip Top.

Seeing how the brewery business is getting dangerous for him, Polizzi decides to see if he can sell his lucrative shares of the *Tip Top Brewery Corporation* located on Davenport Road. By July, a deal was worked out by the Brewing Corporation of America to purchase Tip Top and the Waldorf Brewing Companies for what is being considered the highest price to date for a merger of this magnitude. One million dollars was the offer (equal to $14,362,908 in today's money) and is being considered by Polizzi. According to the proposed agreement, both the Tip Top building, which makes 800,000 barrels capacity a year, and the Waldorf who makes 200,000 barrels capacity a year will remain in full operation.

BEER BOTTLING IN 1944

(Courtesy of the Authors collection)

The new year was not any better for Al Polizzi. After an in-depth investigation by a Federal Grand Jury, Polizzi was now being accused of and facing indictments in a gasoline scandal. For their help in the war effort of WWII, six men had appeared before Federal Judge Freed on charges of illegally obtaining gas T-stamps for over 350,000 gallons of gas. As a result of the gasoline rationing, all forms of automobile racing, including the famous Indianapolis 500, were banned. The six people included Alfred Polizzi, Richard Allen, a former Ohio Department of Transportation District Manager, and Robert Dissauer, a former chief clerk of the Federal ration board. Then there was Myron Bernstein, who operates a rubber company on Rockwell Avenue, Mrs. Eleanor Minnery formerly a clerk in the ODT office in Cleveland, and Fred Garmone, a former City assistant prosecutor.

GASOLINE RATION STAMP

(Courtesy of Wikipedia)

The extended charges consist of planning to conspire to make false statements to the ODT board so that their business could obtain additional gas stamps, and then controlling the distribution of ration coupons. The Feds are looking to charge them all with twelve other counts of fraud. No ruling was ever found for this accusation.

The case of illegally selling whiskey finally came to court in October of 1944, as both Polizzi and Garmone have been accused of selling over $83,000 in liquor sales. Both men plead guilty to a lesser charge of having dealt with the purchase of a large volume of whiskey without first getting the simple low-cost $127 required dealers license.

In Judge Freed's Federal Court, U.S. District Attorney Frank Steel made his opening statement, which included they have sufficient proof and can eagerly show the government how Polizzi and Garmone visited Ulrich (Sonny) Vogt in Chicago. The whiskey shortage in Ohio was at its peak as the men purchased over 1,751 cases and acquired them in April 1943. The out of state liquor came from *the Peerless Liquor Company* and then sold illegally in Ohio, for a substantial profit. The government noted how Polizzi's *Tip Top Company* was successfully solicited by a courageous group of 54 bar and restaurant owners for his help.

The government did not apparently have enough substantial evidence, and the plea deal was soon conceived as the men plead guilty in Judge Freed's Federal Court to a lesser charge of engaging in the wholesale of liquor business without having the license. The people were free of charges of having violated the OPA regulation of operating an illegal black-market whiskey distribution center until their upcoming sentencing in November.

TIPTOP BREWERY 1941

(Courtesy of Cleveland State University Archives Division)

At the same time, both Polizzi and Garmone; are being accused of lying to Federal Judge Emrich Freed about the amount of money they profited from the sales of the abundant supply of illegal whiskey. Garmone claimed he only made $825, and Polizzi declined to say how much he actually made. Judge Freed was furious after being informed by a liquor probation department that the actual amount of cases of whiskey sold, should have gained the men at least a profit of $156,000 to as high as $250,000.

At their hearing, Judge Freed called Garmone up to the bench first and stated, "Your statement Mr. Garmone is that you only made $825 from the sale of the whiskey. I'm going to give you one last chance to tell the probation department an accurate figure, so I know how to sentence you?"

Garmone quickly turned and softly spoke with his Attorney Parker Fulton when Judge Freed exploded and yelled, "There will be no secret conferences in this court. You can tell me right now whether you would like additional time, to speak the truth, or want to be sentenced on the face of things as they stand right now." Polizzi and Garmone looked at one another as both stood and asked for the additional time to review their earlier figures. Reluctantly Judge Freed granted their request until November 15.

When November 15 came around, Polizzi with his attorney Elmer McNully, and Garmone with his Attorney Parker Fulton arrived in Federal Court in downtown Cleveland, and in front of Judge Freed. Judge Freed soon opened the sentencing hearing before either man could speak with saying, "It is my considered judgment that both of you men were in these operations jointly. You either made significant profits than you have admitted, or you turned the profits over to others who identities you are still concealing." Each of your sentences will be eighteen months in jail and a $5,000 fine, as both men were quickly taken out of the courtroom and being sent to the Federal prison in Milan, Michigan.

Before the end of the year, Polizzi found himself convicted of income tax evasion, as well. It was at this time, he decided to move his family to Coral Gables, Florida. By this point in his criminal career, U.S. Senate investigators described Polizzi as "one of the most influential members of the underworld in the United States."

1950

It was the end of June as Al Polizzi, and his family has been living quietly full time now in the amazingly beautiful and sunny Miami, Florida, in the community of Coral Gables. Until recently, Polizzi has filed a libel lawsuit against *Cowels Magazine Inc.* of New York who publishes the very popular *"Look Magazine."* The straightforward lawsuit is based on the May 23 article, which named Polizzi as a member of the Grand Council of the Mafia leaders in the United States. The article was titled, *"The Super government,"* which defiantly mentioned Polizzi as a part of the national and worldwide criminal organization of "La Cosa Nostra." The article claimed this group of powerful men has long and vigorous arms, stretching and reaching into many different political pockets and reaching into the Senate, the Cabinet, and even the White House itself, along with every state capital building in the country.

Polizzi filed the wrongful complaint saying, *"Look Magazine"* made several false, combative and defamatory comments as well as outrageous, libelous statements about him. He courageously and immensely denied ever being a part of or a member of this so-called Mafia. Polizzi admits that he had once been a "counselor" for a group of Italians and denies ever participating in any of its illegal activities. Polizzi and his attorney filed a $1 Million lawsuit against the magazine.

Polizzi brilliantly defended himself and stated, "He is proudly invested in the construction business and established his residence here in Florida back in 1945 and has been an honest and upright citizen who is law-abiding and trustworthy.

16

1951

As we look into the personal connection of Alfred Polizzi and the famous Kefauver hearings that took place in Cleveland, Ohio. In regards to Polizzi, the committee already knows of his meaningful relationships across the country and exceptional close ties with Milano. Frank Milano has been alleged to be one of the biggest and one of the most influential men in organized crime throughout the United States.

Polizzi had served six months in jail and paid a $1,000 fine for bootlegging charges against back him in 1936 and then again in 1939 when he was the President of the *Lubeck Beverage Distribution Company* and then in 1944 when he was the President of the *Tip Top Beverage Company*.

In a bold and brave move to protect his good name, Al Polizzi at first refused the Government polished invitation to come to Cleveland from Florida to testify in front of the Kefauver national crime committee. However, he did offer instead to attend the Washington D.C Committee hearing where he would testify. In this unexpected and decisive move, Polizzi escaped being the fourth man in Cleveland to be indicted for not answering the specific and often difficult questions asked of him. In DC, Polizzi took his Fifth Amendment rights about the illegal actives that he or his friends may have or may not have been involved in Cleveland or other portions of the country.

Polizzi was now regarded to be a good, honest family man and churchgoer who is also a well-dressed and respected member of the community and often seems to be well-connect. A successful builder in the construction business in Coral Gables, Florida, where he aligned with men like Attorney Samuel Hass from Cleveland, Mickey McBride, Tommy McGinty, Charles Bernstein, and A.E Gordon a lawyer with Hass.

Now back in Cleveland on January 17, Parker Fulton, who is representing Al Polizzi told the Senate committee, that he has been severely thinking of filing a lawsuit as he objected to answering specific questions and the scope of the combative, foolish subpoena asking his client to attend the criminal hearings. Fulton pleasantly objected to the court's single-action asking Polizzi to turn over all his personal and business financial records since 1945, as well as all of his income tax reports filed in his name.

Polizzi stated he is not involved in any type of organized crime or other illegal activities in Florida or across the country for that matter. Fulton firmly proclaimed and filed a formal objection to his client's current affairs and these tiresome and outrageous questions, which falls way outside the committee's purview and does not involve Mr. Polizzi at any level. Making a courageous gesture to the committee, Polizzi has turned over his property deeds listing his ownership in a boat named the *"Wood Duck"*(which he purchased from McBridge) along with his partnership with *"The Sands Hotel"* in Miami, Florida. In addition, Al turned over other related Cleveland properties he still owns or has sold along with his current home in Coral Gables.

Forced to testify, it was now Thursday, January 18, and viewed to be "Big Al" Polizzi's turn on the tension-filled courtroom inside the Federal Building in downtown Cleveland. Polizzi, with his Attorney Parker Fulton at his side, seemed well prepared for the rapid-fire of the problematic question coming from the committee members.

Mr. Polizzi asked if he may first address the court with an opening statement, which was readily allowed by Senator Kefauver, hoping that Polizzi would incriminate himself. Polizzi stood tall in his designer suit and proudly spoke openly and professionally as he stated, "Senator, I had led a peaceful life ever since 1944 when I left Cleveland. I went for one purpose, and one proposes only, and that was to get all the way, away from all the

"Old stuff and accusations," which has been thrown at me repeatedly over the years. I had had nothing else but heart-aches and anguish when I lived there. I haven't made all of my money illegally, over the years, most of it was made legally, and I did have some to start with. I perhaps may have begun my life in the wrong way. However, that has changed and changed for the better."

With Kefauver leading the line of questions, the Government was ready to attack Polizzi. Joseph Nellis led the list of Attorneys and Senators, including Senator Kefauver and Charles Tobey from New Hampshire, who was licking their lips to ask and to finally hear what Polizzi had to say about his personal involvement in organized crime.

Over one hundred questions were asked during Polizzi's stress-filled session. The first seemed to be how much he was worth and where he obtained his vast fortune. Then most of the others had to deal with people or criminals he knew or knows, and if he was in business with them and his role as the so-called mob boss in Cleveland. The committee asked if he knew note-worthy people like Frank and Anthony Milano, Mickey McBride, the brothers John, George Angersola, The committee then asked about Vincent (Doc) Mangine, a local gambler, Sam, and his brother Morris Hass. They even inquired about the famous Al Capone, Detroit criminal boss Peter Licavoli and his brother James Licavoli who is a well-known racketeer in Ohio. Polizzi was then asked, "If he knew Mickey Cohen when he was in Cleveland, or now that he is living in Los Angeles." Additional questions included, "if the Mayfield Road Gang was really the so-called The Black Hand Society."

The committee was now interested in an assortment of issues dealing with his relationship with the murder of "Slot Czar" Nate Weisenberg and his involvement in the slot machine business along with his partnership with Buckeye Catering Company. Their interest moved to Charles Polizzi, who has been called his cousin, and Morris Klienman, a notorious gambler associated with some of the top Jewish gangsters like Moe Dalitz.

The anxious and nervous Polizzi and his attorney answered some of the questions with as few words as possible. Many times, a simple yes or no was his tense response. Others were responded to with I am not sure, or I cannot remember as they denied and refused to answer over 35 percent of the questions asked of him, with "a very vague response or I prefer not to respond to that question, or I just refuse to answer." As many of his answers were vague and did not reveal much if any information to the select committee. Nevertheless, he did omit that he was arrested for bootlegging back in the 1930s during Prohibition and was in the slot machine business for a short time. Attorney Parker Fulton often told Polizzi not to answer the question and usually bitterly protested to the Senators on how their problems were stated and attacking his client's good name and that the issues they are interested in, were in his past and not of any importance to what his client is now aligned with.

By the end of the long and grueling session, Polizzi and his attorney looked to be both physically and mentally exhausted and could not wait for the questioning and the day to end. Kefauver and the other Senators seem wide-eyed with concern over Polizzi's election to not answer all of their questions honestly and truthfully, and they would be filing a Federal Contempt of court charges against him, for not co-operating.

It was announced in the Detroit Kefauver Committee session, how they would allow Polizzi to testify once again in a closed-door meeting in Washington D.C. on February 18. Again, Al Polizzi dressed in an impressive dark silk suit, as he sat quietly with Fulton next to him as the men whispered to one another. Polizzi looked very nervous and yet charming seated in a chair and seem to be ready to answer all the questions and co-operate with the group of Senators in the Kefauver Crime hearings. The same issues he had refused to respond while in the Cleveland Hearing where now haunting him once again. Polizzi told the Senate Crime Committee he is now worth an estimated $300,000 and that in the last six years in the building and construction business, his assets have doubled, and his income tax has been about the same.

Polizzi, however, did deny any connection to or in business with organized crime members. His construction company is a legitimate business venture, and his collaboration at the time is with Forrest Thompson and James Licavoli, who was paroled from the Ohio Penitentiary after Thompson promised the parole board, that he would hire Licavoli to work in his company. Polizzi also stated how his business has built a prominent shopping center, which included a grocery store and a theater for Arthur "Mickey" McBride, who was an old-time taxicab magnate and is now in the middle of building a $400,000 school for the city of Miami.

In a threatening voice, Senator Tobey attacked Polizzi, raising his deep voice and almost considered yelling at him, "How much money will you make on the deal with McBride?"

Polizzi sat calmly and stated, "He did not know."

Tobey retaliated with vigor, "will it be $300,000 or $52,000?"

Polizzi stated he thought that the figures were too high.

Tobey now asked, "If he knew Moe Dalitz, who had operated mainly in Detroit, Cleveland, and Las Vegas?"

Polizzi remained calm and relaxed, and his simple response was, "the last time I saw Dalitz was when I went on a hunting trip with him to Mexico back in 1932, and he was with Morris Kleinman."

During his testimony in the highly explosive Kefauver Hearings, Polizzi stated he and his stepbrother Chuck were involved in several of the old casinos in Ohio.

It was now late June in Washington D.C. as Frank Costello was the focus for the members and seen as a significant milestone by many of the Senators on the Committee. Costello seemed very confused at times and did not come across as the "Boss" as a few of his comments and answers dealing with the Cleveland connections, which did not seem to be well thought out. Costello informed the committee he was, in fact, a partner in the Desert Inn Hotel in Las Vegas with other men from Cleveland including Morris Kleinman, Moe Dalitz, and has had some business dealings with a construction firm in Florida owned by Al Polizzi, Mickey McBride, and A.E Gordon. He also stated he has been in business with Morris Wexler from Cleveland, who operates the Empire News Wire Service, and another Clevelander Sammy "Gameboy" Miller, who is in the casino business with him in Miami's Island and the Francis Club's.

It was now August 22 as more trouble, and unwanted publicity was in-store for the 52-year old Al Polizzi as an article written by Joseph Guilfoyle reached the national newspapers.

He is a hotelkeeper, builder, and real estate developer while entertaining friends from Cleveland to Miami; as "Big" Al Polizzi alias Albert Allen who was once jailed for rum-running and was sought as a principal suspect in connection with a double murder. Polizzi served a short prison term for violating alcohol tax laws; however, since 1945, he has been on the straight and narrow path.

In his profitable real estate development business with his partner in Coral Gables, Polizzi has helped the community by building theaters, beautiful homes, supermarkets, and even schools. Believe to be a partner in the exclusive Sands Hotel on the beautiful Florida coast of Miami. Al's hair is still dark and well-groomed, and his voice is soft and sweet and does not sound like a harsh and rugged mobster. When asked about his earlier days in Cleveland as a Mob boss and his recent issues with the Senate Crime Commission hearings, he seems to winch. In one statement to the committee was "Senator, I don't like to answer those questions about my past; it just takes me back to a sad and terrible time in my life, and it tears me apart."

The Senate Crime investigators have combined their records on Polizzi and disclosed his criminal record:

1920: he had four cases against him involving a robbery with a revolver, no charges were filed

1921: was arrested as a suspicious person and released

1926: In regards to the National Prohibition Act, where he was found guilty and served six months in jail and paid a $1,000 fine

1927: arrested on a suspicious person charge and held in conjunction with the murder of Hyman "Nate" Weisenberg, a known slot machine baron. The charges were later dropped against him with a lack of evidence.

1928: he was arrested on a suspicious person charge, just on general principles and nullified by Judge Sawiski

1930: Cleveland Police Chief Jacob Graul distributed a circular among his prescient. "Wanted as a suspect in connection with the double murder." The wanted poster bore a picture of him and included a detailed physical description along with two other men. The order stipulated to, "Hold until other officers can arrive to interview the men in regards to the Joe Porrello and Sam Tilloco murder on July 5th inside Frank Milano's Restaurant on Mayfield Road." No closer or records can be found in regards to this poster.

1932: Al was arrested once again by a suspicious person on general principle, and was later released

1935: In Detroit, he was picked up as a suspected person and listed as a "Fugitive" and was published in a police notice, he was soon arrested. The next day the police had found there was no actual warrant for his detention, and he was released.

Al Polizzi found himself as a partner in "Buckeye Catering" which installed slot machines and cigarette machines in stores, taverns as well as other places around Ohio. Al's job was as a salesman where he would pay a friendly visit and ask businesses to allow his company to set the machines inside as they will share in the profits; "Who could dare say no to Big Al." Polizzi stated, "He sold his shares of the Buckeye Company in 1938 to his other partner, including the late Nate Weisenberg, John aka "John King" Angersola."

When asked about the Sands Hotel, Polizzi stated, "This hotel is for anyone and everyone to enjoy and relax in. It is a beautiful vacation location for the whole family to enjoy and has not been a hangout for gangsters of any kind, and we cater to between 5,000 and 7,500 people a season."

A POSTCARD FROM THE OLD SANDS HOTEL ERA 1950S

(Courtesy of Card Cow. Com)

17

1952

As the Kefauver hearings informed, millions of wide-eyed Americans. At first, the "Reality style" television show was welcomed with open, curious minds. Daily Americans would watch their B&W television screens, which brought these high-profile criminals right in front of their wide-open eyes. Yes, very few of the honest citizens knew some of the men they watched. While others only heard or read their names in local newspapers or about the so-call criminal institution called La Cosa Nostra or the Mafia.

Like so many other gangsters after the crime committee meetings, Al Polizzi was facing a hard-uphill challenge to clear his good name and the admired reputation while in Florida. The surreal possibility of deportation leered over his head as he openly reported a mistake in his earlier testimony. Polizzi testified, "he did not use the $300,000 of his old racket money when he moved to Florida." The reality was he did use it to set up his legal construction business. Polizzi is also accused in Federal Court in Miami of perjuring himself when he filled out and applied for his U.S. Citizenship many years ago.

Attorney Ernest Duhaime has filed a petition with the U.S. Court for stripping the dark-haired handsome, 52-year old, Italian-born Polizzi of his naturalized citizenship, which he received back in 1928. Polizzi directly swore on the federal affidavit, "that he had never been arrested, and did not have a police record at the time." This is in complete contradiction to his previous sworn testimony in the Kefauver hearings.

1953

By April, Polizzi's lawyers in Cleveland, James Paduano, and in Florida Parker Fulton are feverishly working diligently to help him survive this latest attempt at destroying his lavish lifestyle. Working together, they filed an assortment of plea deals asking the government to erase the old charges in his ancient past. Polizzi is enthusiastically asking to have his 1926 police arrest for bootlegging conviction expunged along with the outrageous 1944 charges of operating a Black-Market whiskey operation.

It was now the end of April, as the second request, which was filed in March, and then sent to the White House for review, was now depressingly left unanswered. This could only mean his proud and helpless plea for leniency never got past the powerful Justice Department and into the President's hands to read and to consider. This was the second time the fifty-three-year-old Polizzi sent his plea to President Truman directly. The first was in 1948, which did not go past the Department of Justice as well.

This new hopeful plea was sent directly to President Eisenhower; and was blocked once again by INS agents, as either a strange request for mercy, which had not been made public before today. Polizzi, with his attorney in Cleveland, James Paduano at his side, announced to the media, "He was surprised at how fast his clemency plea was turned down. These false accusations against Al from his past have already been clear-up. We really thought he had an excellent chance for a Presidential pardon." Paduano went on and stated, "He and Polizzi are looking to gather up between two to three hundred business and personal friends across the country who will be willing and able to testify to his sparkling impeccable moral behavior and good-hearted character as a good man and proud citizen."

It was now Tuesday, December 22, as two INS investigators; John Northup and James Heathermom testified at the denaturalization trial of Al Polizzi in front of Judge John Holland. Their carefully worded statements had to deal with Polizzi, who had merely and falsely signing his naturalization certificate; Northup stated, "He lied about never being arrested, or jailed and about being a dishonest and powerful racketeer figure while living in Cleveland, Ohio."

It was now the defenses turn to prove Polizzi as an honest, reliable man and honorable citizen. A group of influential, impressive character witnesses came from Florida to his aid in the all-day court battle. Two men merely came in to testify to Al Polizzi's respectable reputation in their beautiful city. The first man was a soft-spoken Dade County Circuit Judge Vincent Giblin, who elegantly testified, "He has known Polizzi since 1947, and his reputation in the community is "splendid." Next on the witness stand was Monsignor Thomas Comber, a priest at the Church of the Little Flower in Coral Gables, who testified, "Al has a solid reputation, in our church community as a good and moral character. I have personally known the Polizzi's for over six years. Al and his wife are among the more active members of our loving community."

It has taken a long year to finish the trial as it was closing in on Christmas. On Wednesday, the lengthy court battle of Defense Attorney's and the government facing off against one another finally concluded. Polizzi standing nervously in the courtroom next to his Attorney Louis Sabatino, listened carefully as a delightful Christmas gift was given to him, and his family by the Federal Government led by U.S. Attorney James Guilmartin. "The Federal Court had listened carefully to all the arguments and testimony in the problematic case both for and against Polizzi criminal past." After lengthy consideration, the final ruling by Judge John Holland graciously dismissed the lawsuit, which will now allow Alfred Polizzi to keep his American citizenship despite his recent testimony. With this judgment, the Government cannot bring up any new charges against Polizzi's naturalization situation.

Judge Holland proclaimed, "The government had boldly failed to show by a clear and convincing manner, and give adequate proof that Polizzi had committed a fraudulent claim of his acceptable behavior. The case had no facts collected after his initial 1938 questioning by agents."

Polizzi clearly stated, "I am just very thankful for the Judge's well-thought and important decision. My prayers have all been answered, not only mine but the prayers of my family and friends. I am thankful to everyone for their continual support."

1964

In late November, a memo became known to the FBI and listed by the Federal Bureau of Narcotics. It stated, "Al Polizzi is confirmed to be the most powerful underworld leaders currently operating within the United States, with multiple connections in the underworld."

1970

By the 1970s, Polizzi's influence reportedly extended across the country from Ohio to Central Florida and to Southern California while his old friend, Anthony Milano's son, Peter, was now the leader of the Los Angles crime family. Polizzi operated a very profitable construction company named the Thompson-Polizzi Construction Company. During Polizzi's career after 1944. Polizzi was never arrested or accused of any crime dealing with a narcotics violation while living in Florida.

1971

It was now October, and a single independent bid to build a shopping center by the Thompson-Polizzi Construction Company became a fantastic news story across the country. "*Newsday*," a Long Island, New York newspaper quoted Millionaire Bebe Rebozo, a close friend of President Nixon, has awarded a significant and impressive contract to Al Polizzi's firm. It was one of the six contractors bidding on the project. Polizzi's proposal to build the elaborate shopping center was the lowest at $673,839 (this is equal to $3,981,000 in today's money).

The story was about how Rebozo and the U.S. Loan Company have both capitalized on his close friends in Florida. During their intense investigation, *Newsday* found out that the loan to build the shopping center was secured by the Government.

REBOZO, HOOVER AND PRESIDENT NIXON

(Courtesy of the National Archives)

Rebozo quickly became a best friend and trusted financial and real estate advisor to Nixon. In 1968, Rebozo changed his political party from Democratic to Republican, to assist his friend.

In 1976, Rebozo was the subject of an intense bank fraud investigation. The loan application Rebozo filed was with Hudson Valley National Bank, located in Yonkers, New York. It stated that the loan was for residential real estate development when it was actually used for his business. Rebozo repaid the loan with interest, and the bank did not file a complaint against him.

Alfred Polizzi died peacefully of natural causes with his loving family by his side in May 1984 in the city that he loved and adored, Coral Gables Florida.

As a matter of fact, his good and trusted friends enjoyed being near one another. Morris Kleinman moved to Bay Harbor, Florida, just north of the Surfside community when he retired. In 1949, after the fascinating Newport Kentucky Club closed down, Sam Tucker moved to a lovely Surfside community just north of Miami Beach, while old pal Tommy McGinty lived in West Palm Beach.

18

ARTHUR B. "MICKEY" MCBRIDE

(Courtesy of the Cleveland Police Museum)

Born on March 20, 1888, and died on November 10, 1972, 18 months after his wife Mary Jane passed away in Coral Gables, Florida. McBride was the brave and ambitious founder of the Cleveland Browns in 1945 and controlled them until 1953. He was born in Chicago, and by the age of six, he was working for the publishing tycoon, William Hearts.

Arthur moved to Cleveland in 1913 to become the circulation manager of the *Cleveland News*, with a starting salary of $10,000 (equal to $255,900 in today's money.) His primary job was to organize the young and sometimes innocent paperboys, newsstand vendors, and street corners around the city, which abundantly turned violent with the Circulation Wars. One of McBride's young fighters was Alfred "Big Al" Polizzi, and a friend named Morris "Mushy" Wexler. Both men would have a long and prosperous relationship with McBride.

By January 5, 1926, Municipal Judge Alva Corlett helped Police Chief Jacob Graul prepare arrest warrants and subpoenas, which were made in complete secrecy. McBride was charged with violation of the current gambling laws and with contempt of court. By the tenth, his attorney Sylvester McMahon won his release by fighting the charges with Chief Justice John P. Dempsey.

Making a small fortune in the newspaper business, he purchased his first apartment building in Lakewood, Ohio. In 1930, McBride went into business for himself, and in 1931 buying a majority share of the *Zone Cab Co.*, which operated 300 cabs at this time. By 1934, McBride's good influence on the city grew, as violence erupted between the taxi drivers of the *Yellow Cab* Company. Mayor Davis even ordered the *Yellow Cab* company off the streets to prevent further fighting between the cabbies. McBride was optimistic and gleaming with pride and in complete control of the Cleveland streets.

McBride used the information he received from an inside source that the *Yellow Cab* Drivers were the aggressor in the fights between the two companies. Many public officials in the city hall believed that McBride used his friendly personality and powerful influence with Mayor Davis to get this quick action and response. The local Taxi Union Local 555 went to bat for the Yellow drivers. Soon a hard-fought battle was worked-out, between the union and Yellow Cab lead by J. T. Smith and McBride's Zone Cab.

By July, McBride took a strategic step and merged Zone Cab with Yellow Cab Co to form the most significant taxi company with over 500 cabs on the city streets. McBride also owned taxicab companies in Akron and Canton, along with real estate in Chicago and Florida. By the end, McBride's rained as the "Taxi King," and controlled over 1,200 taxicabs in Ohio. It was common knowledge that the cab rates were regulated and noted that the current price for a cab driver to pay the company was 5 cents a mile. Sadly in 2017, the Yellow cab company closed and went out of business.

MAYOR HARRY L DAVIS

(Courtesy of Wikipedia)

By the late 1930s, McBride leveraged his astonishing newspaper connection to launch a wire service to help bookmakers across the country. His goal was to inform his customers of the updated horse race results. This necessary but straightforward business model put him with a direct link with a multitude of crime figures across the country that operated gambling joints. He invested his own money into the *Continental Press* and *Empire News*. Both were based in Cleveland and run by local mobsters Morris "Mushy" Wexler and Sam "Gameboy" Miller.

As a smart businessman, McBride purchased several buildings over the years. In 1939, he bought a building on Euclid Avenue and East 85th Street. McBride continued to expand his growing empire and purchased a construction company as well as several apartment buildings around the city. One was on the corner of Woodland and South Moreland Road, which he purchased for only $6,000 in 1942. Then in 1947, he sold the property at 333 Euclid Avenue for a pleasant 1 million dollars, an unheard-of amount at this time. One of McBride's trusted allies was Captain John Fleming of the Cleveland Police Department, who became a partner in one of his apartment buildings along with a paycheck from the Yellow Cab Company until 1941. Fleming became a trusted adviser for McBride and Al Polizzi as he negotiated many business deals for them. By the mid-1940s, McBride owned much of the residential and retail land on the north side of Lorain Avenue from West of 117th Street to West 130.

In April 1940, a federal grand jury indicted McBride and Morris Wexler. Both had worked for the Cincinnati-based *Western Union Telegraph Company* along with his father-in-law Thomas F. Kelly. Kelly was the former branch manager of the *Baltimore National News Service,* along with Lionel C. Lens. The *Baltimore National News* was considered a front and dealt with supplying information used in gambling. The allegations were based on the current federal laws that forbid the interstate transmission of lottery or horse racing results. McBride hired Martin McCormack to represent him, along with Kelly and Lenz, as well as Harry Payer and Morris Wexler. Attorneys fought to prove that phrase racing does not in any way constitute a lottery and dissemination of news concerning the outcome. Their encouraging argument was, their business did not in any way conflict with the current federal laws of a lottery statute. McCormack fought for the first amendment, "Freedom of the press was at stake under this indictment." McCormack stated, "Twenty-eight states have made pari-mutuel betting legal. Sending out the results and the prices paid to the winners is not against the law. The results are truthful, as they send out the daily results about these races and are legal under the law. His client cannot control what people or bookmakers do with this information after it is sent out and is of no concern to him. If the government continues to fight this case and file an indictment, then it would have the power to indict every press association in the country."

The Continental Press released a statement, "We transmit news and horses race results in which millions of law-abiding American citizens are interested in. In 1941, McBride purchased the *Sandusky Daily News*, which started its daily publication back in August 1934.

Spreading about his empire across Ohio, McBride bought the newly developed Cleveland Browns franchise and helped to spearhead the new All-American Football Conference in 1945. The enthusiastic and intelligent businessman hired the hometown's favorite Ohio State Coach, Paul Brown, as his leader and coach of the organization. Brown essential no-nonsense leadership skills were showcased when he became successful in bringing Ohio State University to the National Championship title in 1942. By 1955 McBride sold the Browns for an estimated $600,000 (equal to $5,569,000 in today's money) after winning five league championships and reaching the championship game two more times, making it the most successful Cleveland Sports team at the time.

In September 1946, McBride faced more unwanted interest from the government. His close friend, James M. Ragen, the former general manager of the *Nationwide News Service,* was killed in a gangland-style ambush in Chicago. In his will, Regen named McBride as the trustee of his estate.

Ragen left an estimated estate worth more than $555,000, and his share of the *Continental Press* worth 2 million dollars to his two children and McBride to manage it for them. One year earlier, Ragen had accused that some former Capone gangsters were threatening him for control of his wire service.

1950

McBride faced more charges of corruption from his *Continental Press* empire on February 14, 1950. Earlier, McBride had added his son, Edward, as a managing partner in the wire service. McBride stated he purchased 1/3 of *Continental Press* in 1943 from James Ragen Jr., and in 1947, he bought the remainder of the company from his dear friends' estate.

On the same day, Continental's public relations consultant, A. E. Bergener answered a claim filed by the *Cleveland Plain Dealer* on February 11.

On Saturday, a story on the organization and operation of the race wire service has prompt this statement to you on behalf of Continental Press. In your, article Continental assumes you had referred to it when you mentioned the race wire service since Continental is the superior wire service in the country. That Continental is controlled by various hoodlums and crime syndicate from the West Coast newspapers to St. Louis- Post-Dispatch. Both have sought to attach Continental to the old Capone syndicate. Even the press in Miami operated by John Knight has claimed that Frank Costello is controlling Continental business in the interest of his organized crime network.

Continental has no relations of any kind with Frank Costello or the so-called old Capone syndicate and never has. Continental does not serve bookmakers and has no ties to hoodlums and thugs of any sort.

Continental is under the sole control of Arthur McBride and goes about his daily tasks of gathering factual information to post on his service to radios and newspapers across the country, free from the influence of any kind, and from anyone.

1951

At this time, Arthur McBride and his son Edward were subpoenaed to appear and testify at the Kefauver hearing in Cleveland, Ohio.

By the late 1960's Arthur Bernard "Mickey" McBride retired with his wife Mary Jane to the beautiful and peaceful community of Coral Gables Florida, near his dear close friend Alfred Polizzi.

Sadly, he died of a heart attack at the esteem Cleveland Clinic and was buried in Cleveland's Holy Cross Cemetery. The couple had three children: Arthur B., Jr., Edward and Jane.

19

GEORGE ANGERSOLA

(Courtesy of Cleveland State University Archives)

This portion of Cleveland Gangland Style; is dedicated to the Angersola Brothers, John, and George, who were hugely instrumental in the development of the dominant Cleveland Crime Syndicate, known throughout the nation.

1929

It was April as the Cleveland police were kept extremely busy with their frequent raids on bootleggers and the many prohibition criminals actively working around the city. The criminal element lost once again, this time in the courtroom of Judge Oscar Bell, who proceeded to charge eight of the twenty-one criminals arrested as a suspicious person at the so-called "Liquor Dock" at the foot of the East 105th Street.

The police, with their limited allegations, concluded that the men assembled in the early morning hours to accept an unusually large cargo of illegal sugar cane coming into Cleveland north shores from Canada. One man, however, remained in police custody, John Angersola, who had used his alias John King when he was arrested. Angersola was at the whiskey wharf when the massive 32-ton ship full of corn sugar was seized during the defiant raid. John was arrested and is still being held in the Cuyahoga County jail, pending his expected disposition on Federal liquor violation charges.

1930

The Cleveland police force was boldly taken by surprise on July 5 as a double murder took place. The men were known as "The Sugar Cane Baron" Joe Porrello and his trusted friend and close associate, Sam Tilocco. During the intense criminal investigation of the double murder, John Angersola quickly became one of the prime suspects in their carefully planned investigation. For some unknown reason. Cody and other detectives investigating the deaths are at a strange loss to find any relevant or reliable evidence against the men, which they had suspected in the pending case.

A disturbing, an unforeseen incident soon accrued, which upset the police force and the prosecutor inside the police headquarters. In a hastily made-up police lineup, Angersola could not be identified as being at the scene of the crime, by their principal witness, Frank Joiner. Joiner, who initially told the detectives he was present in the Mayfield Road café when the two men were killed. To their dismay, Joiner failed to recognize anyone in the lineup of people inside the restaurant at the time of the double murder.

JOHN "FRED" ANGERSOLA

Then on July 29 Safety Director, Edwin Barry and Deputy Prohibition Administrator John Wright took quick and drastic action in what they believed to be an emergency situation as they defiantly instituted a 24-hour police motorcycle patrol of the city. Their orders were simple, to follow all trucks within the city limits when they leave the corn sugar warehouse. Their primary purpose was a simple one, to put a stop to the increasing rate of the highjacking of the corn sugar trucks, which is the prime ingredient used to make illegal whiskey.

Safety Director Barry was thrilled when he found out that Common Pleas Judge Harrison Ewing took a brave and groundbreaking decision to have the corn sugar building owned by Marco Chipetta at 2500 Woodland Avenue to remained padlock. The police saw this bold action and a dramatic show of the cities' unlimited power; in an attempt to stop the illegal trafficking of whiskey's main ingredient to the suspected hundreds of family home stills located around the city limits. With this intense action, the city of Cleveland executive leaders had come together in the fight to stop once and for all the prohibition whiskey production made around their town.

It was now August 22 as acting Police Chief George Matowitz opened up on his professional agenda as he proclaimed war on all gangsters and racketeers. Within days of his order, and under the careful supervision of Inspector Emmett Potts. The first list of individuals criminals included; John Angersola, who is still considered to be the primary suspect, even without enough substantial evidence to hold him on in the double murder of Joe Porrello and Sam Tilocco.

1931

The New Year started out to be a peaceful one and showed a promising future for the criminals and the country. It was on January 26 as a spray of bullets rang loud and clear around the crowded streets on Central Avenue S.E and East 4th Street as an attack on the blacklisted racketeers who had made a sufficient number of enemies among his former criminal friends. The fierce attack was viewed by the police as an attempt to take complete control, or a stronger piece of the giant monopoly of the profitable, "Policy Rackets" business.

The powerful attack was made against William Richardson, a notorious black policy kingpin who proclaimed he was no longer involved in the racket business and was frightened to death. Richardson told the police, he was in a fistfight earlier in the week and struck by several men who attempted to force him into a car, for what they called a "conference" on his lucrative gambling business. With the constant threats of danger, torture, beatings, bombing, and of course, assignations have been happening in the "Roaring Third" area known as the home ground of the policy game in Cleveland. Since the abolition of the old "Clearinghouse" lotteries, the operators reluctantly agreed the game was not very healthy or profitable anymore for anyone staying in the racket business.

Police reacted immediately as they issue arrested warrants for John Angersola and Charles Colletto. Both men had been named on this so-called "Blacklist" of public policy operators in Cleveland. There was no surprise when they discovered the car was titled to John Angersola, and identified as the car trying to abduct Richardson by force.

On February 4, Angersola and Colletto, who has been hiding out for eight days now and were considered the primary suspects in these "Shakedown" efforts against William Richardson

Angersola has repeatedly denied the current ridiculous allegations against him. He had proclaimed he had nothing to do with the attempted kidnapping of Richardson or trying to kill him. Richardson had violently fought to save his own life. At the end of the lengthy and frustrating investigation by the Cleveland Police, Richardson and several other witnesses had failed to identify any of the men in the car, which included Angersola and Charles Colletto as his attackers.

1932

On March 25, twelve men suspected to be racketeers were finally arrested from a one-year-old case. This was a brave attempt to clean-up the rising crime rate in Cleveland. The men detained under the weak suspicious person charges where Alfred Polizzi, John and George Angersola, Frank Milazzo, Frank and Angelo Cellura, Frank Brady, Mike Arizone Joe Fatica, Joe Marinelo and Phil Sidarto as they were gathered inside the Milano and Polizzi Italian Import store.

William Richardson, who earlier was arrested for perjury when he accused Angersola of shooting at him, has now changed his dark and scary story, once again. He previously testified he could not positively identify the men who shot at him. He now has told the police he remembers and will prove he does recognize Charles Coletti as one of the men who shot at him over a year ago. However, Coletti had earlier died in a city jail.

By early April, the twelve men handsomely appeared in a jam-packed courtroom dressed in their best Clark Gable style suits, silk shirts, and ties, and elegant Fedora hats. The men looked to be all professional men of honor and well-distinguished members of the society with their Attorney Martin McCormick at their side. McCormick carefully and pleasantly took good care of the nasty technical arrest complaints filed against his clients by the police and seemed ready and willing to fight a short battle for their acquittal and quick release from all charges filed against them.

McCormick filed three active motions on their critical defense in front of Judge Oscar Bell and Prosecutor Dennis Lyons. The first two proposals were to dismiss all the charges against his clients because the ordinance about being a suspicious person is against the current Ohio and the United States Constitution. He then added the state must be entirely precise about how a defendant was a suspicious person and for exactly what reason.

His strong objection was, "Former criminals cannot be construed to be actively associated with other known criminals, in as much as the American Law assumes a man who has paid the penalty and debt for his crime is no longer a criminal and has been rehabilitated."

It was now July as Police Chief Matowitz's latest fight to arrest known criminals Matowitz ordered Detective Captain Potts and Detective Lieutenant Alfred Jones a simple common task known to all police officers; to "Frisk" all known racketeers and pick them up. Then place them under arrest if they could not give a prime substantial reason for their presence or account for themselves and why they are present in this location.

20

1939

It was now April 26, as John Angersola was involved in the gambling business in one fashion or another. After a long, secret, and intensive police investigation, twenty-one men, had been, round-up and arrested on specific criminal charges. This gang of men gathered together in an attempt to muscle their way in on the popular and very profitable numbers policy rackets. Some of the top men in Cleveland's crime circle where listed in the multiple arrests. They included John and George Angersola, Alex (Shondor) Birns, Angelo Lonardo, Charles Polizzi, Little Angelo Sciria, and his brother Dominic, John DeMarco, Victor Maunion, Milton Rockman and Dominic Sospirato. Some of the men have retained Attorneys Thomas Burke and Martin McCormick to represent them in court.

The first criminals brought up before the Judge, was Charles Polizzi, along with nine other men. They reluctantly stood and strolled before Common Pleas Judge Joy Seth. Polizzi was faced with a costly and a ridiculously high $50,000 bond, or he suffered going to jail. (This is equal to $909,949 in today's money) In the total shock of such a high bond, Polizzi could not raise this enormous sum and was sentenced to stay in prison while his case was awaiting trial. His unbearable outcome in court posed a significant problem for the other gangsters. This incredible high bond was too scary for them to face and to raise. Several of the men pondered their next move and made a harsh and selfish decision and choose an alternate course of action. Their choice leads them into hiding and to nevertheless missed their first court appearance.

After returning from a conference in Florida, Safety Director Eliot Ness has now become involved in the extensive investigation to hunt down, up to 50 known mobsters in our area.

John and George Angersola were first thought to be hiding out in bright sunny Florida with his friends before coming up to Cleveland, this was learned by Detective Ernest Molnar. It was now believed the men were hiding from local police in the Cleveland area. The brothers tried to find out ahead of time what their high and impossible bond could possibly be set at before turning themselves in. Molnar had recently been promoted to head-up the Vice Squad. His men have gone on multiple and fruitless raids around the city, trying to get some reliable information on the whereabouts of these people. Another man arrested in the wake of the search included Frank Hoge, a known Policy King in Cleveland, as he received a lower bond of $30,000.

DETECTIVE LIEUTENANT ERNEST MOLNAR

(Courtesy of the Cleveland Plain Dealer)

It was now June 9 as "Big" Angelo Lonardo found himself being arrested by Lieutenant Alfred Jones while hiding out in an apartment building in Shaker Heights. His original excessive bond was harshly set by Judge Joy Seth at an impressive $60,000.

Lonardo, with his attorney Frank Azzarello by his side, pleaded, "Not Guilty" in front of Judge Hurd and intensely negotiated for a lower bond of $35,000 on the charges currently pending against him. The judge finally agreed on the more reasonable bail.

It was a few short days later when the FBI named agent Al Rosen of the local office in charge of this critical cause, and the searched for Angersola, with FBI identification # 98146. Rosen soon became officially involved in the manhunt for the other missing nine men who are now under specific indictments for their involvement in the number's rackets. After the gleaming evidence was reviewed by the United States District Attorney Emerich Freed and the United States Commissioner B.D. Nicola, Federal arrest warrants were quickly issued. The current list of missing men to be John and George Angersola, Milton Rockman, Dominic Sospirato, Angelo, and Dominic Sciria along with John DeMarco, Victor Maunion, and Joseph Artwell. FBI agent Rosen stated, "At this time, we have lowered the original bond, and the maximum penalty on these charges is now set at a mere $5,000 fine and five years in prison. A wanted notice will be placed in all of their files in Washington."

Later in 1949, Detective Molnar, who had led several successful raids and made multiple arrests were now being investigated and found to have frequently helped the city criminals who ran the numbers business along with the *Mayfield Road Gang* for several years. While feeding them critical and secret information about upcoming raids, police activity, or arrest warrants. Molnar allowed his new friends to operate unmolested in return for a handsome payoff. Molnar was later convicted of excepting bribes from criminals and sentenced to serve 66 years in the state prison. Ironically, or with the help of his many influential friends, he was released after four short years.

It was now October as George Angersola found himself in a terrible bind once again. This time he made a hard and hazardous decision, which placed himself in Saint John's Hospital on Cleveland's Westside. His illness was a severe and incredibly painful spinal ailment he endured several years ago. He gave himself up to Cleveland police with his Attorney Frank Azzarello at his side. The frail Angersola pleads "not guilty" to the proposed charges against him. He was surprised when he found his hospital room was guarded by Sheriff Martin O'Donnell on a 24 / 7 basis to ensure he did not try to leave or have some of his lost criminal friends visit him.

Ten days later, Common Pleas Judge Frank Day and County Prosecutor Frank Cullitan agreed to lower the initially higher bonds of five of the seven men held in the County Jail to only $25,000. Their original bond ranged from $50,000 to $60,000. This vital decision and rulings came to light just after John Angersola turned himself in. Angersola bond was set at only $25,000. This motion made both the judge and the prosecutor review the first higher bonds. Was it a case of having a mental lapse of judgment or a skillful and thoughtful maneuver to entice the other men to turn themselves in and face the music? Or could it have been they actually felt it was unfair to have some of the people in jail for $50,000 or more, while others had a much lower bond? No one in the city or the newspapers commented on the motive behind lowering the bail, nor did they hear any arguments from the defense attorneys.

21

1942

It was now June as the trial of the final last twelve defendants in the severe extortion case was set to begin, which started almost three years ago. The court was anxiously ready, to begin with yet another criminal who had profited about $2,000 over eighteen-months while he defiantly waited for his trial to begin. The complaint was filed against the policy operator George Hales. Prosecutor Frank Cullitan has scrutinized the complicated facts in great detail and requested Judge Patrick Walher to set a firm court date for these trials to begin. This long and weary process started back in April 1939. Sadly, it has been passed on from one nervous judge to another, because of one crucial and vital criminal is still reported missing. Safety Director Eliot Ness related; how "Angelo Sciria has still not been located and is believed to be hiding somewhere out of the country or possibly not with the living."

Attorneys for the twelve accused men along with George and John Angersola are the cities, primary defendants. They are seeking to obtain a court petition for the discharge of all charges against them in their criminal racket case. These criminal cases have been held over their client's head for an astonishingly extended period. This impressive motion was filed by Attorney's Frank Azzarello, Howell Leuck, M.A. Picciano, L.E. Appleton, and Selmo Glenn. The attorneys for the defendants have claimed their clients have been bravely willing to proceed with the court case against them.

It was now the end of June as Common Pleas Judge Frank Day addressed the second round of jury selection. One hundred possible citizens nervously appeared in court to see if they would be selected as a juror for the upcoming trial. Six men and six women were formally seated to hear the criminal case.

The trail finally begins on June 25 and is well documented by *The Cleveland Plain* Dealer and written by Anthony Disantis.

This case is about how two armed men held up and took money and equipment, which was used to mark the illegal policy slips while George Hales was calmly working as a cashier on East 39ʰ and Scovill Avenue, while inside his home. The scene was described by one witness, Sterling Willis, who took the stand and looked into the eyes of the hundreds of people inside the Common Pleas courtroom. Willis is the second person to testify in the courtroom of Judge Frank Day. Willis apparently identified Milton Rockman as one of the gunmen who threatened him. Willis previously stated that Rockman told him, "You inform Slim (meaning Hales), don't pull another ball without seeing me first, or his brains will fall out onto the sidewalk." Willis told the court he informed Hales as soon as he saw him.

Under intense cross-examination by the prosecutor, Willis accidentally admitted he had received more than $4,000 from the city of Cleveland to testify in this case. The town gave him the money so he could meet his personal living expenses for more than three years until the case could come to trial.

Hales reluctantly described how the policy business, which he had financed by some lucky hits against other policy operators. It was now destroyed since he was forced to make payments or tributes to the racketeers. Hales then stated, he initially started his business back in June 1932 and was forced out of business by December 1933. The other men Hales said wherein the room was, "Big George King" known as George Angersola and Little Angelo Sciria. Both men told Hales in no uncertain terms, "You are not paying up, and you know what happens to you if you do not pay."

In their defense, George Angersola, Angelo Lonardo, Victor Mannino, and Milton Rockman all testified and admitted knowing Angelo Sciria. All eagerly denied the state's excessive charges of forcing any policy house operator to pay them a tribute.

Hales told the jam-packed courtroom that he did agree to pay

123

the tribute of $25 a week for protection to the men. He would
then take his payment every Monday to Sciria's home, which
Hales believed, was being collected for Angersola.

The three-year-long criminal trial finally came to a close on July 3, as the ten men were found guilty, in the $2,000 policy extortion conspiracy a shakedown and alleging the criminals were demanding a 40-cent kickback of all the wages bet with George Hales. The mobsters are all free on a mere $5,000 bond as the men face a penalty of a $1,000 fine and five years in jail.

After the final verdict was decreed, Defense Attorney Leuck stated, "He will file for a miss-trail on several fronts. One being: the men should have been given separate trials; and not lumped all together, in blocks of four or five." Judge Day stood firm in his decision of not allowing some evidence into the court documents, while the judge fought the defense on many facts they discussed, claiming. "they are set on flimsy grounds that did not seem reasonable to him."

1944

It was the end of August during an ongoing effort to curb the crime in the city. Detective Inspector Frank Story and Lieutenant Martin Cooney proposed a different type of opportunity to Mayor Frank Lausche. Their idea was to post a list of the *"Who's who of top hoodlums"* in an attempt to eliminate or diminish the criminal's profound activities. They explained, by posting their names in the local newspapers, and hoping it would embarrass them and their families, as it compels to drive the gangsters out of the city or out of business altogether. By 1958 John Angersola was listed as a *Top Hoodlum* in Miami as well.

1948

It was New Year's Eve as a threat to blow up Police Chief George Matowitz home, and himself became known to the citizens of Cleveland. This eye-opening event was believed to be the result of the Chief's firm and unmovable stand, and the war on the policy operators in Cleveland.

DETECTIVE GEORGE MATOWITZ

(Courtesy of Allan May and his book "The Sly Fanner Murders")

Detective Charles Nevel had confirmed the bombing took place at 3:45 in the afternoon when the phone call came into the detective's bureau, which threatened the life of the Chief. The actual quote from the caller was soon released, "Chief Matowitz's house would be blown sky-high, and there'll be no more chief unless he stopped giving protection to certain individuals like Johnson and Buster."

Matthew Johnson is twenty-seven years old and has testified for the state against Ernest Molnar, who was convicted of taking bribes with a former Police Officer, Buster Johnson. Johnson had once been suspected to be a partner in the most prominent policy syndicate in Cleveland.

1951

John and George "King" Angersola, soon found their name on the long list of the twenty people from Cleveland, including Al Polizzi, Chuck Polizzi, Joe DiCarlo from Youngstown and James Licavoli. All were invited, no mandated to testify at Senator Estes

Kefauver, crime investigation hearings that will be taking place in Cleveland in the middle of January.

It was now March 23 as both John and George Angersola have still not been located and served their warrants to testify in front of the crime committed. The brothers are believed to be living big in the Miami, Florida area and into the exuberant gambling operations there. The FBI would later learn that John Angersola was a partner in the fabulous *Gold Hotel* in Miami.

On August 4, the announcement finally came in as Senator Herbert O'Connor, the Crime Committee Chairmen, stated, "Both John and George Angersola were living comfortably in Miami, Florida will now come forward and testify before the committee at a closed session to be scheduled shortly."

The Cleveland Plain Dealer article, written by Edward Kernan told the country how the Angersola Brothers court hearing date was finally set. It was held on August 6 in Washington, D.C. Both George and John testified in front of a closed-door session in the Senate. Both men noted to be working and living in Miami. They sat proudly and spoke softly and told little of their life and occupation to the committee.

One of the Crime Committee counselors Downey Rice mentioned, "John appeared to be the "Kingpin" and refused to answer, or he answered too vaguely, and his statements were meaningless sentences to us, that often ran together without any meaning and amounted to saying the same thing over and over again."

Rice told the reporters; both brothers have the same defense attorney, Fred Kaplan, who regularly works in New York and in the Miami area. Rice stated, "It would be up to the committee if they wish to bring up Contempt of court charges against the two brothers." The Angersola Brothers have been the central figure in other inquiries years earlier when the committee was investigating the old criminal group, "Mayfield Road Gang," which had their headquarters in Cleveland, Ohio. Their names are also listed, revealing reports on the intense

Cleveland Syndicate investigation of gambling and racketeering operations. They're known to be associated with gambling operations in Kentucky, Nevada, Pennsylvania, and Florida.

During his visit to the witness stand, John answered only a few simple questions from the committee that were asked with considerable hesitation. John bluntly refused to answer many of their concerns, and often pleading and taking his Fifth Amendment rights. John did admit, however, that he owned "The Grand Hotel" in Miami, as he then refused to answer a multitude of other questions dealing with other hotels, clubs, or interests he may have in the Miami area. John also seemed to have lost his vivid memory when it came to answering multiple questions about "The Buckeye Catering Company," which he was listed as a partner.

Defense Attorney Rice boldly told the Senate committee, "John Angersola has not been involved in the racket business for over ten years and lives as an ordinary everyday businessman in Miami."

For George, his memory was just as bad as his brother John' had been. There were too many questions asked to him without any attempt to recall his memory or answers, which he happily said, "I can't remember, or his favorite response was, "I do not know." George could not even remember or tell the powerful committee where he lived a few months earlier while he was hiding out from Senator Kefauver and this crime commission.

As for George's employment history, it only states he worked as a union organizer and was paid only $100 a week from the Cleveland Cleaning and the Dying Union.

1956

It was now March as George "King" Angersola was known and listed as a "Mob Contact" with many of the unions in Cleveland. George has been named by some of the New York racketeers who can apply "extensive pressure" on labor unions in Cleveland and

New York to, *"tow A-line"* with regards to the massive health and welfare insurance business which has become a prevalent and lucrative investment with gangsters over the country.

The New York Grand Jury has recently released explosive information from an earlier testimony of Louis Saperstein, a Newark insurance broker and an unnamed New York mobster who has been in the union insurance field since 1952. Saperstein told the story of how George Angersola was his primary contact overall and has several phone conversations dealing with meetings with William Finegan. Finegan was the Executive Secretary of the Cleveland Federation of Labor when he was seeking to handle some of their insurance business from Local 436, which was headed up by a union official, Louis "Babe" Triscaro.

In an unfortunate surprise for the New York Grand Jury, Saperstein, unsightly blood-soaked body was found. He had been shot four times in the torso back on March 10th after he appeared before a New York Grand Jury and the proceedings testimony were made to the public. Finegan stated, "That he, in fact, "Kicked Back" fifty-percent of the $299,000 he made on the insurance scam to the local mobsters." Saperstein's personal attack and murder were labeled as a "Mob style hit" in all the local newspapers. By the end of the year, Attorney General William P. Rogers named Angersola as a prominent underworld figure in the country.

"L TO R: EDWARD F. MURPHY, PRES. TEAMSTERS DISTRICT COUNCIL... T. W. ROBERTSON, FEDERAL LABOR CONCILIATOR... WILLIAM FINEGAN, PRES. CLEVE. FEDERATION OF LABOR

(Courtesy of Cleveland State University Memory Project and the Cleveland Press)

22

PART III

JOHN "BARON" DEMARCO

John Anthony DeMarco; was born on February 28 in 1903 in Licata, Sicily, and became a Naturalized citizen in Cleveland, Ohio, on August 24, 1926.

In the later years of John's life, he was considered by many in the Cleveland mob to be the "Consigliore" during the middle portion of John Scalish regime in the late-1960s or so, after the "Old-Man" Anthony Milano retired his role. John was a cousin of Joseph Lonardo, one of the first crime bosses in Cleveland.

1929

During October, while the Cleveland police were investigating the murder of yet another criminal of the "Sugar War" victim Vincente "James" Porrello, who was killed on September 29. The 26-year-old John DeMarco found himself in jail once again and in the middle of the intense investigation. He was subsequently arrested under a suspicious person charge along with Charles Cassaro. Both men were soon inside the courtroom of Judge Mary Grossman, one of Cleveland's first female judges. Even though DeMarco believed he was innocent of any wrongdoing, he remained in custody under a strange and enormous $15,000 bond (estimated to be worth $221,676 in today's money.) He was considered a material witness in the murder case against Charles Cuini and Louis Cangelosi, who is being tried for Porrello's murder.

JUDGE MARY GROSSMAN

(Courtesy of the Cleveland State University Memory Project)

1932

It was now March 1, as the Trumbull County Grand Jury finished hearing the closing arguments in the sad, dismal kidnapping case of a young boy. The eleven-year-old, James De Jute, who was the son of a wealthy and respected Niles contractor. This just so happened to co-inside on the same day as the famous kidnapping of Charles Augusts Lindbergh Jr. The son of the well-known aviator Charles and Anne Morrow Lindbergh, and one of the most highly publicized crimes of the 20th century.

In Niles, the two men accused of this horrible crime gather together as they received a copy of the papers while the signature of the Prosecutor G.H. Birrell was still wet. Judge Lynn Griffith quickly indicted the two criminals. Angerly, the horrified judge announced, "the men will be facing kidnapping and extortion charges, and sad, lonely life in prison for their hideous crime." The men were named as twenty-nine-year-old John DeMarco and thirty-one-year-old Dowell Hargravee, both of Youngstown, Ohio. Nine dedicated police officers, most from Trumbull County, helped to save the child and apprehended the two criminals quickly while they hid in a back room of an old gambling casino named the *Hillside Club* on the outskirts of Youngstown.

According to documents, the two men were not looking to harm the child in any way, but looking for a fast and easy score as DeMarco and Hargrave could now be facing a lifetime in a Federal prison, because of the boy's young age of eleven. If they had only waited three more months to take the child, the men would be looking at a much shorter sentence of from ten to thirty years. It seems young Jimmy will be turning twelve on June 16. At this time, the men remained scared, motionless, and were nervously looking to go to prison for the rest of their natural lives!

While the Grand Jury was busy hearing the minimal amount of evidence against the two men, a group of federal agents, and a local police officer from Mahoning and Trumbull counties worked side by side with the police force from the city of Niles for several weeks. Multiple leads came to their attention from concerned citizens that could potentially lead them to an impressive bootlegging team from both local counties.

It was now June, as a strange turn of events arose. A Youngstown father of five children, Anthony Lauri, found himself captured back in the middle of May. It seems he was on the run from the Trumbull County authorities and found hiding out in a small town in West Virginia. Lauri was accused and later convicted of assisting in the kidnapping case of the eleven-year-old boy James De Jute from Niles, Ohio. After a lengthy deliberation period by the anxious jury of five men and seven women and in the seventh round of balloting, Lauri was found guilty and given a life sentence.

In return, the Grand Jury decided to offer mercy to the other two men, which meant they were now looking at a mere ten to a thirty-year prison term. Expert defense evidence provided the jury with a significant breakthrough for John DeMarco. By a strange twist of fate, and the graces of God, DeMarco was not in the car or on the sidewalk when the boy was taken. Even later in his jittery, nervous testimony, little Jimmy himself stated the same defiant facts when asked several questions about his abductors by the prosecutors. He openly proclaimed, "that two men picked him up on the sidewalk, one was Hargravee, and another was a man he could not identify."

Nervously, and looking to save his life, DeMarco calmly testified how he went to a vacant building, known as *The Hillside Club*. He merely intended to pick up some liquor for a few friends when suddenly a gun was placed in the back of his head, and he was being held captive like the boy. Neither of the two guilty men has hired an attorney at this time to represent them. Because of his reliable testimony, the judge had believed DeMarco, as he left happy and free to go.

1936

According to the book *The Rise and Fall of the Cleveland Mafia,* by Rick Porrello, Dr. Romano, the skillful surgeon who had saved Frank Brancato's life four years earlier, became a problem for the Cleveland crime family, namely for Anthony Milano and Angelo

Lonardo.

Romano lived on the Eastside of town in the city of Willoughby. One or possibly both of these men actively felt Romano was becoming a little too greedy and bitterly thrived on obtaining more power and status in the organized crime world and became a downright threat against the Mayfield Road Gang.

On June 11, 1936, a county worker found Dr. Romano's helpless body inside a car alongside the Chagrin River Road in the peaceful community of Moreland Hills south of where his home was located. Dr. Romano's mutilated body was found face up in the back seat of his car.

At this time, only a few people were brought in for questioning by the local police. It was no surprise to the police when no one was ever convicted of the brutal murder of Dr. Romano. It would not be until years later that the FBI would find out from a reliable informant, who had committed the crime, and who the responsible triggerman behind Romano's death actually was.

1939

The Cleveland Plain Dealer had an article on April 27, "Twenty-three figures in the money-making policy rackets were finally indicted!"

In a two-year-long investigation that encumbers some twenty-three men, all of whom are well-known criminals were all indicted by the Grand Jury on charges of Blackmail and extortion. Their pictures, along with the names of these die-hearted hoodlums, consisted of a comprehensive policy cleanup by local police officials on the thundering corruption in Cleveland. The people mentioned are, Alex (Shondor) Birns, Dominic Sospirato, Angelo (Little Ange) Lonardo, Charles Lavocco, Solly Hart, Milton Rockman, Joseph Tampiro. John (King) Angersola, George Angersola, Frank Hoge, Victor Manning, Dominic Scerria, Angelo Sciria, John DeMarco, Joseph Atwell, Albert (Big Al) Polizzi, Charles Lardomita. Elsworth Jewell, Nick Satulla, and 4 members of the black policymaking rackets. The man considered being the head man in town, William Richardson, followed by Tommy Boyce,

Herbert Oliver, and Larry Gaskin. Later, John DeMarco; was found guilty and severed close to four years in prison.

It was mid-August when Detective Lieutenant Ernest Molnar was cruising around the town near East 55th and Broadway. He soon recognized a car owned by Vincent Dylinski, an associate of the high-level policy mob who had been indicted. Keeping in touch with his headquarters, he asked for assistance, as Keith Wilson, Chief of Investigators for the Office of Safety Director Eliot Ness, took up the tail on Dylinski. The detectives continued to follow the car through the community of Huron near Sandusky and Lake Erie. The vehicle stopped at a summer cottage in Willow Grove, just two miles west of Huron, it was now 6 PM.

Both officers rushed into the cabin with guns drawn and were surprised to find DeMarco and his wife in bathing suits ready to go and relax at the beach or take an early evening swim. Two other men and three women were also in the cottage. DeMarco was dragged back to the Central Police station, booked, and placed in the County Jail until he could face a judge.

DeMarco's apprehension now left just eight men out of the twenty-three still at large. Angelo and Dominic Sciria, John and George Angersola along with Milton Rockman, Dominic Sospirato, Victor Mannino, and Joe Atwell.

1943

Moving into a new year found the same old courtroom appearances of the men arrested and tried for extortion in the 1939 policy operator's extortion case. The defendants have fought hard to win their appeal and to overturn their guilty verdicts by the court. However, they found themselves in the same old predicament, guilty as charged in the newest trial lead by Cleveland's robust County Prosecutor Frank Cullitan. Cullitan has been riding high on a long winning streak, as his conviction rate is now a record high in Cleveland at 92 percent for the last five-year period from 1937 until 1941.

FRANK CULLITAN, WITH PROPERTY, SEIZED FROM A 1936 RAID ON THE THOMAS CLUB.

(Courtesy of Cleveland State University Archives Division)

Cullitan stood proudly and declared, "The city of Cleveland has enjoyed a peaceful environment since these criminals have been in jail, as the crime rate has gone down dramatically.

The ongoing circus-like atmosphere of constant delays has gone on for almost four years now. Nevertheless, it kept being push back time after time and repeatedly rescheduled by the court system. It was almost like no judge in the county wanted to be a part of this tense and controversial criminal case against several of the most influential gangsters in Cleveland.

23

1957

It was a chilly November day as John Anthony DeMarco was approached by the New York State Police Department. It was November 14, just several miles from the home of an ailing friend Joseph Barbara and many powerful and influential men. Barbara estate was the location of the famous Apalachin meeting was to have taken place. Driving the car was John Scalish. The two men stayed at the Parkview Motel in New York, located on Route 17, before being arrested on that fateful day.

1958

It was now June as rumors have been floating around Washington D.C. and Cleveland, stating that Scalish and DeMarco will be subpoena to appear in yet another Senate hearing on the famous organized crime case, which will now be investigating the botched syndicate meeting. The Senate committee is very interested in finding out first hand what if anything organized crime has to do with the escalating trouble with labor racketeering as concerns radiated across the nation. U.S. District Attorney Sumner Canary stated, "The Senate committee will probably issue several subpoenas, and for the sake of security, they would not go through any of the local marshal's offices to serve them."

1959

A new battleground against organized crime came forward as the Federal Government began the criminal hearings of the sixty-plus men arrested in upper Apalachin, New York, on or near the Barbara estate. Growing court actions continue to build across the nation and forcing several union officials to bring in their personal as well as private records from their union funds before a Federal Grand Jury. The jury in Cleveland consisted of nine women and three men in the courtroom of Judge James Connell's.

1961

It was February 21, as John DeMarco found the weight of an elephant lifted off his shoulders and his weakened heart. The New York Justice Department officially informed him that Assistant United States Attorney for New York has re-considered the current criminal indictment against him on the conspiracy charges from the Apalachin meeting. The charges were dismissed by U.S. District Judge Alexander Bicks.

It was now July, as DeMarco faced yet another personal and severe allegation in local newspapers. This time it was not the police, but from a jealous husband, Joseph Artino. Artino eagerly accused DeMarco of stealing his wife Josephine away from him as she filed for a divorce. In Artino lawsuit, he was looking for a $500,000 payday against DeMarco, for allegedly taking his wife away from him. Henry Levine, DeMarco's attorney, stated, "I have heard many things about John over the years. However, he has never been accused of being a Casanova. John is living happily with his only wife in Shaker Heights, and I don't believe a word of this frivolous lawsuit." The suit soon fell apart and was dismissed as the alleged wife denied any involvement with DeMarco.

1962

It was now February, as the FBI carefully watched DeMarco's every movement and became increasingly aware of John planning a short vacation with his close friend John Miceli, who is a significant partner in the local Miceli Dairy Product Company. The flight was scheduled for San Francisco, California, and was booked to arrive back in Cleveland three days later.

The FBI noted how DeMarco's long history of crime, and as a prominent figure in the Italian Criminal element in Cleveland. Since DeMarco suffered two significant heart attacks, one in 1950 and the other in 1958, his position of power has been lessened considerably. This could have been an order from Scalish or on his own accord. However, DeMarco remains a vital part of the large organization. His physician has stated that another heart attack might prove to be fatal to John. Therefore his activities were significantly curbed. DeMarco is regarded to be a Top Hoodlum given his valuable contacts and called upon as a counselor to many underlings in the organization.

1968

John's cunning and long career in crime, he had only one prison record. That was for four years in 1943, when he was accused and convicted with the numbers rackets along with Angelo Lonardo for extortion in muscling in on the local policy rackets.

John later died from yet another major heart attack on October 25, 1972, at the age of 68

JOHN DEMARCO'S ARREST RECORD

1. Cleveland, Ohio charged with murder on September 26, 193, Charges were dropped.

2. Cleveland, Ohio July 31, 1931, investigation of suspicious person charges. Charges dropped on August 1

3. Cleveland, Ohio August 13, 1939; Extortion. On August 14, he was held over to a Grand Jury. On August 10, 1942, he was sentenced to 5-years in the Ohio State Penitentiary on charges of unlawful flight to avoid prosecution for extortion accompanied by threats of violence.

4. The Ohio State Penitentiary Columbus, Ohio On August 15, 1942, he was charged with Blackmail and given a sentence of 1-5 years and was paroled on October 1, 1944.

5. Cleveland, Ohio. August 23, 1948, was picked up as a suspicious person and released the same day.

6. District of Columbia, Washington Bureau of Narcotics on May 21, 1959. Arrested him on 18 different United States Code # 371. Dealing with Narcotic violations.

7. United States Marshal Service in Cleveland, Ohio, on May 21, 1959, charged him with conspiracy to commit Perjury in the Southern District of New York dealing with the Apalachin meeting in November 1957.

24

FRANK BRANCATO

THE STREET BOSS

Francesco Brancato was born on September 27, 1897, in Licata, Sicily. He was the middle of five sons of Ninfa and Giuseppe Brancato. Giovanni was three years older, Giuseppe two years younger while Salvatore and Samuel were three and four years younger, respectively. Three sisters, Antoinette, and twins Mary and Sara rounded out the large Brancato family.

In June of 1927, Salvatore Vella was becoming a leader in the community and operated his own small-time bootlegging business out of his home and was also known as a police informant who would often inform the police, reasonable stories about the Lonardo's lucrative business transactions.

One day, Vella parked his car in front of Piunno Funeral

Parlor on Woodland Ave. Waiting for a friend to meet with him. Not concentrating on the activities behind him, another vehicle pulled up next to him and then stopped. Vella looked at the man through his window, the driver smiled back at Vella with a nod of his head that seemed to say hello. Not thinking anything of it, Vella then smiled again, not knowing the man, then without any warning, another man strolled by on the sidewalk next to Vella's car. He stopped, looked into the driver's window, with Vella's face only a few inches away. Shots were fired into the car, hitting him in the stomach. Panicking, Vella tried as hard as he could to get out of his vehicle when several more shots struck him by the man he never saw coming. The killer ran from the side of the car and jumped into the waiting car just ahead of Vella's car, as it quickly sped away.

A few days later, police were actively looking into any possible suspects and picked up several men for questioning in Vella's murder. These people included Frank Brancato along with Antonio Lando. Brancato was known as a friend of both the Lonardo's and Porrellos', and with a lack of evidence, he was soon released before the end of the day. Lando was later convicted of the shooting since the police had an eyewitness who had recognized him. However, Lando was later acquitted of the charges against him. The eyewitness was now not 100% sure it was actually Lando standing next to the door firing the shots into Vella. The police believed Brancato was to have been the driver of the other car, but again, they had no substantial evidence, and no one could identify him.

On February 25, 1932, the Porrello boys were playing their usual card game in the corner of the back room. They choose that table for protection since they could easily see if anyone entered the room. They played with their friend and bodyguard Dominic (Guelli) Mangino, also known as Terra-Terra.

Ray Porrello suddenly looked up, and to his surprise, he saw what seemed to be an assassin squad standing there with shotguns and revolvers in their hands. Joe Todaro dashed behind the counter as Ray Porrello jumped up, pushed his chair back, and tried to pull out his gun.

The gunmen sprayed the room with bullets. Ray fell to the floor with a bullet in his head, while Rosario stood up and was shot three times in the head. Guelli was in the middle of the room when he was shot through his brain. The tough-minded bodyguard refused to die for two hours. Another man was killed who just happened to be in the room; it was believed that he was murdered only because dead men tell no tales.

Inside the cigar shop, a grotesque crime scene unfolded with pools of blood scattered around the small room as the trio laid dead on the ground. It would soon become a spectacle in the neighborhood. After hearing the gunshots, plenty of curious people in the community came running over to the cigar shop from nearby stores. Within minutes, reporters came running to snap a few photos or get the first scoop of who the dead gangsters were. By this time, the police were trying desperately to secure and to close down the crime scene so they could start their investigation.

THE CIGAR STORE ASSASSINATION

(Courtesy of Dennis Sutcliffe)

The *Cleveland Press* reported on February 26, 1932, that police continued to question and interrogate Frank Brancato, as he was under arrest while fighting for his life at St John's Hospital, a few hours after the triple murder. Brancato's wife, Virginia, appeared at the hospital and ran to Frank's bedside. She threw her arms around him and exclaimed, "Frank, Frank, tell me what happened!"

The police guard said the two whispered in English for a short period, and then they both quickly changed to Italian. Virginia later claimed to the police in broken English that Frank had been home with her that evening before he was shot.

Frank later informed the police he may have gotten some medical attention from his wife, but he was too weak to recall for sure. Little hope was held for Brancato's life at this time, as he was not expected to survive the night or the upcoming surgery, scheduled for the next day to remove the bullet deep inside his abdomen.

Inside the operating room the next day, Dr. Romano worked diligently for several hours to locate the hidden bullet. However, he found it lodged too deep for him to reach in a typical operating fashion. If he continued the procedure, Brancato would surely die from massive, uncontrolled bleeding. Dr. Romano decided to close up Frank's stomach for the day and to review the X-rays of his stomach area once again after he stabilized him.

The next morning, Dr. Romano brought Frank back into the operating room to try something different than he had thought of overnight. Romano decided first to take out Brancato's intestines to get to the bullet. It was a bizarre thing to try. This procedure was never heard of before in the operating room or in the medical community. Unsure whether it would work, Dr. Romano took his time in a five-hour surgical procedure. Dr. Romano was then able to finally locate the bullet and take it out while repairing eight damaged areas of his stomach and intestines.

Romano then worked delicately and diligently to fix the holes in the patient's stomach linings. Dr. Romano slowly and methodically placed Frank's intestines back inside his slim body and hoped for the best.

The police and Inspector Cody hoped that Frank Brancato would live through the night so the City of Cleveland could prosecute him for these three murders.

On the morning of March 4, a story in the *Cleveland Plain Dealer* declared Brancato was at the scene of Porrello killings. It mentioned the bullet that was taken from his stomach area, which came from one of the weapons used in the shooting of the men.

After a lengthy trial and no witnesses, Brancato was only charged with perjury and giving a false statement on where he was at the time of the shooting. He spent the next few years in prison

1951

It was on January 15, an article from a Sandusky, Ohio, newspaper article said that Frank Brancato, continued to be the subject of searching examination by the Kefauver Crime Investigating Committee, according to reports.

The Sunday *Plain Dealer* described the developments of hearings in Cleveland in connection with the criminal probe as "Brancato Day." *Plain Dealer* stories published:

> *Brancato, a reputed Prohibition-era gunman, an ex-convict, gambling club operator, and now a Spumoni king, trudged down the long corridor to the closed-door hearing room in the early afternoon for the second time in three days. Under his arm, he carried a bundle of personal records, apparently missing from the first batch he had delivered on Thursday. Brancato spent a few minutes with his attorney and then left the room without comment to reporters. Brancato never testified during these hearings.*

1955

Brancato was now waiting outside the downtown office of his attorney, Henry Levine, located in the Williamson Building when Levine arrived there shortly after nine. Together, the two men walked into the Federal Building, which was located across the street, and then went to the fourth-floor headquarters of the immigration service.

Brancato freely surrendered to John M. Lehmann, Cleveland's Chief of the Immigration Service. Levine left the room and walked down to the third-floor office to file a writ of habeas corpus with the federal courts on Brancato's behalf.

As Levine disappeared down the staircase, Brancato sat quietly when he was quickly hustled out of the office by several INS agents to a waiting elevator, and then whisked to the basement, then into a waiting car with its engine still on. By the time his attorney Levine was able to file his writ for Brancato, the agents were already speeding toward Cleveland Hopkins Airport in Brookpark.

Back upstairs to see his client, Levine heard what had just happened to Brancato. Levine was angered and shouted, "They shanghaied him! This is jungle law, not American justice."

Horrified, Levine rushed to see Federal Judge James C. Connell, but Connell refused to handle his complaint and case, saying he was currently trying a patent lawsuit, and not involved with this case.

After hearing this, Levine actually ran to see Judge Charles McNamee, who agreed to look into this matter. He quickly summoned Lehmann and U.S. Attorney Summer Canary into his chambers. Lehmann proceeded to inform the judge he was under direct order from the Detroit office, "to take Brancato as soon as Levine left the office, and before the writ could be filed in federal court."

Judge McNamee asked, "Is it true that the man was spirited away and kidnapped?"

Lehmann bowed his head to the judge and just replied, "The writ had not been filed at the time we took him, and Brancato was in our custody, so we took him to the airport."

BRANCATO LANDING IN BOSTON WITH INS AGENT BECK

(Courtesy of Cleveland State University Archives)

Judge McNamee order Brancato back to Cleveland after a heated and lengthy court battle Brancato won his freedom as his deportation was later withdrawn.

1958

In an FBI file dated January 3, a confidential informant advised that Brancato, Scalish, DeMarco, and others regularly met to play cards and gamble in a back room at LaMarca's barbershop on Kinsman road. Nevertheless, the police had not been able to catch the men gambling. The informant also told them that he could not be sure, but in his opinion, these were local high-level meetings of the Italian hoodlum element.

1959

A *Plain Dealer* article on October 20 by J.C Dasohbach discussed the possibility that four witnesses were called before the Federal Grand Jury and cited for contempt of court. Mentioned in the article were John and Sam Scalish, John DeMarco, and Frank Brancato. All refused to answer questions put to them by Max H. Goldschein, an attorney in the criminal division of the Department of Justice. Goldschein came to Washington to challenge these men in the grand jury investigation into labor union leaders and activities of vending machine operators.

THE POPULAR CAPTAIN FRANK'S ON
THE EAST 9TH STREET PIER

(Courtesy of Cleveland State University Archives)

1962

FBI spoke with Frank Visconti, part-owner of the evening hotspot named "Captain Frank's Seafood House located on the East 9th Street Pier. Visconti informed the police, "Frank B, was extremely well-liked by the Italian community and "would give you the shirt off his back if you needed it." Visconti told agents that he knew of an instance where an individual came to Brancato to borrow some money, and Brancato did not have it on him, but he went to some of his friends to borrow the money from them and lend it to these individuals. In other words, "If Frank did not have it, he'd go and get it for you." Brancato had done many favors for many people in Cleveland. Brancato's close friend and *compare* was DeMarco. John was apparently on the payroll of the Fulton Fish Company as a salesperson. Visconti said he believed John was connected in some way with the Miceli Dairy Company but was unsure whether Brancato was linked to either of the businesses.

1963

On May 5, the FBI reported that they found another massive dice game or barbut game in Cleveland, located at the Ohio Plating Company on Second Street and High Street. The game was held on the third floor. They noted seeing Brancato going into the building and staying for several hours. Among the guests were DeMarco, Logatto, Cassaro, and young Frank Lonardo Jr.

During a meeting with an informant on October 7, 1963, the FBI asked him who would be likely to take over as the boss when Scalish died. The source told them that because of their age and experience, Brancato could be considered at this time, but because of his health and heart condition, DeMarco likely would not be considered.

A source advised the Cleveland FBI on November 18 that he had never heard of the title La Cosa Nostra ("Our Thing"). In his mind, the organization was always known as the Outfit, and at no time has the men involved with the outfit used the name "Mafia" when speaking of their friends or organization. This was merely a term the newspaper used to describe them. As far as he was concerned, the leaders of the Outfit in Cleveland were Al Polizzi, who now lived in Miami, Anthony Milano, John Scalish, Jack Licavoli, Frank Brancato, and John DeMarco.

25

1965

On March 18, an FBI informant advised them that he had heard in Steubenville, Ohio, Mafia Boss Dino Cellini came to Cleveland and visited with Brancato and John DeMarco every month in a Murray Hill restaurant. The informant was unsure whether it was to give them their share of the profits from his gambling interests from his area of Ohio, but in his opinion, it had to be.

The same informant said he and a bunch of the younger Mob guys who called both Brancato and DeMarco a couple of "Dons." Many were waiting for the old men to just die so they could move up the ladder in the outfit, but none of them had the "balls" to try to kill either man.

1970

The man brought in by Brancato to help him with some collections was Carmen Semenoro, who moved his wife and young son into an apartment complex in Warrensville Heights, Ohio. Located just outside of Cleveland on the southeast side, many of the city's underworld members chose this area of Cuyahoga County as their home. On his FBI record, Semenoro was officially listed as a salesperson for the Munroe Lighting Company of Cuyahoga Falls, for which he earned a salary of $200 a week. Selling light bulbs. However, it was not the reason Semenoro was asked to come to Cleveland.

On May 15, Brancato, Mike Romeo, and Semenoro were arraigned before Federal Judge Thomas Lambros. The strike force attorney described Brancato as the brains of the operation but exposed that Semenoro made the actual threats. Bail was set at $10,000 for Brancato and Romeo, and each was soon released. However, the judge places a higher $100,000 bond on Semenoro, and he was returned to jail.

At the same time, Brancato was taking additional heat from inside the Cleveland family on two fronts. Members that were reportedly incensed with him for allowing himself to become associated with Semenoro; and those who were furious because of his failure to disassociate himself from him. Brancato was well aware of the danger Semenoro posed as being a co-defendant in the upcoming extortion trial. Nevertheless, what concerned Brancato the most were the whispered rumors that Semenoro had just become a stool pigeon, and talking to the Feds.

While Brancato contemplated what had to be done. Semenoro seemed to be waiting to see what was going to happen in his trial. He told a young custodian at his apartment, "Take my word for it and don't wind up like me. I got in with the wrong crowd, and my life isn't worth anything now."

The following night, September 23, 1970, Semenoro spent with his wife Sharon and son Kevin who was only 4. Late that evening, he was painting a ceramic lamp in his first-floor apartment. At 10:15 PM, the telephone with an unknown number in the bedroom began ringing. Sharon Semenoro went into the bedroom to answer it with her son Kevin following her. When Sharon picked up the phone and said hello, the only sound she heard was someone hanging up on the other end.

In the living room, Carmen Semenoro could be seen through the sheer window drapes from outside the apartment. He hunched over, concentrating on his work when the first of three shotgun blasts were fired. All three shots hit Semenoro in the head and face, killing him instantly.

A mafia historian in Cleveland strongly believes that an enforcer for Brancato, Bob Boggess, was given the "Hit" order on Semenoro.

1973

This year Frank Brancato was sick on and off most of the time. By November, he was in University Hospital dying a slow and painful death, from Cancer. Brancato died peacefully with his close family by his side on December 17, 1973.

151

FRANK BRANCATO'S ARREST RECORD

F.B.I. Records on Frank Brancato's arrests with Federal ID Number 137835; Cleveland ID Number 29063:

Cleveland, Ohio: Arrested on May 13, 1926, on suspicious person charge; released.

Cleveland, Ohio: Arrested on June 13, 1927, on suspicious person charge; released.

Cleveland, Ohio: Arrested on December 11, 1927, on suspicious person charge; released.

Cleveland, Ohio: Arrested on August 21, 1930, for the murder of Frank Alessi; later found not guilty and released.

Cleveland, Ohio: Arrested on March 8, 1932, on suspicious person charge; released.

Cleveland, Ohio: Arrested April 9, 1932, for perjury. Held in jail on June 2, 1932, when he was found guilty of perjury and sentenced to the Ohio State Penitentiary in Columbus, Ohio, pending his appeal. He was later released on bond until his next jury trial.

Cleveland, Ohio: Arrested on July 28, 1932, on suspicious person charge; found not guilty.

Columbus, Ohio: State Penitentiary ID Number 66919 on April 24, 1933: convicted of perjury for the

Porrello brothers' murders and sentenced to 1 to 10 years in prison. He was discharged from the Ohio Penitentiary on December 2, 1936.

Buffalo, NY, at the INS office ID Number 2544646, registered as an alien on October 1, 1940.

Pittsburgh, PA: Allegheny County ID Number 17141: Arrested May 28, 1945, on a suspicious person charge and discharged on May 29.

Cleveland, Ohio: picked up for questioning on August 25, 1950, questioned and released.

U.S. INS office in Cleveland, Ohio: Number 0707-K-2129 on August 28, 1951, for violation of immigration laws.

Los Angeles, California: ID Number 362369 on October 5, 1956; Registered with the city as an ex-con, given ID Number 40146. Not arrested.

Cleveland, Ohio: ID Number 90341 on July 29, 1957, brought in for questioning and released.

Las Vegas, NV: ID Number 72377 on September 19, 1963; registered as an ex-felon per the county ordinance.

Cleveland, Ohio: June 23, 1968; brought in for questioning in the case of Peter DiGravio murder in Chesterland, Ohio. Released the same day.

FBI, Cleveland, Ohio: ID Number 5041 on April 28,

1970; charged with extortion and conspiracy per the Anti-Racketeering Hobbs Act, Title 18 Section 371. No trial date was set. Later in the year, charges were dismissed.

Cleveland, Ohio: September 25, 1970: Questioned in the murder of Carmine Semenoro.

FBI, Cleveland, Ohio: ID Number 8174 on September 29, 1972; for violation of Ohio gambling laws. No trial date was set.

26

THE UNDERBOSS

ANTHONY "OLD MAN" MILANO

The Milano brothers found a new home in Ohio and settled in the community of Cleveland around 1916.

Only a few people alive today knew who the real Mr. Anthony Milano was in Cleveland from the 1940s until his death by natural causes in 1978.

Yes, he started the first Italian Brotherhood Club (IAB) as well as The Mayfield Imports Company located on Mayfield Road on the east side of Cleveland across the street from the center of Little Italy, and of course, Holy Rosary Church. Yes, his brother Frank was the "Boss" of the Cleveland crime family for several years, known as "The Mayfield Road Gang."

Yes, Anthony Milano was the "Underboss during most of his

life for his brother and then for their friend Alfred Polizzi and counseled John Scalish and retired in 1972, when John DeMarco took over the role.

Yes, Mr. Milano and his brother Frank operated a well-known and stylish gambling house in Richmond Heights, Ohio, referred to as the elaborate Ohio Villa Gambling Club.

Anthony was an Italian mobster who rose to power in America working for the Cleveland Crime family in what was named "The American Mafia." He was the godfather of future Cleveland crime family "Underboss" Angelo Lonardo, the son of Big Joe Lonardo

Anthony was born on December 5, 1888, in Reggio Calabria in Southern Italy to Pietro and Grazia Milano (née Mazza). His family eventually immigrated to the United States and made their first home in Buffalo, New York, for a short period until the family found themselves on their way to Cleveland, Ohio, by 1913. Anthony married Josephine DiSanto and had four children, John, Peter, Frank, and Carmen.

Anthony Milano and his brother Frank were active in the profitable extortion rackets and bootlegging during prohibition years in Cleveland.

1912

On September 21, two men were being held on federal counterfeiting charges. Both men wanted to be released, but at last, only one could be that lucky.

Both Milano and Turone were arrested on Thursday by U.S. Secret Service agents. Their attorney was A. E. Bernstein, as bail for each man, was set at a high cost of $2,500. The only bail, bondsman in the city at the time, was Vincent Dandrea. He only had enough money for one $2,500 bond, which would allow the release of one man that night. Sadly, the other man would have to wait for another Bondsman on Monday to help him get out of jail.

Inside the United States Commissioner, Court Judge Walther authorized the release of Frank Turone, the cousin of Anthony Milano. Turone was chosen to be released from prison because his wife was sick, and his sister was expecting a baby very soon. Milano thought of his family first and accepted his fate and slowly walked back to his jail cell, smiling while Turone walked out of jail.

Arrested the day before in Cleveland was Domineo Barletto, who spoke very little English and was detained by Patrolman Michael Harwood for passing counterfeit coins to his wife while she worked at the nearby store. Barletto was placed on a $2,500 bond as well and could not make bail.

It became a cloudy day in early October for young Anthony Milano as Domineo Barletto pled guilty to charges of passing counterfeit money in front of Federal Judge William L. Day. Barletto testified to the agents from the Secret Service that he was forced to do this by several men and felt compelled to name, Anthony Milano and Frank Turone.

During his prior arrangement in front of Judge Day, Berletto told the brave story, which convinced the federal officers that he was threatened, and would lose his life if he did not co-operate. Barletto continued and said he was a victim and used by the men. Barletto's story continues as he said he left Chicago on his way to New York when he stopped at the Union Station Depot to wait for his next train to New York. He stated, "He was approached by Milano and Turone, who promised him some work." For the next few days, he went around the city and purchased an assortment of items with the fake coins the men gave him. He then refused to do more work for the two men when he was told by a vendor the coins were counterfeit.

According to Barletto, Milano held a razor to his throat as he warned him that if he turned them into the police, he would be killed. Barletto was sentenced to one year and one day in Leavenworth, Kansas. Both Milano and Turone were released on bond before their final hearing and quickly disappeared from the city.

In early October, the Cleveland Police and the Secret Service found it strange that Mr. Milano sold his busy neighborhood saloon at 2263 Orange Ave. in Cleveland and disappeared for a short while.

Agent Washer, who was on detail for President Taft, was brought in to search for the missing Milano Brothers and Turone. Washer soon traced railroad tickets that Frank Milano purchased to Pittsburgh, PA. Washer, then found that the three men got off the train in Youngstown, Ohio and quickly double-backed across Ohio and ended up in Chicago. Before an arrest could be completed, the trio left Chicago and stopped in St. Paul, Missouri. Washer reacted quickly and sent photos of the three criminals and a detailed description of another man to Agent, T. R. McManus stationed in St. Paul. By the time McManus received the photos of the trio, they astonishingly vanished once again. Agent Washer dug into the case and found the trio could be headed for Duluth and ordered McManus to go there and apprehend the men.

By November, a mere six weeks after their first arrest, Milano found himself being questioned by the U.S. Treasury Agents for his involvement in passing counterfeited coins in over a dozen cities and for jumping bail. By Thanksgiving, the Milano brothers were arrested inside a home in Duluth, Minnesota. Tony was escorted back to Cleveland to face his changes along with the confiscated coin molds used in the counterfeit scam. For Frank Milano, he was placed in a jail cell in Duluth, awaiting charges of his own.

By December, after the intensive three-month investigation, the Secret Service arrested who they believed to be the "Chief" of the counterfeiting ring. The man was Rocco Straniero from Pittsburgh. The Secret Service Agent, who stopped Straniero, was J.F. Nye, who consistently kept in touch with the Italian community. Nye was assigned to observe and question Stranerio.

During the intensive interview, Stranerio was unable to satisfy Nye's curious nature as he placed Stranerio under strict surveillance.

U.S Attorney Alburn then learned that Straniero gang consisted of nine men, including Anthony Milano and Frank Turone, who had manufactured the coins for him. All nine people have been arrested and are awaiting their sentencing.

Straniero was brought to Cleveland, and sentenced in Federal Court by Judge William Day, to seven years in the federal prison in Leavenworth, Ks. After Stranerio's conviction, Detective Martino, an Italian himself, spoke freely and openly on how the "Black Hand" operates as many Italians in Cleveland have been made to "Pay a Tribute" to men like Straniero. Many families have been impoverished because of "fear of death" by the man who they call the "Chief."

By January 19, 1913, Milano found himself acquitted on the counterfeiting charges by a federal jury and released.

Even with his colorful criminal past, Anthony Milano became a naturalized American citizen on June 27, 1924. He married the lovely Josephine DiSanto. Years later, his wife Josephine and their children moved to Los Angeles in the 1940s while he split his precious time between his family in Los Angeles and watching over his lucrative business ventures in Cleveland and Las Vegas.

27

1930

By this time, the Milano brothers were growing their "*Mayfield Road Mob*" based in Cleveland's Little Italy, as they replaced the Porrellos as Cleveland premier criminal group. The Italian Mafia faction was even mentioned by its old name in the movie "*The Godfather II*" as the "Lakeview Road Gang" as Lakeview Cemetery borders Mayfield Road Hill, which marks the beginning of Little Italy in the heart of Cleveland. By the summer, the slot machine business was becoming more significant than any other crime in the city of Cleveland, along with the other cities across America.

Anthony Milano acquired additional strength and clout in the Cleveland organization and helped in building a strong union movement through a little-known business transaction or what is known as a swap. Milano agreed to help organize the voiceless truck drivers throughout Ohio at the Commission House if he was promised that future officers of the new unions would all be, "Italian boys." After this effective agreement, Milano was able to place other men of Italian descent into critical labor union positions, one man being John Felice senior, the father of later Teamsters powerhouse John "Skip" Felice. By the end of the same year, Milano was involved in an auto accident and driven to the hospital by his trusted friend Al Polizzi, where his left leg was found to be broken. This incident held Milano up for many months while he recovered.

At the same time, little know Jewish Teamster leader William Presser became a known loyal friend of Anthony as he accepted full credit for getting Presser Sr. his first job in a union position. A former Teamster officer mentioned that for an extended period, Presser got his daily orders directly from Milano. However, by 1973, Mr. Milano opposed Jackie Presser to run for the top position in the substantial union. He announced that Jackie was a spoiled brat and that he would not support him or the advancement of other Jewish personnel in the Teamsters Union.

Then it was in 1931 when the Milano brothers gained such a stronghold in the Ohio region, they were asked to join the National Crime Syndicate with many of the powerful criminals around the country.

On March 23, 1932, another assignation took place that was linked directly to Milano. The murder of Fred Capillo, a former corn-sugar man and a promoter of the modern-day clearing house or better known as the lottery operation. His lifeless body was found slumped over the steering wheel of his car located in front of 2915 East 54th Street. He had two bullet holes in his forehead.

1938

On May 5th, *Cleveland Plain Dealer* writer Chad Skinnee wrote how Safety Director Eliot Ness has obtained crucial evidence which he hopes to use to smash the influential "Mayfield Road Gang" and send the men and their leader Anthony Milano to prison for good.

Ness is tired of the gang running their illegal gambling operation virtually untouched since the end of prohibition with little interference from the police. Ness then reported, he will be turning over the secret evidence he has unveiled to County Prosecutor Frank Cullitan and his assistant Charles McNamee for the submission to the Grand Jury to review.

Ness is diligently seeking accurate answers to three questions that have been plaguing him for some time.

First, how was the Mayfield Road Gang, able to muscle their way into the very lucrative numbers racket over a short period without any interference from the police or a fight from the other mobsters in the city?

Second, how could this be allowed by the police? Was it because of their lazy attitude towards gambling and how was this able to grow to the massive proportions that have attracted the racketeers from "The Hill."

Third; What is the full strength of the Mayfield Road Gangs activities since the bootlegging days ended, and the "Corn Sugar" business was put out of business.

The Mayfield Road Gang has become the dominant force in the city by cutting out its competitors by just killing them. Many of their members were even harassing or paying off policemen until they left the men alone so they could go back to doing business as usual.

28

1933

By May, over 1,000 prominent citizens of Cleveland attended the most elegant dinner party of the year. Held at the new Brotherhood Country Club to mark the special dedication ceremony while hundreds of people were turned down because they did not make a reservation in advance.

The close group of men from the Italian Brotherhood Club acquired 100 acres of land on Highland Road in a quiet community of Richmond Heights. Their future plan is being developed to create a community for their proud Italian-Americans friends. After the completion of the building, the ballroom was well lite as it measured 120 x 84 feet and colorfully decorated in the traditional Red, White, and Green; the colors of the Italy Flag as well as Red, White, and Blue for the American Flag.

Michael Picciano's grand dedication ceremony clearly marks the advancement of the proud Italian people have made in Cleveland. Their ambitious plan and goal will not stop until they develop, a recreation center and a family-friendly park, a home for the older Italian community, and a school for the arts. Mayor Ray Miller, of Richmond Heights, extended his cities welcome and congratulations and the massive undertaking in these trying times. He even introduced Stefano Ardito from the Italian Consulate to the roaring crowd of spectators.

Salvatore LoPresti is a local produce leader in the community. He mentioned that this vast undertaking was the vision of Anthony Milano, who has become the treasurer of this outstanding organization.

Attending this celebrated event and sitting at the head tables where County Prosecutor Frank Cullitan, Assistant County

Prosecutor Frank Celebrezze, Municipal Judge Frank Day, Charles Cavoto, and Lucian Nardi along with police prosecutor Samuel Lograsso.

1938

By July, Anthony Milano was named in a civil lawsuit filed in Common Pleas Court on behalf of Mrs. Ann Ratty, who claims her husband Leo lost an incredible $35,750 gambling in the Arrow and Thomas gambling clubs from July 1937 until October 15th, 1938. Mr. Ratty is an attorney who has been indicted for emblazing the cash from his multitude of clients. Others charged in this lawsuit were Thomas McGinty, Sam "Game Boy" Miller, Harry Potter, Morris Kleinman, Morris Dalitz, aka Moe Davis, John Angersola, and Louis Rothkopf. All of these men were known gamblers, and have worked together and jointly with Milano to keep peace in the Cleveland area.

In early October, Eliot Ness led yet another raid against the Cleveland Mafia's largest known numbers bank, operating out of a private home on East 36th Street. The evidence seized their secured indictments against many of Milano's men, including George and John Angersola, Angelo Lonardo, Chuck Polizzi, Angelo Sicria, Shonder Birns, Masihe Rockman as well as sixteen others.

By the end of 1944, the new "Boss" of Cleveland would become the young John Scalish who lasted unchallenged and untouched until his unexpected death in 1976.

1945

The story of sixty-year-old Nate Weisenberg, who was best known as the "slots baron, kingpin or czar" in Ohio, was murder in his own driveway on Silsby Road in Cleveland Heights, Ohio on February 24, 1945.

At this time, detectives are unsure if Anthony Milano had Wesienberg killed or another theory by investigators is that out of town mobsters who knew Weisenberg had wanted these new machines for themselves without buying them.

According to Allan May's *Crime Town USA*, Weisenberg was alleged to be aligned with the *"Mayfield Road Gang"* for the last twenty years and was looking to move his slot machine business into the Ohio counties of Mahoning, Summit, and Trumbull.

1950

By this time, Anthony Milano is known affectionately as *"The old man"* since he was in his early sixties and fought diligently to change the American conception of Italians. It was that all Italians wherein the so-called mafia and could not be trusted. Over the next two decades, *"The Old Man"* still held considerable power and influence in Cleveland and across the country.

Anthony Milano had many legitimate and criminal businesses across the country. Later, his eldest son Peter became a member of the Los Angles crime family, and the Milano's relationship strengthened the ties between the two large cities and powerful crime families.

According to *"To Kill the Irishman"* written by Rick Porrello: by the early 1950s, Tony and brother Frank Milano were in a close relationship with the Los Angles, Mafia crime "Boss" Jack Dragna, Johnny Roselli and future "Boss" Nick Licata.

1952

According to Rick Porrello *"To Kill the Irishman,"* a confidential informant told the FBI that Anthony Milano, who was mentioned as being a person of interest in the government's *"Top Hoodlum Program." Anthony Milano is the head of the Los Angles Mafia, and even though Milano may be residing in Cleveland, Ohio, he remains in control of the "Italian Group" in Los Angles as well. In a confusing statement, the FBI informant related that Anthony Milano is the "Boss," and Jack Dragna is only a "Puppet."*

Dragna has been connected with the Chicago Syndicate and under their thumb as well. Milano holds all the power over the Italians as he resembles that of a king, and his word is the law to his loyal followers. The informant continued and stated, "Milano maintains a resident at 9451 Sunset Boulevard, in Beverley Hills, while residing in LA. He has up to 60 henchmen ready to gather at moments noticed to carry out his orders. The informant noted that in his opinion, Mr. Milano was probably the most powerful man in the United States insofar as the criminal element among Italians is concerned. Milano has been able to avoid publicity and the spotlight that other influential people search for. Milano keeps to himself and stays in the background and is not as well-known as many other Italians in the country.

29

1959

By January, to coincide with his move to California, Anthony Milano decided to sell his Mayfield Road Imports building, which he purchased back in 1948 for $22,500 to Joseph Taddeo, who is a well-known attorney. It seems Milano owned back taxes of $30,916 on this building, and to help satisfy the internal revenue, he sold the building to pay off the debt. Taddeo mentioned he purchased the building for his client John Miceli. Miceli is a reputable produce and dairy broker in the city. Milano has been known for a long time as "The banker of Mayfield Road."

The Government states that Milano owns back taxes of more than $11,175 for the years of 1946, $2,417 for 1948, $4,339 for 1949, and $11,988 for 1950. This current financial business troubles with the government seemed to motivate Milano into an early retirement stage of his life to help take the increased heat and pressure off of him.

1970

Earlier, Anthony's niece married John Nardi, whose legal job was listed as Secretary-Treasurer of Teamsters Vending Machine Local 310. Years later, Nardi became an essential associate of the Cleveland, crime family. Nardi went against the other Italians in the Cleveland family in the mid-1970s and sided with the Irish gang led by Danny Greene.

1973

In August, Leo Moceri mentioned that he believed that Anthony Milano was anxious to get his son Peter who was now a Capo in LA, back to Cleveland from Los Angeles. He wanted Peter to work alongside his nephew, John Nardi. Milano had hoped that Peter could one day take over the helm of the Cleveland, crime family when Scalish decided to retire. With John DeMarco dead of a heart condition and Frank Brancato having a severe health condition of his own, there could be no one strong enough to control the city that was currently having significant problems with Danny Greene.

On September 23, 1973, *The Plain Dealer* had an article written by Mairy Jayn Wege.

Mister Anthony Milano continues to be seen at his Italian American Brotherhood Club located on Murry Hill for over 40 years. Mr. Milano will usually visit the club for their traditional monthly meetings on Tuesday for a dinner that costs only $7, which is often packed to capacity. Milano is joined by the Sargent in Arms, Mickey Rini, as many candidates seeking votes will come and visit Milano and look for his substantial support in the Italian community. Milano and Rini are currently helping mayoral candidate Ralph J. Perk who has been a member of the club for nine- years and Rini for 25- years.

Old police records describe; Milano as being involved in gambling and multiple shooting, which happened in and around Murry Hill. Milano denies being a part of any bootlegged connections that occurred in Cleveland during the explosive prohibition years. Milano is now 87 and still denies the existence of the society known as the Mafia, even though the FBI insists they see an extraordinary amount of evidence. If this is the case, why don't they do something about it? Milano stated, "Valachi is full of baloney, he just told them what they wanted to hear."

"The Hill" residents lovingly refer to Milano as "The old man or Mister Tony" as he is still loved by the supportive, friendly, and loving Italian community. Cleveland Police says Milano has a clear-cut teamster connection and has the power and clout to get anyone a job in one or another labor union in the city.

Milano is a humble and quiet man. He only says, "I get favors done for people." I just recommend people for a job. I do not take money from them, and if they try to pay me, I tell them to leave, I just like to help people in need. Milano states a few of his protégés are Ohio Teamster William Presser and famous Italian singer Perry Como who often sang in the Ohio Villa Club during his career.

Milano recalls once, "He helped Jackie Presser when he went to talk to the current Teamster AFL President District Council Edward Murphy. I knew Murphy was going to be leaving his critical post in the union, and I only asked him to put Presser in, he did." Milano had unyielding ties with the Jewish network of criminals, including Moe Dalitz.

After an in-depth investigation, it seems that Murphy had a mysterious past obligation to Milano. The story is told that back in 1932 when Murphy could not organize construction workers until he visited Milano for his help. Because of Milano's powerful influence in Cleveland.

Milano has been able to get his nephew Jack Nardi a post as a Secretary-Treasurer of Local 416 and another Italian Brotherhood member Nick Francis a post as President of the Union. Francis replaced the previous President Patrick Catalano, who was slain in his garage, and his body found dumped elsewhere.

After a full investigation into the Cleveland Unions, local Federal agents have declared that because of Milano's influential friends in high places across the country, he has been able to put mob associates as representatives in at least 15 different union locals.

Earlier in the 1930s, investigators were able to uncover that Anthony Milano helped to finance the building of the sanctuary of St. Anthony's Church in Akron, Ohio. Milano has also contributed money to aid in the construction of John Carroll University, on Cleveland's Eastside.

In Milano's Brotherhood Loan office, he proudly has it hanging on the wall. A picture of President Nixon who signed it, "To Anthony Milano with best wishes," Milano admitted that while President Franklin D Roosevelt was in office, he was placed on the now-famous national "Black List."

Milano continues to deny, that back in 1951, he approved a loan for Los Angles mobster Mickey Cohen. Cohen was given a $45,000 credit from his Brotherhood Loan Company to purchase his new home in the beautiful upper scale area of Brentwood, California.

1975

It was a Sunday, June 15th, as *The Plain Dealer* posted an article written by Thomas Andrzejewski, which revealed the elegance, and charm promoting the small Italian community named Little Italy seated just south of the prestigious Case University.

The small Eastside neighborhood known as Little Italy has two items of controversy to its name, one is the 6 Italian restaurants of the Golden Bowl, Mama Santo's, Guarino's, Rene Cremona's, the Roman Gardens, Theresa's and Minnillo's. They are always built to be an excellent restaurant for all of Cleveland to come and enjoy a home-made style of Italian cuisine. There is, however, an unwritten law in Cleveland, where these traditional restaurants are not allowed to be downgraded for any reason at all. The other controversy is what could be called "The Organization. This does not exist" or as others may like to call it and referred to by the Fed's like the "LCN" (La Cosa Nostra) and a person most mentioned by "The I" (short for FBI) is the "Old Man" himself, Anthony Milano.

The United States Justice Department is entirely against Organized crime in Cleveland, which has been active in Little Italy and at times, even concealing Federal agents hiding behind trees and bushes.

1978

It was a somber day in Cleveland, Ohio, on August 6, 1978, when the easily loved "Old Man" Anthony Milano passed away quietly. The former Murray Hill businessman described by local citizens and federal law officers as a senior advisor to the Cleveland Mafia over his long career in organized crime. The Justice Department, two years ago, even posted that at the age of 88, he was still a trusted advisor and consultant to the criminal organization, which many called the Mafia, but was just the "La Cosa Nostra," just a group of friends working together. Milano died at the peaceful age of ninety.

Most Cleveland residents publicly knew Milano, as a friendly grocer, an importer of fine Italian foods and gift items are known as Mayfield Imports for so many years with its home on Murray Hill Road and the founder of the Italian American Brotherhood Club.

Regrettably, only a few people knew who the real Anthony Milano was and how he enjoyed life and the Philosophy's of life through his own eyes, his thoughts in business, his feelings about life, love, and happiness.

It is believed by many, who really knew Anthony Milano, that he wrote these inspiring notes while relaxing in the city and community he loved so dearly. The town he helped to build in the 1920s to become known as the center of the Italian community in Cleveland, Ohio, Little Italy on the street known as Murray Hill.

The following Philosophical Quotations were written by Mr. Anthony Milano.

Cleveland's own Street Philosopher and poet, Mr. Doug Rutti, bring this list of inspirational quotes for you to enjoy.

➢ To know poverty is a great accomplishment.
➢ He, who thinks he is so great, suddenly falls.
➢ When upon entering, you read "charity" inside, you
   find neither charity nor laws.

- To become dominated, it is necessary to give the people discipline, education, liberty, and bread.
- The secret of power is desired.
- Hunger is the teacher of life.
- The support of life is hope.
- Study first the penal code, and then go swimming.
- If you want to live and be healthy, take the world as it comes.
- Nobility is acquired by personal deeds, not by birth.
- The mirror of the mind is the face: and the mirrors of the heart are the eyes.
- He who lives in a mansion must realize that he also may live in a stable.
- He, who knows how to talk, knows how to win.
- It is better to educate and discipline the mass rather than punish them.
- The progress of man: (1) be punctual; (2) mind your own business; (3) don't promise to do more than which you are able.
- To understand man, one must study a lifetime.
- Women are like a piano; it is never possible to understand her.
- Do not be overcome by snobbishness, wealth, and power.
- The duty of many is to support the family; the duty of a woman is to be economical and maintain honorably the family's name.
- Never belittle any man, for as small as you may think he is. He may someday be useful.
- Losing wealth, nothing is lost, losing health, something is lost, losing trust, all is lost.
- If you cannot do good for others, do them no harm.
- Success or failure on man's destiny is dependent upon the influence of a woman.
- If you want to live in peace, look, listen, and be quiet.
- The smile is the clearest and most faithful impression of the man's sentiment.

- ➢ Grace, courtesy, and elegance are the arts that contribute to making life more pleasurable and beautiful.
- ➢ Courtesy is the flower of humanity.
- ➢ Empty the glass that is full; fill the glass that is empty. Never keep it full; never keep it empty.
- ➢ Weapons and wealth are good only in the hands of those who know how to handle them.
- ➢ He who is served, cannot command unless he learns first to obey.
- ➢ Do everything you can do not spend all you have; do not believe everything you hear and do not tell everything you know.
- ➢ Do not put off until tomorrow that which you can do today.
- ➢ Remember the past, see the present, and study well in the future.

30

(Courtesy of Cleveland State University Memory project)

MILANO'S OHIO VILLA ERA

It was early in October 1935, when the birth of the *Ohio Villa Club* became known as a favorite notorious gambling hotspot in the heart of the quiet east side community in Richmond Heights.

1938

On January 26th, as luxurious looking, attractive, and upscale gaming club was in the newspaper. A *Cleveland Press* article on March 24th was written by Eugene Segal. *"Society Note*: at the Ohio Villa Club, the *Mayfield Gang hosted some of the elite high-society people in town as their special guests last night, at the spectacular reopening of the colorful Ohio Villa Club on Highland Road. It was an elegant affair, almost as good as the New York society parties put on by the famous socialite Ms. Elsa Maxwell.*

Over the winter months, the Ohio Villa, enlarged the grand dining room along with an exciting new casino area so that guests would no longer bump into one another when they would be standing next to someone at the crap tables. The enlargement made room for a shiny new assortment of green felt dice, roulette, and card tables. While some people might suspect that financial considerations prompted these improvements, others who attended the rededication ceremony were treated to elaborate dignified manners of their host. All felt the Cleveland boys enthusiastically wanted to make their guests more comfortable and possibly stay a little longer, and of course, to lose more money.

The entire Villa dining room, including a spacious bar and casino area, which has been plush carpeting of a lovely color of a blue and yellow pattern, giving a feel of style and elegance.

While it is not polite for a guest to mention such a thing, it is reported that the "Mayfield Road Gang" or should I say the Milano Brothers spent over $35,000 (In today's money that is equal to $627,000.) A few more nights like this reopening night would more than pay the Milano's back their investment as at least 1,500 guests attended the spectacular gala evening festivities.

Being an exclusive, glamorous club, *The Ohio-Villa* is hard to find, since there are only a few signs posted a half a mile before you get close to the club's main entrance. Then there is a giant neon sign at the entry of the vast grounds, as it lighted up the complete area around the barn, making it look as though it was on fire. Many of the guests were met at the entrance by a brilliantly uniformed doorman who ushered and welcomed them with a grand smile. The guests were next invited into the fantastic, beautifully decorated dining room, as they enjoyed an impressive dinner. Stewarts in the finest of evening clothes wearing a nice southern vacation tan. Women paused to congratulate Frank & Anthony

Milano on their beautiful establishment and to wish them well, and all the success in the world, as they often gave them a kiss on the cheek.

The dining room, including a new and significant dance floor which became jammed packed with dancing couples enjoying the big band sound from a live orchestra. During the early hours of the evening, several gaming tables and chairs were set up for the men and women to play Keno. The Keno players overflowed into the casino area and into the simple yet elegant bar area

When you finally reached the elaborate casino floor from the rear of the dining room, you could see how fantastic and exclusive the club had actually become. The entrance was now marked *"Members Only"* as an assortment of beautiful women dressed in an elegant evening gown politely asked the guest whom she did not recognize for their credentials. If you were unable to produce any, the man would be asked to step aside then be quizzed by the manager in a quiet, very gentle, and professional manner.

Some wise players slipped a chip or two into their shallow pocket when he won or moved it to a companion playing next to him; saying "this is for coffee and a donut in the morning," while his friend replied, "That's all you have left is this?"

By June 30, *The Ohio Villa* was considered to be one of the *"Big Three"* gambling clubs in the area. The club temporarily moved out all of its gaming equipment on Tuesday because of dissension among the Richmond Heights City Officials and an eruption of concerned residents over the club's flamboyant and flagrant operation of the organization.

By September 24, *The Ohio Villa* has long operated as a wide-open gambling joint in Richmond Heights, now advertises itself as "The Showplace of America."

An advertisement printed in the *Lakewood Courter* and T*he Rocky River Call* on Friday gives explicated directions on how to reach the exciting nightclub and asked those who wish to make reservations to phone "John Itta at Kenmore-1205." The ad also emphasizes "no cover charge" and eloquently added a fabulous floor show with the music provided by a local favorite This week it was Freddie Carlone and his fantastic orchestra.

One story told is how Freddie Carlone, a popular dance band in the Ohio / PA area, helped to promote a rising new star. Carlone and his orchestra were playing outside of Cleveland and invited anyone in the audience who thought they might have the talent to come up and sing with his band. A handsome young barber named Perry Como was terrified, but his friends urged him and pushed him onto the stage. Carlone was so impressed with Como's performance that he immediately offered him a job.

HANDSOME 29-YEAR-OLD PERRY COMO

(Courtesy of Wikipedia)

Chief Deputy of The United States Marshal service J.J. Wein related how one of his agents went to the *Ohio Villa Club* to serve notice to them on a Federal Court lawsuit. Wein claims he would not know until tomorrow whether the Agent was successful in helping the warrants. The officer, who was identified as female, notified Wein that she successfully served the defendant in the lawsuit of both *The Ohio Villa* and *The Thomas Club*. The agent identified herself then gave the warrant to Morris Kleinman, while he was leaning against the bar in the *Ohio Villa Club*. She politely notified him that he was to appear in Federal Court on August 19. Kleinman also accepted the subpoenas for the other defendants of the Brotherhood Country Club, Michael Piccano, Ralph Dodero, and Joseph Taddeo

On December 12[th,] the unwanted announcement came from several employees, "it was going to be the last night for *The Ohio Villa.*" The club would soon be hauled before the United States District Court.

The Cleveland Press announced on December 17, how Sheriff Martin O'Donnell was put squarely "on the spot" in connection with the gambling in Cuyahoga County when a motion was filed in U.S District Court seeking authority to question the sheriff about the wide-open gambling casino.

Also, subpoenaed was Mayor Ed Williams and Marshal Yaro both from Richmond Heights so they could testify in the current lawsuit against the exclusive high-class gambling resorts. This action was yet another in a series of legal maneuvers undertaken by Russell Bleecher, who represents the insurance company Lloyds of London, to padlock the clubs and to recover thousands of dollars stolen from a bank and later lost at the Ohio Villa and Thomas Clubs

On December 20, Attorney Russell Bleecher asks Federal Court Judge Paul Jones for a direct order to compel Morris Kleinman to answer specific questions about the operation. At a deposition hearing before Henry Gabriel, a court reporter told the story of how Kleinman refused to respond to every question addressed to him by Bleecher except for one, that he informs the court his name. Calculated legal action against the gambling resort was regarded to be filed against Michael Picciano and the other club officials."

Picciano is a former police city prosecutor, along with Morris Kleinman, who is a well-known racketeer. Both men were named as co-defendants in the $17,000 lawsuit filed in Federal Court several weeks ago to recover gambling losses.

THE ELEGANT OHIO VILLA

(Courtesy of the Authors collection)

31

1939

On January 19, Federal Judge Paul Jones set January 27 for the first court hearing on a motion in regards to the lawsuits. The judge is asking once again that the *Ohio Villa* and *The Harvard Club* be closed down as immoral and a grave public nuisance.

The depositions were sought from Cuyahoga County Sheriff O'Donnell and Mayor Edward Williams of Richmond Heights. Requests for these statements were made to five additional defendants listed in the lawsuit. Sam Tucker, Morris Kleinman, John Croft, Harry Potter, and M.A. Picciano, who is listed as the club president.

On March 17, *the Cleveland Press* stated, a confidential memo was sent to Sheriff Martin O'Donnell. It merely read; "On March 29[th,] the Ohio Villa will reopen its gambling club.

The Press told its dedicate daily readers; P.S; You can get to the Ohio Villa by driving out of Euclid Avenue to Euclid Creek and then turn south on Highland Road. It is on the left-hand side as you approach Richmond Road.

P.S.S; you can't win!

Sam Tucker, Morris Kleinman, John Croft, Harry Potter, and M.A. Picciano met with Attorney Leonard Danaceau, who represents the Richmond Heights resort. Danaceau firmly believed the lawsuit would be dismissed by the court for lack of evidence against his clients.

Michael Picciano is a former trustee of the Brotherhood County Club. He decided last week to dissolve and turn the property back over to the Brotherhood Loan Company, of which

Anthony Milano is listed as the treasurer. There is a current loan listed of $116,000 on the mortgage, which is currently in default. It was learned that the jittery shareholders would be given notes against the Brotherhood Loan Company, notifying them they would receive a mere twenty cents on a dollar of the face value of their stock value.

A second lawsuit was filed back on January 18 and named the defendant's Morris Kleinman, John Croft, Harry Potter, and the Brotherhood Loan Company.

While the second court battle continued, on April 17, *The Plain Dealer* once again announced the reopening of *The Ohio Villa* in the eastside suburb of Richmond Heights. As almost five-hundred men and women, most of whom appeared to be persons of wealth, enjoyed themselves in the elaborate club. By 10 PM, the Bingo games started.

The guests were treated to the fantastic music of Freddie Carlone's Orchestra featuring Mickey Katz on clarinet, along with a fabulous floor show. Gorgeous floral arrangements and horseshoes filled the lobby where a doorman in formal attire welcomed the patrons back into the club for an evening of entertainment.

The club was forced to close down early last December after being sued by Russell Bleecher, an attorney for Lloyds of London, to recover $17,000 that was allegedly lost, thereby a disgruntled gambler Fred Herbison, a former bank teller now serving a three-year term in federal prison for embezzlement. It was reported last week that this lawsuit had been settled quietly out of court.

1940

Closed since last Christmas, *The Ohio Villa* "nightclub" reopened for its 1940 spectacular season on April 17. The night was chilly and raining, but the vast crowd overflowed into the beautiful lobby as the elaborate doors open. The guest enjoyed a spectacular floor show, fabulous food, and plenty of beverages along with bingo, as they listened and danced the night away to an eleven-piece orchestra.

For this reopening, the expensively printed brochures were mailed to their long list of established clients'. It delightfully announced the start of a new season where keno, dice, roulette, and stud poker are played in the wide-open for high stakes. The grand invitation saying, "We are open once again, presenting for your pleasure the finest floor shows, the most pleasant music, and excellent food in the area."

Judge Frank Lausche and George Baer are currently working on a strategic plan to permanently close down the illegal gambling clubs in the county under the closed eye of Sheriff Martin O'Donnell, "home rule policy."

"Home Rule Policy" currently allowed small communities such as Richmond Heights to govern themselves. "Home Rule" created the mindset for these communities of "it's *your* problem, *you* fix it."

The operators of *The Ohio Villa Club*; has promised to end their gambling activities after another visit by Mayor Edward Williams and Marshal Earl Richmond. This visit to the club came after Judge Lausche attacked bingo as a "lure or decoy" the victims into the club to later play blackjack, roulette, chuck-a-luck, or other gambling games. Both Williams and Richmond have promised to close the resort down and discontinue gaming there for the last time.

By October 19, under the compulsion of a search warrant issued by Common Pleas Judge Frank J. Lausche, three deputies of Sheriff Martin O'Donnell raided *The Ohio Villa*. They returned with outrageously less gambling evidence than that would be found in orphans home!

It is very curious to wonder what possibly could have happened between 4:30 in the afternoon when Judge Lausche signed the search warrant and gave it to Clearance Tylicki, the Chief Deputy Sheriff. At the same time, the eager County Detective Harry Brown, along with Deputies Joseph Krupansky and Francis Boyle, left the court. However, they did not reach the club until five hours later. This mystery is not known?

An observer noticed that by 8:00 PM, the employees of the club got the word. Soon they were busy carting up the large bingo cage, balls, ball rack, and an assortment of large boxes believed to contain bingo cards and other gambling items out of the club through the back kitchen door. Several other pieces of gaming equipment were then carried out, another rear room believed to be the chuck-a-luck and playing cards used in all the other table games.

Several reporters on the scene were given conflicting reports on when the gambling equipment was moved off the premises by John Itta, the catering manager. Itta claims the gambling stopped when all the fuss began, about three weeks ago, while another tale states, "the equipment was moved out only two nights ago." Itta seemed to not be alarmed or surprised when the detectives arrived at the club. Itta appeared to be happy as he took the men around the club and through the complete building, including the back rooms where some fifty empty tables, a cashier cage. A barbershop located on the second floor, kitchen, and cellar remained utterly abandoned, as the frustrated deputies found no signs of gambling equipment.

Most of the energetic patrons who arrived at the same time the deputies were told there would be "no bingo tonight." One loyal supporter proclaimed, "You got to be kidding me" some left immediately while other eager players stayed and listen and then danced to the music of Maurice Spitalny's Orchestra, who played "It's a Lovely Day Tomorrow" and watched the floor show.

Sheriff O'Donnell claimed, "There was something funny going on," as more than 250 people seemed to know and enjoy watching us. They stayed only to see the fun and the wild look in the eyes of the police when they walked into the building as well as what was happening. They all seemed to be amused and enjoying themselves while we looked totally frustrated and annoyed."

1945

According to Allan May's *Crime Town USA*, a Cuyahoga County deputy sheriff noticed an assortment of vehicles parked during the day at the Ohio Villa and investigated. He diligently wrote down the license plate numbers.

The automobiles found to be listed and owned by several major known underworld criminals around Northeastern Ohio. It could be speculated some men from Cleveland came along with additional people from Youngstown included Charles Cavallaro and Howard Aley, from Akron, was Michael Adella, and Carl LaFatch and from Lima was George, Joseph, and Louis Guagenti.

This critical meeting was alleged to have been planned and organized by Milano to make the necessary actions to take over the hugely profitable slot machine business in northern Ohio.

32

THE JEWISH SYNDICATE

Some law enforcement officials have labeled a group of men as the Jewish Syndicate, while others said they were merely a fun-loving group of people who were happy to bring joy, laughter, and entertainment to their multitude of friends across the United States.

These men consisted of Morris Kleinman and Moe Dalitz (aka Moe Davis), who were known as pullers. "Pullers" are known as a group of people who pulled-whiskey and beer from reputable dealers in Ontario, Canadian bottlers, then bring the product into the United States by using Lake Erie as their primary avenue. According to the local police, some of the men who worked closely with them are Sam Tucker, Max Diamond, Harry Bremmer, Ben Nobel, Harry Katz, Solly Hart, John King Angersola, Art Anders, and Sholem Cohen. It has been said that Max Diamond spent up to $50,000 to buy the best and fastest boat he could find in the area. The ship was named the *Sambo G*. The shipments would be substantial, and he would sell his superior goods to the highest bidder. Often, the boat would be lined with a reinforced hull, as machine guns were added for protection from smugglers or rival gangs.

Often larger ships would leave Ontario with the proper papers for the Canadian boat patrols to inspect and view the cargo. The boat would then head for Point Pelee, the longest stretch of land from Canadian towards the United States. Many times, they would then land and unload the massive ship into smaller speedboats, or they would just head out to Pelee Island just a short distance from the US border. Pelee Island was across from what is known as Avon Lake, Ohio. The cargo would then be separated into smaller boats, which would head for different ports on the vast coastline of Lake Erie. Locations would include Sandusky Bay, Avon, or other small inlets in Lorain or Elyria, or they headed to the East of Cleveland and as far as Lake County, where the goods would be unloaded. Of course, all of the trips would take place in the quiet darkness of the moonlit night, and often would be completed by five in the morning. Before the sunrise and police or citizens would awake and notice the rumrunners in action.

Once the boats landed, they would be quickly unloaded by using a hoist assembly to bring the valuable cargo. The load was typically Hiram Walker or Seagram's liquor, to the waiting trucks, then onto their destinations. Of course, there were times when a boat was highjacked or lost by a raid from the border patrol officers, the Coast Guard, or a rival bootlegger. Klienman even tried to write off the purchase of one of his boats on his personal income taxes as a business loss. However, it was noticed then rejected and not allowed as a business expense by the IRS.

From the run running days, the men went into the illegal gambling business, loan sharking and racketeering as a group. Others came on board, while others left the group. However, they worked together to develop an active and astonishing organization, men like Tommy McGinty, Louis Rothkoph, along with a few other men. Over a short period, Moe Dalitz had developed a stable relationship with the dominant Meyer Lanksy.

This firmly determined team of men helped to forge an unstoppable charge into the new legal world. The world of lights, glimmer, games of chance, and live entertainment, a city that never sleeps which, we all know as Las Vegas. The elegant hotel named the Desert Inn, and then the Stardust Hotel became two of the significant resorts the group partially owned.

MORRIS BARNEY "MOE" DALITZ, aka "Davis" as he was known in Cleveland in the early days, was born in Boston, Massachusetts, on December 24, 1899, and raised in Michigan. As a young man, Dalitz worked in his family's laundry business early on in his young career. However, he began his new career more profitably as a bootlegger when prohibition started in 1919 and capitalized on his access to the laundry trucks in the family business to deliver the goods. He became known as the headman in the leading criminal organization of Jewish American gangsters. "The Cleveland Jewish Syndicate," which was known for their violence and courageous illegal ways.

Additionally, he developed a partnership with the Maceo Syndicate, which controlled Galveston, Texas, as they supplied liquor from the Gulf Coast, Canada, and Mexico. Although he admitted under oath during the Kefauver Hearings in 1951, that he had been a bootlegger and had operated illegal gambling houses. Amazingly, during his lifetime, Moe was never convicted of a single crime.

It has been stated that Dalitz arrived in Cleveland around 1928, where he formed strong ties within Cleveland's Eastside, Little Italy community. Included were the brothers George "Freddy King" and John "John King" Angersola, Alfred Polizzi, and the powerful Frank and Anthony Milano of the "Mayfield Road Mob" to form the leading underworld organization in Cleveland. While converting his incredible profits into legitimate businesses, he also owned a portion of several illegal casinos in Cleveland. Some of Moe's other friends in business included Joe Massei, Sam Tucker, and Abner "Longie" Zwillman.

According to Allan May's *"Crime Town USA,"* since Dalitz was initially from Detroit, he helped to bring together the Cleveland Syndicate (or the Italians) with the Jewish men from Detroit to form what became known as, "The Combination." The Combination worked together in a very effective manner as they controlled gambling in Toledo, Cleveland, Youngstown, Buffalo, and Pittsburgh and in Port Clinton.

According to the FBI, Dalitz owned a share in many of the gambling clubs in Ohio. *The Famous Jungle In*n, located in Trumbull County, *the Mounds Club*, *The Thomas Club,* and *the Pettibone Club*, and in business with Anthony Milano, in the *Ohio Villa Club*. Near Cincinnati, he invested in the *Beverly Hills* and *Lookout Club*.

Moe's initial investments in Las Vegas began in the late 1940s with the Desert Inn when the original builder of the resort, Wilbur Clark, ran out of money. Dalitz took over the massive construction project as he and his friends reportedly held 74 % of the stock. When it opened in 1950, Clark remained the public face of the organization and frontman of the new luxury resort.

In July 1966, the Justice Department became involved in the Gaming Commission with appointed Chairmen, Milton Keefer, who brought the hearing to order. The investigation started back in

1963 where the *Chicago Sun-Times* stated that six Las Vegas Casinos, the Desert Inn, Stardust, Flamingo, Sands, Fremont, and the Horseshoe have lost an average of $70,000 to $100,000 a month through skimming. Believed to be, behind the significant operation where Clevelanders, Moe Dalitz, John Scalish, Morris Kleinman, Al Roen, Louis Rothkopf, Rudy Kolod, along with George Gordon, Sam Tucker, and Tommy McGinty.

Jimmy Hoffa had testified to his longtime relationship with Dalitz through union representation of his dry-cleaning empire.

It is interesting to note that Moe Dalitz and Al Polizzi were such good friends, Dalitz was Polizzi's best man at his wedding.

Mr. Dalitz, once healthy and full of energy, was now weakened by an old heart, cancer, and kidney disease. Moe has used a wheelchair for a lengthy period. Morris (Moe) Dalitz died peacefully on August 31, 1989

33

MORRIS KLEINMAN was born on September 18, 1896, in Cleveland, Ohio, and by 1919 Kleinman took over his father's poultry business and soon became bored as he turned to boxing. He became known for his incredible and powerful "One Touch" knockout. Early in his career, Morris married his first true love, Gizella, and the couple had two children, Mandell and Allen. Morris won the Cleveland Lightweight championship and went on to win the featherweight national amateur championship twice. After he had retired from the fighting game, Kleinman became a fight promoter, bookie, and strong-arm bootlegger and gambler.

In the 1930s, Kleinman was a suspect in the murder case of Morris Komisarow (a known rumrunner) along with Moe Dalitz and Louis Rothkopf and Max Diamond. Kleinman did whatever he needed to do to maintain a low profile, but had a solid reputation as, "The king of contraband."

During the bootlegging wars, Kleinman dominated the field as he controlled what territories his rivals did and who they sold their liquor too. Only one year later, the Internal Revenue Service estimated Kleinman had accumulated over $1.6 million in assets, and they wanted their fair share of it in taxes.

By 1950 after investing in Las Vegas with the Desert Inn and Tropicana Hotels, Kleinman found himself investigated by the I.R.S. for Income Tax Evasion and would be arrested very soon. After his Las Vegas investments, the times changed, as it would lead him to make significant investments in Florida, in the legitimate real estate business, and their many profitable gambling enterprises.

The FBI had given him the ID number of #731237, and in 1963 Klienman released the news that he sold his stock in the famous and top-rated Ice Capades show for three-million dollars on what was believed to be only an original meager investment of $323,000.

The flamboyant Morris Kleinman died comfortably in Florida on May 5, 1989, at the age of 93.

SAM "SAMBO" TUCKER, was born in Lithuania on July 11, 1897. His parents were Louis and Jennie, and Sam was one of four children. The Tucker family moved to America from Russia by October 1912. Sam became a U.S. Citizen, and by 1926 he found himself living in Akron, Ohio. His smooth, calm, and persuasive manner impressed many, as he became known as the "Gentleman" of the syndicate.

SAM TUCKER

By 1926, Tucker and his friends, who included Max Diamond, who was operating a fleet of boats on Lake Erie. A few of their fleet could handle as much as 1,500 cases of whiskey bringing it into Cleveland from Ontario, Canada. As their bootlegging and rum-running business grew, so did their large fleet of boats. Their fleet of the fast ship became known as "The Big Jewish Navy."

In January 1930, Tucker, known as the "gentleman of the Jewish Syndicate" along with his friends, Dalitz and Kleinman, was indicted in front of a Buffalo N.Y. Grand Jury for a violation of the Tariff Act in 1922 and conspiracy to defraud the U.S Government. Tucker was the smooth, friendly, smiling the frontman and was always the man who represented his friends in meaningful negotiation and in a peaceful and demure yet persuasive manner.

In 1935, Tucker was named as a part-owner of the *Thomas Club,* along with Dalitz, Rothkopf, and Marty O'Boyle. Some of their hired help included Solly Hart, Ben Nadel, and Harry Brenner, along with Albert and Charles Polizzi and John Angersola from the Italian mob. These men were responsible for several vicious beatings, shakedowns, and unsolved murders.

In 1936 while dealing with the U.S Tax Court, Sam described his new "Syndicate friends" for some years before and stated, "I have been in business for various companies, with Dalitz, Kleinman, and Louis Rothkopf. They included different laundry business, real estate, nightclubs, and casinos."

In 1940, Tucker moved from Cleveland to Kentucky to supervise the famous *Beverley Hills Country Club* as the casino manager for Dalitz and his group of powerful cronies. The club sadly closed when a massive fire destroyed the remodeled club in May 1977. Regrettably, over 165 people died that Memorial Day weekend.

According to Michael Newton, the author of "Mr. Mob," Tucker was arrested by U.S. Marshall in 1944. His crime was for violating the "OPA" las, which regulated the price of whiskey, served at the *Beverly Hill Club*. Jurors, however, failed to reach a verdict and a conviction for Tucker. The government quickly ordered a second trial. Nevertheless, the trial never took place as the FBI continued to have on record in 1958 that the next hearing was still "pending."

By 1948, Sam was living in a luxurious Surfside community, located near Miami, Florida. Other friends who lived in the area where Sam Cohen from the old Purple Gang from Detroit. The men started up a company named S&G business.

While under oath in 1951 at the Kefauver hearings, Sam admitted that he had been friends with Moe Dalitz for the past 26 years and that he knew Kleinman for about 30 years and Louis Rothkopf for 15-19 years. Sam Tucker continued to be involved with many, if not all, of Moe Dalitz's projects and with the "Cleveland Four."

LOUIS "UNCLE LOU" ROTHKOPF was born on June 12, 1903, in Cleveland, Ohio, and later died in 1956. Lou married Blanche Morgan in 1929. He became a Cleveland mobster, at the young age of twenty, he was overseeing construction of several illegal distilleries. With his mind on business, Louis often traveled to other cities to become aware of their style of managing. It has been alledged that among the men, he spoke with and became friends within New York was Frank Costello. He then moved his attention to controlling some of the illegal gambling and other criminal activities from the 1930s until the early 1950s.

A longtime associate of Meyer Lansky, Rothkopf Cleveland, was given criminal ID # 1126584 and was involved in illegal gambling operations in New York for well-known "Bug and Meyer Mob" during the 1920s. Following the end of Prohibition, Rothkopf became involved in running syndicate gambling operations in Cleveland, Ohio, with Moe Dalitz, James Licavoli, Maurice (Morris) Kleinman, and Thomas McGinty.

In December 1935, Federal agents followed Louis to Kansas City for a meeting with other bootleggers. On December 16, wiretaps overheard his wife Blanche strongly suggested to her husband to return to Cleveland, where his partners wanted to discuss an agreement. The Federal agents indicted Rothkopf, Max Diamond, and 10-others. Lou was arrested by a U.S. Marshal for income tax violations in Cleveland on February 23, 1937. Rothkopf was then convicted on May 22 and sentenced to four years imprisonment and fined $15,000. Later Rothkoph received a gift from the Judge, the wiretaps used to convict him of the crime, were ruled inadmissible, and he was set free.

Suspected by authorities to have ties with top organized crime figures (particularly to Mickey Cohen and Abner Zwillman), charges were dropped by a United States District Court against Rothkopf on January 9, 1940, regarding racketeering charges with Max Diamond, Maurice Kleinman, Albert Philips, Morris Phillip, Kulius Kater, and Tony Scalise.

Within several years Rothkopf had gained increased control of the gambling operations in the city of Cleveland. Rothkoph has been mentioned and suspected to have been one of the men helping to finance Bugsy Siegel's Flamingo Hotel and Casino. In 1947, when Siegel was ordered to be killed by Lucky Luciano. It has been reported that Lansky called Rothkopf and request him to contact Mickey Cohen on his behalf to arrange protection for Siegel. Luciano reportedly said, "I want you to tell Mickey Cohen to stay close to Benny at all times - never let him out of his sight. If anything should happen to Benny, Cohen will have to answer to me." However, despite Rothkopf's attempts to honor this request, Siegel was murdered several weeks later, on June 20.

In February 1949, Rothkopf was reportedly in telephone contact with Los Angeles Italian mobster Jack Dragna and later with Allen Smiley at the Flamingo Hotel. He would regularly associate with Mickey Cohen and often observed by the local police visiting his home in California.

Then by 1950, Rothkopf became the manager of the Desert Inn Casino for a short while for his friend Moe Dalitz's and the "Old Mayfield Road Gang," namely John Scalish, which including Morris Kleinman and Sam Tucker. He allegedly bragged to an associate claiming the casino declared a reported income of $12 million. However, overall, an estimated $36 million was skimmed from the massive casino profits.

Unfortunately, Rothkopf's wife Blanch became seriously ill and died in 1955, and Louis believed to have been so distraught that he committed suicide, His cold, lifeless body was found in his garage in 1956, but the truth about his sudden death will remain unknown and a mystery to law enforcement officials.

It is interesting to note that at the time of Rothkopf's death, his estate was valued to be more than 740,000 thousand dollars. (In today money this is equal to $6,876,854.) At the time of his death, George Gordon took his rightful place in the Jewish Syndicate.

THOMAS JOSEPH MCGINTY (aka, T.J. - Blackjack McGinty) was born on October 17, 1893. Although he was not Jewish, the Irishman played a pivotal role and a leader in the criminal world in Ohio. Known as a former professional boxer, the proud, strong-willed Irishman, McGinty, was soon hired as muscle for *The Plain Dealer's* {a morning paper} circulation department. Then by 1913, he headed a gang of labor sluggers competing against the rival, *"Cleveland News"* sluggers who believed to be under the control of the "Mayfield Road Gang."

Dan Hanna, the owner of both the *Cleveland Leader* and the *News,* brought in the young and energetic 27-year-old Arthur McBride from Chicago to help protect his papers during Cleveland's "Circulation Wars." McGinty and McBride's army of big muscle men slugged their way to winning over the street business and gain more readership as beatings, stabbings, shootings street battles, and truck hijacking became a daily experience and unstoppable by the local police force.

MCGINTY WITH HIS ATTORNEY AT THE KEFAUVER HEARINGS IN 1951

(Courtesy of Cleveland State University Memory Project)

McGinty had a significant role in the early "Horse racing tracks" were placing a "bet" on a horse was illegal. However, "betters" would soon become able to "Contribute" money on the horse's behalf. If the horse won the race, all the "Contributors" would divide the winnings accordingly to their monetary investment.

Although a longtime boxing promoter, during Prohibition, Tommy became one of the largest bootleggers in the city of Cleveland during the 1920s. Operating from *McGinty's Saloon* on West 25th Street with two relatives, McGinty was then indicted by a Federal Grand Jury in 1924 on charges of operating a "gigantic wholesale and retail conspiracy." Although initially in hiding, McGinty turned himself in after several days in hiding and pleading not guilty. Later convicted, and sentenced to eighteen months imprisonment. After his release from Atlanta Federal Prison, he soon resumed his exciting bootlegging activities without further interference from local authorities.

It was during the 1930s when McGinty found himself involved in syndicate gambling operations as a part-owner of Cleveland's *Mound's Club* located in Willoughby Hills, Ohio, a friend of Morris Kleinman along with Cornelius Jones, who operated the *Harvard Club* at the time.

When Tommy was in town, he enjoyed staying at the Hollander Hotel.

McGinty's gambling operations included investments in Youngstown, Ohio and Covington, Kentucky and as far south as Florida, as well as a principal stockholder of the Las Vegas Casino, the Desert Inn with his friends Moe Dalitz, Morris Kleinman, Lou Rothkopf, Sam Tucker, and others during the 1950s. Later, he was known to be associated with Meyer Lansky's Hotel Nacional in Havana, Cuba.

Tommy became well-known in his West Plam Beach community with his second wife Helen and his children

Thomas Jefferson McGinty died peacefully in March 1970 while living in Florida at the age of 79.

34

THE POLICY RACKETS

With open gambling going on in many casinos and backroom parlors all across Cleveland. Just like so many other cities across the nation, this lucrative business grew into loan sharking and what became known as the Policy racket. Basically, it is a numbers game, AKA, the Italian lottery, or the Negro pool. It is an illegal lottery played mostly in the more impoverished neighborhoods across America. The anxious bettor attempts to pick the correct three digits to match the exact numbers, which will then be drawn at random the following day. In recent years, the "number" would be the last three digits of "the handle." This number came from the amount racetrack bettors placed on a single day at a significant track published in racing journals and major newspapers in New York. The name "policy" is similar to what some people refer to as cheap insurance.

By 1933, Safety Director Martin Lavelle sponsored legalization for all illegal policy games currently operating. Then charging a fee to allow them to operate. The director thinks this affirmative action would also become an excellent source of additional revenue for the city since he thinks gambling takes an astonishing estimated $35,000 per day.

By this time, Lew Wasserman began his show business career as publicity director at the *Mayfair Casino*, which opened in Cleveland in 1935. The Mayfair was actually owned by Moe "The Chinaman" Dalitz, Louis "Rody" Rothkopf, Morris "The Banker" Kleinman, Sam Tucker, Sam Haas, John Angersola, "Big Al" Polizzi, Chuck Polizzi and portrayed as a public front. At this time, the Angersola brothers, along with Al Polizzi's, were considered the leaders of the Mayfield Road Mafia.

In November newly, elected Mayor of Cleveland, Harold

Burton, along with Chief of Police Matowitz, was driving the dark and dangerous streets one night looking over the city he as in charge of. The mayor wanted to ride around the different downtown gambling clubs and visit several bookmakers who operated openly. Several bookmaking businessmen were spotted to be busy passing out flyers promoting their lucrative business along many of the sidewalks as they have done before and during other past administrations.

MAYOR BURTON CAMPAIGN POSTER

(Courtesy of Cleveland State University Memory Project)

In December of 1935, Mayor Burton hired a new Safety Director, Eliot Ness. Ness told a group of members at the annual Cleveland Advertisers Club how local gamblers have illegally earned at least $200,000 weekly, and half of this is from the numbers racket alone. (Note; this is equal to $3,711,000 in today's money.) Ness stayed in his role as Safety Director until April 1942

In 1937 Ness and Chief of Police George Matowitz created a barn new Cleveland Police Academy. Their united goal was to train newly hired police officers, in a profession and proper police procedures. Their intense training would now be a three-month course based on the current FBI training model.

As one of his first acts, Ness declared war on the mob, and his primary targets included "Big" Angelo Lonardo "Little" Angelo Scirrca, Moe Dalitz, John Angersola, George Angersola, and Charles Pollizi. Unfortunately, Ness otherwise remarkably successful career in Chicago withered. Many politicians felt he failed to achieve any success in Cleveland

In early October; 1938, Eliot Ness led a public raid against the Mafia's largest numbers bank operating out of a private home on East 36th Street. The crucial evidence seized in the raid secured critical indictments against George and John Angersola, Angelo Lonardo, Chuck Polizzi, Angelo Sciria, Alex "Shondor" Birns, Masich "Milton" Rockman as well as sixteen others. As you can see, this policy group consisted of a mixer of nationalities who joined together to make significant amounts of money. The peace was not always calm, and quite often came robberies and threats aimed at one another for a more substantial piece of the growing pile of cash.

Some of the men in Cleveland representing the black community were William Richardson, Tommy Boyce, Herbert Oliver, and Larry Gaskin. From the Jewish community were Milton Rockman, Solly Hart, and their friend Alex "Shondor" Birns.

The picture below is from the *Cleveland Plain Dealer* and shows the incredible diversity of people involved in the lucrative Policy rackets in and around the Ohio region.

THE CLEVELAND PLAIN DEALER, THURSDAY, APRIL 27, 1939

23 Key Figures in Policy Racket Indicted

COURTESY OF THE CLEVELAND PLAIN DEALER

(Courtesy of the Cleveland PlainDealer)

35

JOHN T. SCALISH

(Courtesy of Cleveland State University Memory Project)

John Scalish was born Giovanni Scalici, on September 25, 1912, in Cleveland, Ohio. John's father was Francisco Scalici, and his mother was Margherta Fito, who passed away in March of 1941. Both parents emigrated from Italy together. John was one of eight children in the Scalici family. John went on to marry Matilda "Tille" Rockman, the sister of his trusted friend and business partner. Tille unexpectedly passed away in May of 1978. John would use the alias of John Scalise many times over the years.

As a young boy, John did not like school that much and quit school at the age of sixteen, as so many other children did in the late 1920s. John had the urge to work, to earn a living and to find a place that was the right fit for him and where he could grow and prosper, just like many of the other young boys who had dreams of riches and glory.

This section of our essential Cleveland mob history must open with the ascent of John Scalish as the powerful and influential local organized crime "Boss." He ruled for an incredible three decades. John Scalish was known to be low-key, quiet, yet nevertheless, more importantly, the most powerful and successful "Mob Boss" in Cleveland history. During John's tender, he developed strong alliances with significant crime bosses across the country. Some are Meyer Lansky and Tony Accardo from Chicago. John aligned himself with the Genovese crime family in New York, and throughout the Midwest with connections to Kansas City with Nick Civella, Florida, California and Las Vegas.

The 1930s

As a handsome teenager, Scalish was already interested in burglary and being a stickup man for the old Murray Hill mob guys. John found himself arrested and fingerprinted the first time on January 10, 1930, for a robbery in Lorain, Ohio. Scalish; was only investigated for this crime and then released for lack of evidence against him. Police records show that he was involved in the burglary of The First National Bank in Mantua Twp. South of Cleveland on February 5, 1931. This case was then turned over to the Ravenna Sherriff's office; John; was released on probation after being convicted of the crime. He was only asked not to return to the city.

There was a robbery on April 4, 1932, of a Kopperman Bottling and Label Works Company at East 124th and Union. Scalish and three others were brought in for questioning as a suspicious person. Reviewing the case, the Grand Jury had three witnesses to the robbery, that could not identify Scalish and his friends; they all seemed to have a "Hazy Memory," and were all released.

The next robbery took place on June 11, 1932, when John and two other men, Milton Rockman and Alex "Shondor" Birns, went into the office of the City Ice and Fuel Company between 6:30 and 9 AM. The men all had handguns and showing them to the employees as they held the customers and cashiers at gunpoint. The men took $680 in both checks and cash from the safe.

On January 27, 1933, John Scalish found himself brought into the Cleveland Central police stations once again for questioning about a robbery back on June 11, along with his two friends, Rockman and Birns. This time John was indicted, found guilty, and sentenced by Judge Fred Walter, Scalish, was given a ten-year to a twenty-five-year sentence. Scalish served only twenty-one months inside a prison cell before his conviction was commuted by Governor George White. This complicated action took place only a few minutes before the noonday hour on January 14, 1935, when White's term of office would come to an end. How did he get out of prison after only three years? Did his friends in Cleveland, Frank, and Anthony Milano, or Al Polizzi, help him and give Governor White a substantial retirement gift? No one will ever know for sure.

This became the only time in Scalish's dignified and elaborate life that he ever served time inside a jail cell. By 1935, John Scalish, barely 25 years old, the son of poor Sicilian immigrants, was already connected to top underworld figures in Cleveland.

Moving up the ranks and learning in the streets of Cleveland, John soon became a lieutenant for Big Al Polizzi, who was given control of the Cleveland mob when Frank Milano left to live in Mexico.

1945
This is where the new "Boss" of Cleveland would become the young 33-year-old John Scalish would carefully build a stable structure of loyal associates. As the Scalish regime came to power, Tony Milano began spending more peaceful time in Los Angeles, where his family had moved to.

In 1946, Scalish, along with his brother Tom, Frank Embrescia, and John Sanfilipo, owned the popular *Celebrity Bar* located at 10226 Euclid Avenue. The bar was a notorious hang out for the Italian hoodlums in Cleveland and a trendy hangout for people who wanted to be around these powerful men. Scalish was to have sold his interest in the club by late 1949.

In 1947, Scalish and his brother Tom operated other gambling spots known as the *White House*, located at 93rd and Buckeye along with *Dredgers Club* on East 4th Street. His partner was a union man, Louis "Babe" Triscaro, who by now was a Teamsters Joint Council Vice President.

In October 1948, the FBI documented that while doing surveillance on Scalish, he was often in the company of Moe Dalitz. The two men were often seen driving around town, lounging at a restaurant and meeting other people at the lavish Theatrical Grill in downtown Cleveland, or the favorite Hollenden House.

At this time, Cleveland was viewed as a dominant force in the organized American Mafia. Listed third behind New York and Chicago; however, the Kansas City family led by Charles Binaggio was making a strong move to becoming third, sadly Binaggio was murdered in 1950.

The friendship between Scalish, Rockman, and Dalitz moved ahead at the speed of light as it created a well-planned opportunity for the future stability of the Cleveland Mob. With significant influence from Rockman, Scalish was convinced to invest in an up and coming hotel named the *Desert Inn*, in sunny Las Vegas. This financial investment helped to grow the coffers of the mob and assisted in the Union building operations in the late fifties and sixties. The Cleveland Mob continued to skim from the Las Vegas casinos, as it helped created massive financial rewards for many of the men. Soon, Scalish made a significant and hard decision. He enjoyed his life in Cleveland with his family and stayed behind when other close friends, and business partners, Tommy McGinty, Morris Kleinman, and Moe Dalitz, left the cold north coast for the warmth, glimmering lights and growing, unlimited opportunities in Las Vegas.

Years later, the FBI had documented that a confidential

informant stated, "Scalish gets 100- percent of the skim money for the Cleveland Family and divides it up into some of his top men. The count ranged from between $20-$40,000 from the smaller Stardust to $50 -$80,000 from the Desert Inn by the mid-1970s.

In 1949, John Scalish was spotted by Cleveland police having a meeting with William Finnegan, the Secretary of the Cleveland Federation of Labor. This could have been just one of the many informal meetings where the men spoke about joining forces and talking about their future.

The 1950s

It was in the early fifties, Governor Frank Lausche kept a promise he once made and began closing down the local gambling casinos. Years earlier, Scalish, who was forever a business-minded boss, took his profits and invested with his longtime good friend Rockman in the Buckeye Cigarette Service Company. A vending machine firm, changing their earlier business structure of slot machine manufacturing to a variety of vending machines. With the help of Scalish and his men, the company growth came rapidly by muscling routes from its weaker competition.

In January 1955, Scalish found himself proving his innocents once again inside a high-level House Special Anti-Racketeering Subcommittee. One of their findings was that the Buckeye Cigarette Service business was established by forcing other smaller companies out of business. It was speculated they used intimidation and threats of violence to ensure the companies agreed to sell to Buckeye. Scalish's stayed steadfast and claimed they just purchased the companies from their previous owners.

Due to his traditional low-key lifestyle, Scalish was little known outside the underworld until his arrest in 1957. Cleveland Police Lieutenant Martin Cooney knew him and became the lead investigator for the Cleveland Police. He headed up the exclusive racket squad with Safety Director John McCormick, who would soon be looking into the affairs of both Scalish and John DeMarco.

SAFETY DIRECTOR JOHN MCCORMICK

(Courtesy of Cleveland State University Memory Project)

In that memorial November afternoon, John was arrested with some estimated sixty other Mafia members from across the country in the famous police raid on the "national crime conference" at a lavish farmhouse near Apalachin, New York. Scalish had attended the meeting with his chief lieutenant, John DeMarco, who was recovering from a heart condition. Scalish was driving his 1957 Cadillac with DeMarco and a passage later identified as James V. LaDuca, the Secretary-Treasurer of the Hotel and the Restaurant Workers Union in Buffalo, NY. LaDuca lives in Lewistown, New York. LaDuca just happened to be staying at the same motel as Scalish and DeMarco, The Parkview Motel.

Scalish also testified in front of Senator John McClellan's Labor Racketeering Committee in July 1958. The committee learned that nine of the fifty-nine men who attended the meeting in New York had various interests and connections in the coin-operated vending machine business. The court believed most of the criminals were using the vending machine business to laundry their substantial funds through their legitimate activities. While investigating Scalish, the FBI announced that they were not able to obtain any police records about Scalish serving time in prison and why he was outrageously released by Governor George White. It seems his prison files were missing, Possibly thrown out by accident, or maybe even destroyed after 1954.

The 1960s

By early January, one of the defendants in the Apalachin scandal, John Scalish, now 47, has been described to be a very respectable executive and a man who is active in charitable causes and civic projects. However, he has been labeled a crime leader and worked hand and hand with organized crime bosses. After taking his "Fifth Amendments Rights," a total of 35 times, the judge labeled Scalish as brazen, shrewd, cunning, conniving, and contemptuous of society. Scalish was released on a $25,000 bond and was waiting to be sentenced. Police records have confirmed Scalish had kept a low profile in his criminal activities since his last arrest back in 1940, and for armed robbery in 1932 and bank burglary in 1931.

The Buckeye Cigarette Service Company was now under the watchful eye of the Tax Department. The IRS is seeking to collect $13,731 in back taxes from the owners of the company, John and Sam Scalish, Milton Rockman, and Frank Embrescia.

It was August 26, 1963, when the popular and highly respected, "*Saturday Evening Post*" ran an article entitled "*La Cosa Nostra*" This was released two months before the powerful testimony of Mafia member Joe Valachi. As we all know, Valachi became the first mafia member to come forward and tell the raw secrets of the inner workings of the powerful crime families.

MEET THE COMMISSION

(Courtesy of the Saturday Evening Post. John can be seen on the lower right-hand corner)

As you can clearly see, the FBI has collected substantial evidence against the Mafia as they listed the 22-known "BOSSES" from across the country known as "The Commission." Valachi mentions John Scalish as the "Boss," in Cleveland, and how he knew of 40 members in his tight-knit organization. However, Valachi said very little about Scalish as a harsh and respected boss and Cleveland's illegal operation and enormous power and influence.

Throughout the early seventies, John Scalish lived with a pain in his heart. It was weak and getting weaker as the weeks and months went on. He was seeing a heart specialist at Lakeside Hospital who informed him and his wife, Tille. "John would need a major heart operation if he wished to live a longer life."

By Early May 1976, his weak heart was at the point of no return. John received the final word from his specialist, he either had the surgery and took the risk, or he would die in a few months or even a few weeks.

On May 26, a team of heart specialists and dedicated nurses labored for hours to repair his weak heart as they diligently tied together several arteries, to help unsure his possible survival. The surgeons did the best they could for the proud, powerful, and influential man. It was now in God's hands. John peacefully passed away at the young age of 63, a few hours after his critical surgery. John had died as he lived, quietly and without any fanfare, with his loving family by his side.

36

PART IV

THE DEMISE SLOWLY BEGINS

Over the many years, the grand old fashion style Mafia has been derailed. Many bosses have gone underground to avoid the long arms of the Federal Government. The government has turned their once shallow fighting style into an Octopus with the long tentacles reaching in every direction of organized crime.

For the city of Cleveland, many can look at the lack of preparing for the future. John Scalish has been blamed by some for his lack of foresight to bring his town into the next decade of the 1980s. For some unknown reason, Scalish failed to attract or promote energetic young men. People to prove their worth as a leader, and willing to make their way up the hard-fought ladder of his criminal empire to join his organization.

A few years after John took over the reins of his mighty empire in Cleveland, it had been estimated Cleveland, had upwards of sixty-made men in their "Family." By the time of his death in 1976, reports had it down to the low twenties, if not lower. However, no one really knew for sure how many men there were. Many of the men were older and lost the "Tiger Aggressiveness," which would be needed to build up and redefine the defaulting criminal empire.

As we know the history of the gang wars in Cleveland, the two remaining men considered for the high position as "The Boss" was James Licavoli and John Nardi.

THE TEN TOP REASONS FOR THE DEMISE OF THE

AMERICAN MAFIA

1. Breaking their solemn oath of Omerta
2. Assimilation of the Italian-American culture into mainstream America
3. In 1961 Robert F. Kennedy was the U.S Attorney General, with the Justice Department by his side as he declares war on the Mafia.
4. G. Robert Blackly drafts and struggles to pass the robust RICO Act. {Racketeering Influence & Corrupt Organization in 1970, which finally gave the Feds the law they needed to crush the mob.
5. The dedication and hard work of hundreds of FBI and especially special agent Joe Pistone in 1976, {Project Donnie Brasco}as he worked his way inside the Bonnano crime family and learns their inner secrets.
6. 1985-86 the astonishing indictments of five heads of the New York Families of the commission by Attorney General Rudy Giuliani
7. The turning of Mob Bosses and other made men to "Flip" or testify against their families. Impressive testimony from people likes Joe Valachi in 1963 who had an excellent memory for detailed information. Followed by Joe Massino, Sammy Gravano, Cleveland's Angelo Lonardo in 1983, who became the highest boss at the time to turn state evidence and help the Federal Government.
8. The 1950-51 Kefauver Hearings, which took place across the country. The impressive hearings exposed the unique relationship between political corruption, labor, and organized crime. Broadcast on live radio and television. The discussions forced the FBI to changes; it's an excellent notion, "There is no such thing as the Mafia."
9. Internal treachery, which developed into multiple civil wars creating disloyalty and the defiant leap for power

within La Cosa Nostra. Made-Men killing one another, especially; the wild acts of John Gotti, who wanted all the power and money in New York.

10. Naturally, in the end, the FBI defeated the LCN through excessive manpower, determination, healthy finances, wiretaps, the witness protection program, and persistent surveillance. They merely just wore them down.

EXCITING OPINIONS TO CONSIDER IN THE DEMISE OF THE MAFIA:

<u>1957-1960</u> The Senate holds Rackets Committee hearings as the public learns for the first time of the association of organized crime leaders and leaders of several powerful labor unions.

<u>1957-1964</u> A massive intelligence-gathering operation goes underway by the FBI. The McClellan Commission. Most of this came from using legal and illegal wiretaps.

<u>1963</u> President John F. Kennedy is assassinated; Lyndon Johnson takes over, which actually ends the government's war on organized crime.

<u>1968</u> Congress passes, The Omnibus Crime Control Act, which gives law enforcement a stronger enforcement power to combat the Mafia. This included authorizing wiretapping.

(This collection of thoughts has been taken from an extensive source of articles in magazines, books, and newspapers from across the country and put together by Petey Bellini)

37

THE FAMOUS KEFAUVER CRIME

HEARINGS COME TO CLEVELAND

(Courtesy of Cleveland State University Memory Project)

Organized crime was the subject of a vast number of widely read articles in several major newspapers and magazines across the country in 1949. Several local crime investigations began in many cities and states as they uncovered extensive corruption of the political process by organized crime.

It was the spring of 1949, as the 46-year-old Tennessee Senator was desperately trying to make a name for himself. Estes Kefauver decided to take an active but dangerous role an investigate the "Organized Crime Syndicate." Kefauver has promised to dig deeply into these criminals "without fear or favor" and without any attempts to hide the truth from the American people.

By January 1950, Senator Estes Kefauver introduced a bill named Resolution 202, calling on the Senate Judiciary Committee to investigate Mob activities throughout America, which would involve interstate gambling and racketeering activities. Kefauver's plan faced direct opposition from Senate Majority Leader Scott Lucas of Chicago and Nevada's Pat McCarran. As the co-chairman of the Judiciary Committee, McCarran worked diligently to sidetrack Kefauver's proposed resolution. At the very least, he hoped to control the hearings if the Senate approved an investigation.

The Kefauver Committee held its much-published hearings in fourteen major cities across the United States. More than 600 witnesses testified during the informative proceedings. Many of the committee's hearings were seen live on national television, providing many Americans with their first glimpse of organized crime's power in the U.S.

1951

The city of Cleveland was now in the national spotlight across the country. Sadly, the hearings were not televised as others had been, now they would just have to read the daily papers. Al Polizzi became the mysterious man the citizens of Cleveland most wanted to hear from and learn more about. Today's citizens only know of these men or how powerful they actually may be or once were from what they have read in newspapers. The first hearing was slated to start on January 17. It was highly anticipated, as the main attraction would be Arthur "Mickey" McBride.

Cleveland was a prime focus for Kefauver and his select committee, as one Senate investigator mentioned, "Because of the enormous wealth that passes through the hands of the Ohio gambling syndicate...I have become more or less convinced that if Ohio is not the financial capital of gangsterdom, it is surely one of the best sources to gain some easy money."

The impressive list of former and present Clevelanders, who will be involved in a secret closed-door session, will be kept closed at this time. However, the public hearing could be post-ponded until March or early in April, if we do not get all the information we are looking for in January.

Sutton sought for questioning by the selected Senate group of, *"Who's Who"* of known criminals in the Cleveland area. It named Morris (Musky) Wexler, the former head of *Empire News Service,* and the owner of the trendy *Theatrical Grill,* Attorney Samuel Hass. Gamblers, like Thomas McGinty, Morris Kleinman, Sammy Miller, Sam Tucker, along with Louis Rothkopf, Frank Brancato, Alex "Shondor" Birns, Al Polizzi. Frank Visconti owner of the popular late-night spot *Captain Frank's Seafood House.* Chuck Polizzi, who is known to have influential friends in Chicago's crime syndicate. Anthony Milano, along with Harry Brook who is an ex-soldier with Los Angeles Mickey Cohen. Other men indicated to appear where Frank Cammaratta formerly with the Licavoli gang out of Detroit. Sought to give insightful evidence at the hearing as well include retired Police Captain John Fleming, along with Joe DiCarlo, a Youngstown racketeer. The general public, are looking forward to the testimony of the big-time national operator Moe Dalitz. Now comes Joe Aiuppa, who is said to manufacture loaded dice and other specialized gambling equipment for the casino operating around America. Other mentioned criminals included Jerome Milano, formerly of Chicago, and former partner in the slot machine business with the murdered "king of the slots," Nate Weisenberg. James Licavoli, an old gunman from Detroit and the "Purple Gang" and considered to be a close associate of Al Polizzi. Added to the inquest is John and George Angersola, who are also subpoenaed to testify, along with Angelo Sciria, a known policy man, and Angelo Lonardo to round out the group of notorious gangsters in Cleveland.

JOE (THE WOLF) DICARLO

(Courtesy of the Author Collection)

Other witnesses under subpoena are said to be coming from Newport, and Covington, Kentucky, is Police Chief Alfred Schild.

One central question may be, do these men still have their position or the control and power that some left behind in mid-1940? For Polizzi, he became a ligament businessman and purchased a mansion at 1302 Asturia Drive inside the luxurious Coral Gables community. Polizzi now calls Florida his home and attracted very little attention as a man who is working hard to build up his Real Estate Empire and Construction Company.

In the *Cleveland, Plain Dealer* article written by Todd Simon on January 14, announced to the people of Cleveland, all of a sudden, the ex-roughnecks have become prominent in business affairs, money, politics, and possibly gaining ground in the union operations.

However, smudged these men all may appear to be, their money buys more power than a regular citizen could ever possibly imagine. These people drive home from prison now in new Cadillac's, as they have the ears of powerful political influence and public officials firmly clenched in their nicely manicured and soft hands.

Senator Kefauver admits he wants to find out how these men with such a colorful and illegal past in Cleveland have moved on to a better life. They seem to come from the depths of society to now become seen as highly respected and admired citizens of the community. Kefauver admits, "Cleveland looked like the New York Wall Street of the rackets and connected to Miami, Los Angles, and Las Vegas as well as the other main cities across America."

In early January Senator, Kefauver commented that the hearings would be continuing to probe interstate gambling activities in Ohio and will concentrate on Cleveland, Cincinnati, and Newport, Kentucky.

After the first round of Cleveland interviews, Kefauver stated his team plans to have exciting and productive hearings in New Orleans, St. Louis, New York, and Los Angeles and possibly even San Francisco. Kefauver has also commented that the Cleveland Racketeers have powerfully infiltrated into over 100 legitimate business operations in the Midwest and throughout the country, including Florida.

Angelino Ceraldi, the bookkeeper for Cleveland's Italian mob boss, John Scalish for Buckeye Cigarette Company, and Anthony Milano's Brotherhood Loan Company.

By January 3, *The Plain Dealer* article written by Todd Simon told the story of how twenty criminals are wanted to testify in front of the Kefauver committee. They will be given the subpoena to attend the hearings. The discussion has pointed out in other cities that the men who are called before are to provide factual information. Safety Director Alvin Sutton stated, "Joseph Nellis is a Washington Attorney. Nellis will be assisting in the hearing in Cleveland.

By January 12[th,] before the committee was to have begun, Nellis reviewed who was expected to testify. The now-famous inquiry was focused on gambler extraordinaire, Thomas McGinty, who is scheduled to bring in personal and business information to help his attorneys, and to show the court he was an average businessman, that's all. Expected to come and testify was Charles Polizzi, along with his attorney. However, neither man could be found. Investigator Nellis mentioned how the city of Cleveland is like a giant jigsaw puzzle waiting to be put back in order, sine an extensive list of unsolved bootleg murders during the dry spell from 1920 until 1933. Nellis mentioned Homicide Detective David Kerr was compiling a list but refused to discuss further details.

Nellis was informed by James Maxwell that he has just received a piece of paper that states Mike Farrah, a known gambling Czar, and part-owner of the famous Jungle Inn, as well as a political boss in Warren and Trumbull County, would testify if he were called to do so. Nellis posted that he was looking to possibly interview or interrogate 53 known public persons who know about the gambling operations in Ohio. Expected to testify before the committee was Anthony Rutkowski, the Ohio State Liquor Officer, along with his agent James Harrell. Together these men helped to close down Ohio's biggest illegal casinos from the *Mounds, Pettibone,* and *Colony Clubs.*

Still missing and unknown where they could be, were Morris Kleinman, Moe Dalitz, Louis Rothkoph, Samuel Tucker, along with John Croft, John and George Angersola, Morris Wexler, Sammy (Gameboy) Miller and attorney Samuel Hass.

38

It was now January 13, as the city of Cleveland prepares for the invasion of enthusiastic Washington political investigators. The gangsters now look to be a group of legitimate businessmen and dress the part.

Expected highlights of this investigation will be the testimony of Thomas McGinty, a longtime owner of speakeasy's and illegal gambling operations from West 25th Street to the elaborate *Mounds Club* in Lake County and the *Pettibone Race Track* in Bainbridge County. Now McGinty is known as a partner or a stockholder in the fabulous *Desert Inn* in Las Vegas with Morris Kleinman along with Moe Dalitz.

Then there is Alfred Polizzi, who has retired to Florida and considered to be a partner with old-time Cleveland "Boss" Frank Milano. Milano was allegedly among the most prominent commanders of the National rackets in the early 1930s, where he was an importer of olive oil and macaroni.

The next main attraction for the Kefauver Committee hearings was known as the "Underboss" Anthony Milano. Owner of *the Brotherhood Loan Company*, and the *Mayfield Road Imports* as well as the *Ohio Villa* casino located on Cleveland's Eastside. Anthony Milano has been known to have loaned money to West Coast Mob figure Mickey Cohen who once lived in Cleveland.

Milano's brother Jerry was a known slot man and once was the head of the "Buckeye Cigarette Company," which dealt with slot machines and the former partner of murdered slot machine czar Nate Weisenberg.

James Licavoli was the next man of interest and mentioned to be a former bootlegger and known blackmailer in his prime with the Detroit *"Purple Gang"* led by his older brother Pete.

Then came Charles Polizzi, who went from a federal grand larceny charge with fellow gangster Angelo Sciria, John and George Angersola Angelo Lonardo, and Joseph Atwell.

Attorney Alvin Giesey, who was once a government accountant and has now dedicated his skills and wisdom to helping and covering the financial wealth of the gambling giant Morris Kleinman. Giesey has become Kleinman's expert on Income-tax laws as he worked diligently to prove Kleinman's innocence of income tax evasion.

Even a retired Detroit Sheriff, George Timisey, came to Cleveland to testify as to what he knows about organized crime during his incredible 32 years as a veteran Toledo, Ohio police officer. Eighteen of those years, Timisey was the captain of the busy hoodlum squad. Through his extensive career, he helped to arrest top crime figures like Thomas (Yonnie) Licavoli, Pete Licavoli, who served time in prison for murder and then their cousin James Licavoli (aka James White) who was a suspect in the death of slot kingpin Nate Weisenberg in 1945.

The court has speculated that Attorney Richard Moriarty will represent top gambler, Thomas McGinty. According to the court clerks looking over McGinty's extensive and massive collection of records, there could become the possibility of a vast volume of witnesses being called to testify before this committee.

On Wednesday morning January 17, Governor of Ohio, Frank Lausche was called as the first witness before the committee. Lausche is expected to tell his story as he faces many of the men who have crossed paths with him. Lausche is scheduled to tell his story on how he lost a battle in the Ohio legislation, where he was demanding to "kick out" a crooked sheriff who seemed to have refused to act and get rid of the gamblers and racketeers in Summit County. Lausche desperately tried to by-pass the sheriff in an attempt to padlock the old *Arrow* and *Pettibone* gambling Club located on Pettibone Road in Solon while the law officer stood on the grounds where he has authorized "Home Rule Policy" and looked away and did nothing to stop the illegal gambling.

Joseph Nellis was surprised after calling Alex (Shondor) Birns to testify. In a shrewd move, Birns suddenly announced he only brought in some of his documentation of his financial records. Birns had just been released from a six-month prison term for contempt of court charges against him. Birns never testified.

Another newcomer to the rackets is Harry Brook, who confided he has been betting since he was in the military and one who later turned out to be a more prominent interstate operator than anyone had ever known. Brook has also been linked with Los Angeles boss Mickey Cohen. Telephone wiretaps have shown that Cohen depended on Brooks turning in profits up to $24,000 a month.

One of the main events of the day was when the committees Attorney Joseph Nellis questioned at great lengths the influential mobster and wire service operator Mickey McBride. Seated with McBride were his two attorneys Walter Gallagher and William Dempsey. Nellis and Chairmen Kefauver's in-depth interview was estimated to last the rest of the day. Both men went back and forth, questioning him in a detailed fashion with over two hundred questions, focusing on his relationship with several top men in organized crime including, Al Capone.

Then the discussion turned to his efficient *Continental Press* wire service operation and his association with Morris (Mushy) Wexler, John, and George Angersola, Al Polizzi. They were also interested in McBride's connection with Anthony Milano and his brother Frank who McBride admitted knowing for 25-30 years.

For the committee meeting on January 18, Kefauver seemed to focus on accountant Alvin Giesey who worked directly with Morris Kleinman and several other men who were connected with Kleinman. On the stand, Giesey testified he was linked to the gambling operations in Cleveland, Nevada, Florida, and in Kentucky. To the disappointment of the committee, Giesey failed to bring or show any records of bribes, or payoffs allowing Kleinman to enter into these profitable business ventures.

Giesey wisely testified as a tax expert when he prepared and filed income tax returns for Kleinman, and the *Theatrical Grill* owner, and by former Empire wire service operator Morris "Musky" Wexler. Giesey was then asked by committee members about his business dealings with a notorious gambler, Thomas McGinty, who was a partner with Kleinman and several others, in the *Desert Inn Hotel* and Casino in Las Vegas.

By Friday, January 19th, the inquiry brought on the furious questioning of several men and possibly the biggest day of the committee hearings in Cleveland.

First, Kefauver and Nellis seemed to focus on their theory of Interstate crime links between the top known gamblers in the Ohio region. Kefauver stated the first few days have shown links to Interstate connections with other powerful men from across the country. Kefauver referred to one statement as he read; "Mickey Cohen often sends Anthony Milano flowers to his hotel room anytime he comes to Los Angeles." Cohen informed the committee that Milano has lent him money in the past. Milano has denied this statement and said: "He is a liar."

Second, Kefauver states, "Gambling perverts and ultimately corrupts all forms of local government and law enforcement." Sheriffs across the county, in smaller townships as well as the local police, seem to allow a smooth operation for the top gamblers. There is no evidence of bribery, but a strange flow of circumstances, which quickly show up when sheriffs are questioned by county prosecutors.

The third insight is how "Racket money" continues to infiltrate into the business world across our country. The massive amounts of money being made by these gambling clubs allow them to finance real-estate ventures.

Kefauver stated there will be two ways to deal with the people who come up against a contempt of court charge for refusing to answer the committee's questions. One will be a federal grand jury can indict them, which will punish anyone who refuses to respond to a Senate inquiry, or the action can be brought as a contempt of the Senate. These could result in jail time from 30-days to one year in prison, along with fines from $100 to $1,000.

It soon became known to the committee that the most significant money earned by the Cleveland Syndicate of criminals was coming from the Covington gambling Club located in Newport, Kentucky. It appeared that the men in power from the police chief, officers, or sheriff would often act as if, "I do not see anything." In one account, they boasted about wanting to catch these gamblers and throw them in jail.

It now became Anthony Milano's turn to testify in front of the fiery eyes of the Senate committee. Milano sat quietly and calmly next to his attorney Joseph W. Kennedy as the questioning continued. Milano offered very little information, mainly because the men had a hard time understanding the Italian immigrant over his thick accent. Milano openly admitted he was the head of the *Brotherhood Loan Company* as well as *Mayfield Imports Company*, located at 12020 Mayfield Road and was the founder of the Richmond Country Club, also known as *The Ohio Villa.*

The Committee continued to question Milano for a long time on why he has received many phone calls from Mickey Cohen. Kefauver proposed to Milano that they have hundreds of calls made from Milano to Cohen over the past twelve months, and wanted to know why Milano calls Cohen so often. Milano stayed firm and told the committee, "he never called him." Over sixty questions focused on Milano's past history with the Mafia. The committee seemed to be more focused on his association and how he met Cohen. Milano stated it was around 1945 when his wife and child were not well, and the doctor informed him the climate in Cleveland was not good for their health, and he should think about moving to warmer weather. He decided to move his family to

California. Milano stated I met Cohen shortly after arriving there and while I was staying at the Commodore Hotel. Cohen offered to help me find the right home for my family, which he did.

Milano was now questioned about his relationship with Peter Licavoli from the Detroit "Purple Gang." Milano stated how his wife and Chuck Polizzi's wife Angela are sisters, and Polizzi even had Peter Licavoli as his best man at his wedding and has also visited him in Arizona on the Grace Ranch near Tucson. As the family connections continue to surface at the committee meetings, the court found out that Licavoli's sister is the wife of Warren, Ohio Racketeer Frank Cammerata, who is looking to be deported at this time. The committee agrees that the impressive interlocking of these families show how the criminal empire is a significant part of a powerful illegal conspiracy to beat and prevail over the current laws.

PETER LICAVOLI

(Courtesy of the Cleveland Plain Dealer)

39

Two other men took the stand today in front of the Kefauver hearings. James Licavoli a known Purple Gang criminal from Detroit and his brother of Peter Licavoli. Currently, Pete is part owner of the Famous *Jungle Inn*, located outside Youngstown, Ohio, along with Joseph DiCarlo, another know mobster in the Buffalo and Youngstown area. Both men took the stand separately and defiled the committee by refusing to answer the multiple questions brought to them. Even after being warned several times that they are under subpoena to answer the spirated question in complete honesty. If not, they could be charged with contempt of court. Both men stood firm and repeatedly refused to respond to the issues brought to them.

Joseph Nellis, an attorney on the committee, questioned Gerald Eldridge, who was a self-proclaimed activist against gambling. Eldridge proudly informed the court of how he fought against the gaming clubs in the Toledo area for several years. Eldridge claims he did not know of *The Terrace Club*, operated by Frank Brancato back in early 1940, but did know of *The Victory, Chesterfield*, and the *Westwood* gambling clubs. When asked by Kefauver if the Cleveland boys, Milano, Brancato, or anyone else helped in the operation of these clubs, Eldridge proclaimed he believed they did but had no firsthand knowledge or evidence.

By Sunday, January 21st, The Kefauver crime commission investigation came to a close in Cleveland just like the other cities with a lot of fan fair and informal debate about whether their in-depth research found substantial evidence for the American government to establish a link to organized crime across this great country of ours. It is interesting to note that the Cleveland hearings were not televised for one reason or another like so many others had been. Or, was it just a group of criminals acting like businessmen and involved in a highly profitable gambling operation that made most, if not all, a wealthy man?

Many of these men even owned a share in a few of the new hotels and casinos in Las Vegas, so are they really criminals or smart businessmen after all?

The committee's next stop would be down south to New Orleans to speak with the unstoppable and powerful Carlos Marcello.

ACTUAL NOTES FROM THE KEFAUVER HEARINGS ON ORGANIZED CRIME

Filed on February 28, 1951

HOW CRIMINAL GANGS OPERATE

In every large city that was visited by the committee, it found similar patterns of abundant evidence of an organized crime.

These trends summarized as follows:

(1) Groups of individuals who continue to work together to operate, first for-profit, and aligned with many forms of criminal activity.

(2) These persons and organizations do not hesitate to use brutal attacks, murder, bombing, or any other kind of violence to eliminate their competition, or to silence informers, and persuade peaceful potential victims, to enforce their gang activities. They frequently import muscle, or associates from other areas of the country to perform these cumbersome tasks to make detection of the criminals more difficult.

(3) They occasionally used bribery or some other form of corruption to secure the noninterference by local law-enforcement agencies to react to gang activities.

(4) The people maintain favorable arrangements and friendly

relationships with like-minded criminal groups and individuals in other cities, as well as in other areas of the country.

(5) They invest their profits from these illegal activities to infiltrate into legitimate enterprises, to which they bring the operational methods of their illicit business, I. E., monopoly, enforced by intimidation and strong-armed violence.

Then there was Sam Maceo of Galveston, Texas. First, he started out as a simple barber, then he broke into the bootlegging rackets and now owns several Galveston nightclubs, bars, and two hotels. Maceo is also a powerhouse in Texas politics. Biaggio Angelica of Huston, Texas, is Maceo subordinate to the Mafia.

Next is Joe di Giovanni aka Joe Church of Kansas City. Joe is presently the Mafia chief in the Kansas City area, after coming from Brooklyn, New York.

Next in this article is Tony Lopiparo Chief of the Mafia in St. Louis, but tied in jointly with the Kansas City family, he would later be sent to Mexico by Lucky Luciano.

Next mentioned in the intence article is Frank Milano, originally from Akron, Ohio. Frank and his brother Anthony Milano were known as a top dominant force of Ohio Mafia leaders, and intimately connected to Mafia leaders in Chicago and Michigan. He was also the boss of the old Mayfield Road Gang. The Milano brothers were known to be in close touch and connected with West Coast Mafia boss Jack Dragna. Anthony currently lives in Hollywood, California, and owns an interest in a food company and an Italian newspaper in Cleveland.

Mentioned next in the article is Big Al Polizzi formerly of Shaker Heights, Ohio, and now lives in Coral Gables, Florida. Al is considered to be second in command to Frank Milano in the Ohio Mafia. Currently, Polizzi has his fingers into many legitimate enterprises, including olive oil, food-importing, and beer distribution, and lately in the real estate market in Coral Gables.

Many of the Kefauver Committee's hearings were aimed at providing factual information that an Italian–Sicilian organization, which is based on strong family ties, centrally control a vast, organized crime conspiracy in the United States. However, during all the interrogations and meetings. The committee meetings never came close to justifying such a universal claim. Instead, the court uncovered extensive evidence that people of all nationalities, ethnicities and even religions, operated locally within their city or state.

In the Kefauver committee's final report, issued on April 17, 1951, included twenty-two recommendations for the Federal Government and only seven recommendations for state and local authorities. Here are just a few.

1. Among its recommendations were the creation of a "racket squad" within the United States Department of Justice.
2. Then to establish a permanent Crime Commission at the federal level.
3. The expansion of the jurisdiction of the Judiciary Committee to include interstate organized crime.
4. A ban on sports betting via radio, television, telegraph, and telephone.
5. The establishment of a state and/or local crime commissions.
6. A request that the Justice Department investigate and prosecute thirty-three individuals as suspected leaders of organized crime in the United States.

   However, the committee's diligent work leads to several meaningful outcomes. Among the most notable was an admission by J. Edgar Hoover, Director of the Federal Bureau of Investigation, that a nationally organized crime syndicate did, in fact, exist.

The Kefauver Committee was the first to suggest that local civil law should be expanded and use vigorously to combat organized crime. Congress slowly responded to the urgent call to action, and it would not take the situation seriously. It was not until nineteen years later, in 1970, that they would pass the widely acclaimed Racketeer Influenced and Corrupt Organizations Act (RICO) as a direct response to the committee's recommendation. The most prominent action of this Senate hearing was the deportation of over one hundred lesser-known criminals in the United States.

After researching Kefauver's statements, it is fascinating to see that the government selected some of his proposals to combat organized crime.

On August 8, 1963, Kefauver, a heavy smoker, and drinker suffered a mild heart attack on the floor of the Senate while attempting to place an antitrust amendment into a NASA appropriations bill. Two days after the attack, Kefauver died quietly in his sleep in Bethesda, Maryland, of a ruptured aortic aneurysm.

When the Cleveland hearing was over, Kefauver confessed to reporters, "Because of the enormous wealth that passes through the hands of the Ohio syndicate... I have become more or less convinced that Ohio is not a financial capital of the gangster across the country, it is surely one of the best sources of Easy Money."

40

JOSEPH BARBARA SR.

The real mystery is why dozens of men from across the country were summoned to a small city in the upper portion of New York state. As an old movie once said, "They came by planes, trains and of course automobiles." The wealthy men hailed from thirteen states as well as from Cuba and even the small island of Sicily. Membership of the people involved was reported being from over two dozen organized crime families. An astonishing fact was later revealed. Incredibly, above half, the people who attended this secretive meeting were in-fact related in one way or another by marriage. Half were native-born Americans, while the other half were born in either Italy or Sicily. The incredible Barbara estate was located on a lonely McFall Road. Barbara was born on August 9, 1905, in Castellammare del Golfo, Sicily. Barbara used several aliases over the years, "Joe the Barber, Joe Barber, Joe Barbaro."

The vehicles the distinguished men drove was either a friend's or an associate or soldier of theirs wherein, after all, this was the safest way to travel, and leaving no records of a plane or train ticket behind. Many of the men came with their second in command, while others brought trusted loyal Sicily associates or business associates, trusted by their wealthy friends in crime.

Some of the top men in organized crime attended this extraordinary meeting. This included Frank DeSimone and Joe Cerrito from California, Nick Civella from Kansas City, Joe Civello from Dallas, Sam Giacana from Chicago, Joe Marcello from New Orleans, Santo Trafficante from Tampa, John Scalish and John DeMarco from Cleveland, John LaRocco from Pittsburgh, Anthony Gianalone from Detroit, Russel Bufalino from Buffalo. The top men in New York consisted of Joe Bonanno, Vito Genovese, Carlo Gambino, The Olive Oil King Joe Profaci, and Paul Castellano, along with representatives from Sicily, which included Pepi Controni, Luigi Greco, and Giuseppe Settecasi.

Over the years, there has been plenty of speculation on what the real agenda may have been for these men of incredible power, wealth, and influence.

Here are some of the widely thought ideas in no particular order.

1. Continue to raise funds, for increased interaction with political officials, and future legislative growth and opportunities.
2. To discuss possible successors to help replace the aging mafia commission members and their territory. An example of this was mention as to why Nick Civella had taken his underboss Joseph Filardo to the summit.
3. To provide names of possible new members to rise and increase their dwindling membership across the country.
4. To discuss, then to establish new territories for future growth opportunities. Then to expand their profound political influence into more areas across the country.

5.   Discuss significant ways to maintain and grow their ultimate control of substantial beverage and whiskey distributors and distilleries.

6.   Continue to manage a stronger hold in the Women's Garment Industry across the country, not just in New York

7.   Expand the active control of the growing and profitable vending machine business. Noted, was how John Scalish controlled over 50% of the Buckeye Catering Company in Ohio with annual sales of $1.2 Million

8.   Broaden their strength and influence of the various Unions and pension funds across the country, look for possible vital members to help their growth

41

THE SUMMIT

1957

It was a quiet, peaceful, and beautiful day in November as a new Cadillac was approached by the New York State Police Department on November 14. The stop occurred just several miles from the home of Joseph Barbara, where the Apalachin meeting was to have taken place. Driving the car was John Scalish, and his passenger was John DeMarco. It was determined the men stayed at the Parkview Motel in New York, located on Route 17.

Newspapers across America reported, "The raid and arrests of these criminals were like a "Bluebook" of the TOP gangsters from all across the country."

Many believe the particular meeting agenda was to resolve a dispute on top of everyone's mind and to resolve the never-ending question. Who in New York City, would be in charge of the very profitable illegal gambling business, along with the unstoppable narcotics operations?

It is now December 4, and it has only been three short weeks since the sixty-three men were arrested in New York. The Government found its first link to five of the men who held a liquor permit and had a police record, which is a clear violation of the license.

Under questioning on everyone's mind in downtown Cleveland was, "who is John Scalish?" Lt. Martin Cooney, the head of the Special Investigating Unit in Cleveland, stated, John, is commonly known as a partner in the Buckeye Cigarette Company, and said, "John Scalish and John DeMarco were picked up only fifteen miles down the road from the home of Joseph Barbara.

1958

The aftermath of the now-famous Apalachin Conference put the national media spotlight directly on the secretive La Cosa Nostra empire. This triggered multiple state and federal investigations and hearings.

It was early July in Washington, as Vito Genovese invoked his First Amendment rights an astonishing 150 times in the Senate Committee Hearing investigating him of black-market crimes and multiple murder. A Senator from North Dakota, Karl Mundt, sharply criticized the Justice Department as to why "some of the notorious racketeers were freed from a lengthy jail sentence?

1959

The State of New York established a State Investigation Commission to specifically investigate the disastrous Apalachin Meeting and sent Barbara a summons to appear in court and explain the reason for the meeting. In response, Barbara's attorney claimed that he is too sick to testify or come to court for any reason. In direct response to their appeal, the Commission sent a governmental heart specialist to examine Barbara at his home in May 1959. After his detailed examination, the state Supreme Court ordered Barbara to testify in their courtroom. However, in June 1959, before he could appear before the Commission, Joseph Barbara died of another heart attack

By the middle of February, John Scalish and John DeMarco were subpoenaed to appear in Chicago and to testify on behalf of why they have been selected as part of the national inquiry of the November 1957 incident into organized crime. Chicago was the city chosen for this coordinated hearing since Ohio is a part of the Midwest jurisdiction of the grand jury, which includes Illinois, Michigan, Missouri, and Indiana.

It was late in March as DeMarco found himself being questioned by the FBI at his home in Shaker Heights, and accused of being a federal fugitive in the matter of his arrest in New York and near the city of Apalachin back in 1957. DeMarco proudly and calmly told the federal investigators. "He did not care to discuss this matter. I do not belong to a so-called organization, and I have no knowledge of the alleged meeting at Apalachin. All I know is what I have read in the local newspapers and added the papers are not always accurate with their stories. Therefore I do not place any credence in such wild stories. Would you believe me if I told you I did not know the man Barbara? However, I might recognize him if I see him."

FBI agents showed DeMarco a picture of Joe Barbara, who quickly remarked, he did not want to talk about the man or the so-called meeting.

It was now May as trouble for Scalish and DeMarco continued to escalate. DeMarco was soon arrested for defaulting on his original bail of $50,000 from the earlier arrest in New York. DeMarco was listed as one of the twenty-seven men indicted by the Federal Grand Jury, for perjury in his initial deposition about why he was in New York back in November 1957.

Only twenty-seven men out of the original sixty-three were formally indicted by the Federal Grand Jury for concealing information to the Federal Government, and the real reason for the meeting. The government has contended that these men who attended this session were the key members of the "Executive Board of the largest criminal syndicate in the country."

Scalish and DeMarco have continued to proudly take their Fifth Amendment rights and refused to answer questions or testify at all while inside the closed room investigation on organized crime in Cleveland, Chicago, and New York.

In Cleveland, U. S. District Judge Irving Kaufman was informed that John DeMarco suffered his second heart attack in New York City while staying at The Statler Hilton Hotel. He is currently under an oxygen tent inside Saint Clare's hospital, fighting to survive. The judge finally determined that DeMarco will have his own separate trial since he is not able to attend the upcoming hearing with the other notorious delegates.

Until his arrest at the Apalachin Meeting in New York, John Scalish's last arrest was back in 1940, as he continued to keep a low profile from the local police and FBI. Scalish has been out on a $25,000 bond.

One of the significant holes in the government's prosecution's case against all the men came from when they admitted they did not know what actually was to have taken place on November 14, 1957. At least sixty people, many of whom had lengthy prison records, were guests at the vast and beautiful Barbara estate.

After several years, hundreds of thousands of dollars were wasted, and by the time all the inquiries and investigations were complete, a conclusion was made.

The uphill battle to fight the country's top criminals rested on the shoulders of the Attorney General, William Rogers. Inside a courtroom, their final opinions were released by Chief Judge J. Edward Lumbard, Judge Charles Clark, and Judge Henry, all concurred.

There is no definitive proof of an actual violation of our laws to support the unfavorable opinions or substantial evidence, which could prove these people are guilty of a crime. It is clear to see that a case against these men should have never been initiated.

Judge Clark stated, "For in America, we still respect the dignity of all individuals, and even an unsavory character is not to be imprisoned."

THE BARBARA ESTATE

(Courtesy of Cleveland State University)

42

THE POLICY MAN

ALEX "SHONDOR" BIRN

Alex Birn was born **Alexander Birnstein** in 1907 in the small town of Lemes in a section of Austria-Hungry, which became Czechoslovakia under the Versailles Treaty. His parents were Herman and Illon Birnstein. Youngest of three children, he was brought to New York at the age of three months. From New York, the family moved to Cleveland, settling in the lower Woodland Avenue area.

Like most all of the immigrant families, the Birnsteins Americanized their surname to Birn. Alexander's name abbreviated to an English translation of Zander, but the Italian and Jewish neighbors took to calling the boy "Shondor" (as the Hungarian equivalent of "Alexander" is "Sándor" and the name stuck. Like many immigrants during the ear of Prohibition, men turned to bootlegging, working with the Cleveland Mafia Boss Joe Lonardo to supplement their income and better provide for their children.

In November 1920, Birns' mother was tending to the families ten gallons still in their apartment, when a faulty gas connection caused an incredible explosion. Her clothing caught fire, and she soon became engulfed in flames. She quickly ran outside, screaming when a passing motorist came to her rescue and helped to extinguish the fire, he then drove her to the hospital. Horribly burned over 80% of her body, she died the next morning. Shondor was only 13 at the time of his mother's death. Birn was placed in a child-shelter for a time in the old Jewish orphanage.

1925

The eighteen-year-old Alex "Shondor" Birn was arrested for the first time on a felony charge. This was for the theft of an automobile. It was during the late 1920s, Burn found high profit being involved in a prostitution ring as he controlled several brothels, one being located on East 55th Street between Woodland and St. Clair.

1932

Birn; was recruited by local Jewish gangster Maxie Diamond, the leader of the E. 55th Street and Woodland Mob. Diamond would become an associate of Teamsters leader William Presser. Shondor found himself as a trusted member of Max Diamond's gang during the battles for control of the city's dry cleaners and laundry business.

1933

It was January as Shondor was becoming well known in Cleveland as an up and coming criminal and found himself arrested after a wild and crazy seventy miles per hour chase down the busy street of Carnegie Avenue. In the car with Birn was his friend and known Italian racketeer Nick Satulla, and gang leader Max Diamond. The men were all questioned in the attempted bomb explosion of the Majestic Dry-Cleaning Company and then released. The trio seemed to be in the middle of a war with other Dry Cleaners in the Cleveland area.

Later in the year, Birn hooked up with Maxie Diamond as Diamond narrowly escaped death once again from gunfire by rival gangsters in what the police called "a continuation of the city's dry-cleaning racket war." Birns was among those picked up for questioning. He was then released, but only after paying $2 for two overdue traffic tickets.

Max Diamond was born in Russia in 1902 and soon immigrated to America. His first arrest was in 1915. Later in 1937, he was actively involved in the sale of bootlegged alcohol. Diamond had reliable connections and dealings with Tony Milano, George Angersola, and Shondor Birn. In June 1937, Diamond was sentenced to 4 years in Lewisburg prison on liquor violations charges with Louis Rothkoph. Diamond successfully survived an assignation attack on his life two days earlier.

1934

Twenty-seven-year-old Shondor Birns was well on his way to establishing himself as a tough gangster in Cleveland when he was shot on April 5 inside a nightspot brawl near Gordon Park with rumrunner Rudy Dunkin, a muscle man for crime leader and Race Bet Bookmaker Arthur Anders.

Documented in "To Kill the Irishman," written by Rick Porrello, One of Birns's most serious arrests was for the 1934 murder of Rudy Duncan, a 36-year-old nightclub bouncer at the Euclid Avenue Keystone Club. Birns was sitting with two of his fellow gang members when he arose to retrieve some cigars from his overcoat, which he had checked in the coatroom.

The story goes, Birns had misplaced his coat check ticket and could not produce it when asked for it by the coatroom girl. The young lady subsequently refused to give Birns access to his jacket. Over her objections, Birns entered the coatroom, shoving her aside in the process, and allegedly slapping her in the face and retrieved some of the cigars from his coat. He then returned to the table, had two more drinks, and smoked one of the cigars. Meanwhile, the girl became scared and ran outside and summoned Rudy Duncan, the bouncer who also happened to be her live-in boyfriend. She told him about the incident with Birn. Duncan, who was a former boxer with a record in Pittsburgh, Buffalo, and Cleveland, and had experienced previous run-ins with Birn and his loyal gang.

As Shondor was leaving, Duncan came up from behind Birns and menacingly, demanded an explanation as to his presence in the club. Birn muttered something, and the two lunged at each other. In the ensuing ruckus, two shots were fired. One hit Birns in the shoulder, and the other struck one of Birns's friends in the leg. Duncan ordered Birns crew out of the bar at gunpoint.

When the police arrived, they found Birns in his car ready to pull away, while holding a bloody handkerchief to his shoulder. They searched his car and confiscated a revolver, which he had placed in his glove box. He denied owning a gun, and would not reveal who had actually shot him. The police drove him to the hospital. After two days, Birns checked himself out of the hospital. During the criminal trial, Birn testified that he did not see his assailant and that whoever came up from behind him in the club had the gun. Birn refused to identify Duncan as the man who shot him. Likewise, Duncan's recollection of the incident was so vague that he wasn't called to testify as a witness.

Two months later, Rudy Duncan took his 11-year-old foster son, Stanley, to a movie show at the Uptown Theater on E. 105th Street and Saint Clair Avenue. Afterward, they walked to a store for some ice cream. When they got into their car back in the theater parking lot, two men wearing white cotton gloves walked up alongside, one on each side. With a terrified young Stanley crouching in the seat, they fired five bullets into Duncan. Police immediately began a search for Birn. They found him, but they couldn't find evidence to tie him to the murder. He was released. Duncan's death went officially unsolved.

1935

June 29, racebook operator Arthur Anders died in the hospital after receiving a fatal gunshot inside his own nightclub on 1075 E 79th Street in an apparent hold-up attempt. Anders had only $14 in his coat pocket at the time. However, others said he left his bookmaking operation around 5:30 that evening with a pocket full of cash.

Police Detective Cody and Detective Bernard Wolf, who is the head of the homicide squad, brought in Birn for extensive interrogation and questioning in the suspicious attack on Anders. Birn was released later that evening. This murder went unsolved.

1936

On September 2, two infamous, notorious gangsters Shondor Birn 29 and Max Diamond 36 were once again guests of the Cleveland Police inside the Central Police Station and questioned for several hours on their lucrative racket organization. "This time, the men were being held on suspicion of a recent robbery which they may not have committed, but it was a good reason to bring them in," said Sergeant James McDonald.

After this general ordeal, Shondor decided to spend the winter in Florida.

1937

It was in April when Shondor found himself under an order by the police chief. Officers were ordered to pick him up whenever he is found. This brought about his arrest once again for being a suspicious character. Birn had $300 in his pocket, and found himself in a police lineup for a street robbery and then released.

It was now June 29, as Birns found himself being arrested for the fifth time since February. This time he was escorted to the Central Police station after he was detained in an alleged gambling raid in a second-floor apartment on Euclid Avenue Birn was booked on a suspicious person charge. Police found an assortment of betting slips along with other policy evidence.

1938

January 22, Detective Ernest Molnar, a member of the Cleveland Gambling squad, led a raid on two Eastside bookie joints. Four men were arrested, including bookmaker Shondor Birn. The officers confiscated scratch sheets, bet slips, two telephones, a ledger as well as an assortment of other evidence linking the men to bookmaking operation.

It was now October 25 as Birn was surprisingly acquitted after his latest arrest for striking John Sullivan, a police officer. Birn had claimed Sullivan along with Officer John Papp forcefully tried to get him to accompany them to the Central Police Station. The jury acquittal surprised Judge Alfred Steuer and the officers when they found him, not guilty.

By this time, Birn became heavily involved in prostitution as a "vice resorts" as dubbed by the media. Birn operated freely and was well-liked by most, if not all, the prostitutes who worked in his brothels. Many of Birn's clients were judges, politicians, and police officers of high rank. They would serve as valuable contacts for him in the future, and of course, he was always there to help them.

1939

It was now April 26, as the "Big Four" men in the numbers rackets in Cleveland were charged with indictment accusations of blackmail. The men arrested included Frank Hoge, Shonder Birns, along with twenty-one other people for allegedly muscling in on the lucrative policy racket and exacting an enormous "tribute" or payment. The estimated money involved in this crime is estimated to be 5 Million Dollars a year.

Safety Director Eliot Ness has asked for the FBI to help in finding several of the missing twenty-one men, including Angelo Lonardo, and Angelo Sciria. Both men are believed to be operating along with Sciria's brother Dominic. John and George Angersola, Joe Artwell, John Demarco, Dominic Sospirato, Larry Gaskins, Victor Mannino, and Milton Rockman also appear on this list.

It had been speculated that the missing men went into hiding because of the hefty $50,000 cash bond needed for their release while the case is being investigated.

1942

It was May 28 as Birn was under indictment for the last three-years for blackmail, and was now being known as the "Most arrested man in Cleveland." Birn even tried to enlist in the U.S. Naval Reserve as he proudly showed his friends his letter, indicating he has taken this proud step to protect his country. During Birn medical examination, it was determined he had an acute hernia along with his lengthy arrest record, which barred him from enlisting in the Navy.

By the end of September, Birn was known as the Number 1 Criminal in the Cleveland rackets. At this time, he was on trial for two different murders and other crimes, which included bribing a witness, which should have placed him in jail for the rest of World War II, and arrested on a warrant for deportation.

Vernor Tomlinson, the head of Immigration in Cleveland, stated, "Alex Birn never filed for citizenship and is considered an illegal alien. However, he did register as an enemy alien." Birn has been charged with crimes involving extortion. Birn would often go to Canada and re-enter America, which is considered to be illegal because he was "mandatorily excludable" for his extensive police record in America.

1945

It was now April as Birn once again found himself in another altercation with the Cleveland police. This time it was at his popular *Ten-Eleven* nightclub on Chester Avenue in the heart of downtown. Manage by his Italian connections from Murray Hill, Charles Amato, and club operator Anthony Calabrese. Both were charged with selling liquor after midnight to two undercover policewomen.

1947

It was now the end of April, and Birn was successful in transferring his old liquor license from his former *Ten-Eleven Club*, which became known as the *Alhambra Grill Company* to his new updated *Alhambra Lounge and Restaurant* located at 10403 Euclid Avenue. The new restaurant will be found in the basement of the *Euclid-Doan Reality Company* building. Birn maintains he is not the owner of the restaurant, however, he is just the manager. William Kelch, the State Liquor Agency Chief, was diligent in ensuring Birn fill out all the correct paperwork and filed all the proper documents to ensure he was following the state's liquor law. No violations were found during the initial investigation, and the license was successfully transferred to his new restaurant since Alex Shondor Birn name was not listed as the owner.

43

1948

Alex Birns colored relationship with the police department in Cleveland continues to grow. On Saturday, September 18, Birn has been arrested once again. This embarrassing incident happened in the *Doan Tavern* on East 105th Street when he struck an off-duty police officer, Detective Ralph Kennedy, who is a member of the cities racket squad. Police Chief George Matowitz explained how Lieutenant William Halloran was with Kennedy and stated, "I did not see any punches or actual fighting between the two men."

Kennedy's story was that; "He walked partway down the bar and only sat down and ordered a sandwich and beer when he noticed Halloran and Patrolmen Kirk seated at the end of the bar door speaking with a man he knew, Morris Rosen. Five minutes later Kirk walked outside while I was looking out the rear door, I then notice Birns talking with Merrill Cowan, then someone ran in and said Birns was in a fight in the backyard with Patrolman Kirk. Halloran then told me he would handle the incident. Several minutes later, another man ran back in and said they were fighting again, so I ran back outside and found Birn on top of Kirk with his hands on his throat and Kirk holdings Birn tie. I then separated Birn by lifting him off Kirk. Kirk responded, "I want him arrested for assaulting me." I then turned around and found a few police officers from the Fifth District leading Birn across the street to the police station.

By October 30, the trial of Alex Birns began as he is charged with assault, battery, and resisting arrest. Judge Lewis Drucker heard testimony from John Schrink on how he was playing cards in the bar with Lieutenant Halloran, Patrolman Kirk, and Maurice Rosen from 4 until 6 PM. The men admitted they had between eight and ten drinks apiece during their time playing cards. The game broke up a little after 6 PM when Schrink left the tavern. Kirk and Halloran continued to stay in the bar, and by 9 PM Kirk disappeared for about twenty minutes and then came back in

Inside Municipal Judge Lewis Drunker court on November 1, the court found Alex "Shondor" Birns guilty of assault and battery along with resisting arrest, when he for the altercation back in September. Birn was released on a $1,500 bond as his attorney Elmer McNully said he would fight for a new trial. If the new trial is not granted for Birn, he will be facing seven months in the Warrensville Work House on Warrensville Road and a $700 fine.

1949

By May, Birns was out and enjoying his freedom once again. On the evening of May 3, Birn was enjoying the company and hospitality of the Central Police Station after he was picked up as a "Suspicious person" and held overnight, then released. The next day is when he noticed he was being "shadowed" by a police officer in plain clothes. This officer was none other than Assistant Safety Director Alvin Sutton and Patrolmen Edward Willis. Willis soon noticed two off-duty police officers in the car sitting in a parking lot at the Cleveland Indians ball game. Sutton was leaving the stadium at the end of the ninth inning. Appearing in front of them was none other than Birn, sitting comfortably in the rear seat of a detective's car with the two officers as the car pulled away. The detectives look like they were "Chauffeuring" Birns around town and having fun.

Sutton and Edwards jumped into their car and followed them to West 6th Street, where Sutton pulled up next to them and ordered the men to the City Hall and to bring Alex with them.

At the police station, Sutton was so mad he almost threw his hat through a wall as he got the two patrolmen, in his office. After reading the riot act to them and yelling for several minutes, he reminded them they were just to watch and observe him and not to drive him around town like a dame "Taxicab." Sutton told the men, "It is tough to believe that two qualified police officers who are placed in a "Shadowing" duty would not understand that he should not let the person know he is under surveillance."

The only statement and defense the patrolmen made were, "they were afraid they would lose Birn when he left the ballgame, so both men decided, it was best to escort him to the Hollander House where he lives.

It was now late June as Alex Birns found himself in the Warrensville Workhouse once again. This time he was serving seven-months for the earlier charges of assault and battery and resisting arrest on a police officer Kirk. Birns was released on January 20 on a $60,000 security bond and is awaiting his next trial.

It was now September 19, as Alex Birn was back in the Warrensville Workhouse. Birns was currently being investigated for masterminding a bomb threat against a reviled policy tycoon Joseph Allen. Jailed along with Birns are Angelo Lonardo and Joe Artwell. Artwell was also arrested along with Birn back in 1942 on a number's extortion case. Also indicted in this instance were Charles Amato and Nick Satulla. It seems Allen's 1948 Cadillac blew up one week ago when it was parked in the driveway of Allen's home of East 100th Street. Birns sweet-talked and paid a workhouse guard to assist him as a go-between and facilitate communication between himself, Lonardo, and Artwell.

1950

It was December 7, The *Cleveland Plain Dealer* reporter Ted Princiotto; discussed how Alex "Shondor" Birns will try desperately to stamp out his new federal problem as he tried to stall the governmental action to deport him from his previous 1946 deportation order.

> *Attorney Henry Lavine visited Alex Birn several times as the men prepared for the court hearing, as the four-year-old deportation papers have discolored and turned yellow with age because the Czechoslovakia government has refused to allow him back into their country as a citizen.*

1954

Birn now 47, as one of Cleveland's Top Public enemy, and now facing additional action against him from the Federal Government.

It seems a Grand Jury has indicted him for falsifying his income tax returns from 1947, 1948, 1949, and 1950. This four-count action claims he hid over $83,000 of personal income in his filings. The attorney for Birns is Henry Lavine, who said, "Shondor was expecting this action against him." Birn was sent to the Atlanta Georgia Federal Prison, where he would not be released until October 1956.

1957

A front porch was destroyed in an incredible blast on Monday, May 20. It was now Wednesday, May 22, as Alex Birns, Edward Keeling, Willie Jackson and Daniel Boone (all our African American) and have been accused of an ill-fated bombing-blackmail attack on a rival bookie, the 25 years old Donald King, who was at his home at the time of the explosion. Mr. King changed his life around and moved on to a legitimate entity and become a well-known boxing promoter.

When the trial began, King was the star witness for the prosecution to put Birn behind bars. The judge and jury, however, had a tough time to understand King's quick and confusing comments and his rapid, inarticulate speech, which led the local newspapers to dub him "The Talker."

Donald (The Kid) King told the police, "Birn had made several phone calls to me reminding me of my obligation to paying the weekly fee. Then on May 5, King explained, Birns drove to me home and told me to pay up, or else. "I informed him I was low on cash and could not pay, and was leaving the clearinghouse racket for good."

At the trial, King told the jurors that one of Birns men had offered him $10,000 not to testify. "He said if I didn't testify, he would guarantee there would be no more attempts on my life or bombing of my house, and I'd have no reason to be scared anymore." The prosecution even produced a surprise witness who was a former employee of the rackets. On the stand, the *Press* reported. "The lady burst into tears again and again and refused to answer questions about Birn, and the other defendants who glared at her with their critical eyes. Her attorney told the judge she was told that she and her 12-year-old daughter would be killed if she testified." Defense lawyer Fred Garmone called King "a scheming, lying, witness-fixing extortionist himself."

Police Detective Martin Cooney stated, "After these several reminders to King to pay the fee and to live up to his obligation. King refuse, and that is when the bombing attempt on his life accrued. Birn was soon charged and went on trial for Blackmail on July 1.

The trial was in full swing by October as Donald King found himself shot and wounded by a stranger sitting in a passing car.

Just before Thanksgiving, on November 21, the verdict for Alex Shondor Birn and three other men was announced in a jam-packed courtroom led by Judge Benjamin Nicola. Joseph Rubel, the Jury Forman, announced to the silent courtroom, "I don't think we can reach a verdict in this case."

Don King's career as a fight promoter is second to none. His highlights include promoting some of the most prominent names in the boxing world, including Muhammad Ali, Joe Frasier, George Forman, Larry Holmes, and Cleveland's Mike Tyson.

YOUNG DON KING

(Courtesy of the Cleveland Plain Dealer)

44

1959

It was the middle of March as Birns now found himself on the other flip side of the discrete coin as a member of the gambling rackets in Cleveland. Birns surprisingly survived several gunshot blasts when he pulled into his driveway on Judson Drive in South Euclid, Ohio. Remarkably, Birns was not injured. Birns enjoyed holding meetings, or living at the hotel he called his home. The Hollander Hotel was the place that many well-known gamblers stayed when they were in town. Years earlier, even Tommy McGinty kept room # 380 as his own.

THE HOLLANDER HOTEL

(Courtesy of Cleveland State University Memory Project)

After the police investigated and left Birn home, he cruised the neighborhood on the lookout for the man who he believed shot at him until it was daylight. Upon further investigation, Cleveland Police picked up a hood named Clarence "Sonny" Coleman, who owed money to Birns. Coleman was interrogated, then released soon after the lengthy questioning. A few days later, Coleman was shot on a neighborhood street shortly after midnight. Three bullets hit him, but he managed to run-up his front porch yelling, "Let me in, baby, let me in!" At the hospital, Coleman told the police the shooter was a man in the back seat of a car driven by Shondor Birns. Birns was soon arrested and then brought to the booking window at Central Station.

It was no surprise to the police that one month later, Coleman changed his mind and told the cops that he had only speculated that it was Birns in the car. However, the police held Coleman as a material witness. He changed his mind again and reluctantly agreed to testify. At the upcoming trial, a friend and neighbor backed Birns's shaky alibi. He said he noticed Birns arrive home at 12:07 a.m., about the time of the shooting. It took the jurors only four hours to reach a verdict, which resulted in Birns's acquittal once again. The jury expressed their refusal to believe the changing testimony of Coleman, who allegedly was a dope peddler and police informant.

By the end of 1959, Alex Shondor Birns had been arrested 38-times since 1925. His other crimes include attempted murder, gambling, robbery, assault and battery, and blackmail, prostitution as well as Income tax evasion.

1960

An associate and often partner of Birns, Mervin Gold, was being investigated for using stolen Canadian bonds for securing a bank loan.

On July 8, 1963, Gold was found murdered and stuck in the trunk of his own car. He had been severely beaten, then strangled with a clothesline, and shot in the chest several times. A blanket was used and wrapped around his head since he was shot three more times in the skull. The coroner, Samuel Gerber, estimated his time of death as shortly before midnight on Friday.

Anticipating an untimely demise, Gold left behind a signed affidavit claiming that Birns had given him the fraudulent bonds. His wife informed the police that her husband was on his way to meet with Birns that fateful night he was murdered. During their investigation, the police also found an audiotape made by Gold of a phone conversation between himself and Birns. The police wasted no time and placed a pick-up order for Birns arrest, as police were quickly sent out to find him. On Monday, Birns car turned up outside a motel in Toledo. The motel owner said Birns had checked in on Saturday and sought treatment for an injured right hand. He told a local doctor that a firecracker caused the injury.

On Wednesday morning, Birns called John Kocevar, Chief Deputy Cuyahoga County Sheriff. He arranged to surrender at a meeting spot in the suburb of Garfield Heights. He told Kocevar, "I would have been here yesterday, but it was a Jewish holiday." Somebody also tipped off the press. A reporter and photograph were waiting when he arrived. Birns seemed to enjoy his picture in the paper, as he gave an assured smiled when he noticed them and told them, "Thanks for coming, fellows."

Birns was taken to Central Station for questioning by the head of the Homicide Unit, Lieutenant Carl Delau. Amid aggressive interrogation by Delau, Birns insisted he had been dining on frog legs inside a Garfield Heights steakhouse the night of Gold's murder. Besides, Birns claimed that he was at home with a woman he is currently seeing. Birns did not name her but said she was willing to testify for him. His bail was set at $50,000, which he posted with ease.

Then, the *Plain Dealer* reported, "Birns cheerfully walked out of the building and down the front steps to where his attorney, James R. Willis, was waiting for him." All concern on this charge faded away two days later. Birns happily produced a friend, Allene Leonard's, a shy, pretty 24-year-old teacher in the Garfield Heights school system. Ailene confirmed Birns alibi claiming that she had been with Alex the whole evening. This was also verified by the owner of the steakhouse the couple ate at. Birns would soon divorce his first wife, Jane, and would quickly marry Allene one year later. He had married Jane back in 1952 and had one son, Michael.

1967

It was early January, and after a long hard fight with the unstoppable IRS, Birns was sentenced to serve three years in prison for lying and making false statements regarding his income since 1961.

1968

Over the next several years, Birns was continued to be in jail for his past sins, until he was released on June 1, 1971.

1971

Alex Birns found himself, linked up with yet another criminal in the Cleveland area. This time it was a former defiant Longshoreman's union boss named Danny Greene. Greene's life was saved by a freak moment in time when a bomb exploded. A single stick of dynamite was thrown into his car by a passing auto. Greene has been linked to Cleveland most arrest numbers boss, Birns, for several months and believed to be his muscle for any delinquent payments. Their working relationship was bound by the same greed and contempt for their enemies.

1974

The relationship between Danny Greene and Alex Birns began to sour fast. Greene envied Birns's control of the number and policy rackets. In their early days of working together, Greene even looked up to him as a friend and mentor. Greene looked forward to the day when it would be all his. Greene was also jealous of Birns's immense wealth and popularity with the Cleveland media and public. Within a few years, and the death of John Scalish in 1976 had put Birns and Greene on opposite sides of a Mafia dispute with Greene supporting John Nardi, while Birns supported the apparent heir to the thrown, James Licavoli. Greene was soon willing to take on Birns.

The long told story goes Greene had asked Birns for a loan of $70,000. Greene wanted the money to set up a "cheat spot," a speakeasy and gambling house. The smart businessman that he was, Birns was not willing to put his own money into the project. Birns then arranged a loan for Greene through the Gambino crime family. Somehow, the money wound up in the hands of Billy Cox, a runner for the New York mob and the operator of a numbers game, who used it to purchase narcotics. The police raided his house, arrested him, and seized the drugs along with what was left of the $70,000. The Gambino family, from whom Birns had borrowed the loan, wanted all their money back. Birns pressed Greene, but Greene flatly refused to return the money. Greene stayed firm. The men argued over this as Greene; instead, he never received the money and that it was not his fault that it got lost or taken by the police.

In retaliation, Birns gave $25,000 to an associate to hire a hitman so Greene could be murdered. Before Greene could kill him. Several minor underworld characters soon took on this challenge. This agreement would result in well documented failed assassination attempts on Greene.

Not long after, Greene found an unexploded bomb in his car when he pulled into a Collinwood service station for gas. The explosive vehicle was wired improperly and failed to detonate. Greene disassembled the weapon himself, removed the dynamite, and brought the rest of the package to the Cleveland police lieutenant, Edward Kovacic. Kovacic offered him police protection. The arrogant Irishman refused. He also declined to hand over the bomb, telling him, "I'm going to send this back to the old bastard that sent it to me." Greene decided to retaliate.

1975

It is now March 30, 1975, as the *Cleveland Plain Dealer article* written by W. Joseph Campbell

Alex (Shondor) Birns, the number one arrest numbers man, racketeer, was blown to bits around 8 PM last night, just seconds after he entered his car parked behind a West Sidebar. Police, who made the identification stated, "Birns was hurled through the roof of his 1975 Light Blue Lincoln Continental Mark IV. His upper torso was found beside the opened passenger door." The car was parked in the lot behind Christy's Lounge, which was the former Jack & Jill West Lounge known as a go-go spot at 2516 Detroit Avenue, which Birns owned.

Police have speculated that Birns car ignition may have been wired to several sticks of dynamite. The current belief is that the explosive was placed under the front seats of the expensive vehicle.

Although many details were sketchy, the police have outlined the circumstances of the explosion. "At 8 PM, Birns accompanied a man identified only as Ed, who was a part-owner of a bar and walked from Christie's lounge to the parking lot. Ed left Birns just as Birns got into his car. Ed just turned the corner block only a few steps away when Birns turned the key to start the engine when Ed heard the ear-deafening blast. Several callers told the Plain Dealer the blast was heard at nine blocks away."

Parts of the destroyed car were found 1,000 feet away near St. · Malachi's Catholic Church at 2459 Washington Avenue, where approximately 100 people were waiting to enter the church for evening service.

Ed told the police, "Birns came in about 7 PM last night and bought drinks for everyone. The operator of a black number game said, "It's dumb to talk about blacks doing Shondor. "Shon wasn't a bad fella." He was white, but it didn't make any difference. Shon

had a dark soul. He was black through and through. Shit, there wasn't any racial prejudice in that goddamn Shondor Birns at all.

He was a helluva guy... No, No. There ain't gonna be no more Shondor...."

ALEX "SHONDOR" BIRNS LINCOLN

(Courtesy of Cleveland State University Archives Department)

45

JOHN NARDI

John Nardi was born Giovanni Narcchione in the Eastside Little Italy community. Sometime before John's birth on January 21, 1916, his father changed the family name to Nardi. He was the third of eight children. His parents were Lucian and Clara DiSanto. It is interesting to note that John's father, Lucian, was working as a Deputy Sheriff in 1932. Lucian enjoyed a long life and died in 1973.

Nardi began his early mob work as an enforcer for the local vending machine workers union. John is the cousin of fellow mobster Anthony Delsanter and had brothers Robert and Nicholas Nardi. John had married Lillian and had two children, John Jr. and a daughter Carol.

Nardi had earned his first police record entry in 1939 at the age of twenty-three, where he was charged with blackmail. At this time, Nardi was employed by Musical Employee Union Local 442 vending workers union. His job was to sell the services of their repair technicians. Sometimes he was too enthusiastic about his work. One incident stated, "Nardi threatened a bar owner with bodily harm and destroying a jukebox if he did not hire his union man to service his jukebox." Safety Director Eliot Ness ordered him to be arrested; eventually, the charges were dropped.

1946

Nardi soon became business partners with the mighty Ohio Teamsters official William Presser. Mr. Presser had a reputation of being a mob associate and the father of future Teamsters President Jackie Presser in several Jukebox companies. Police say it was Anthony Milano, Nardi's uncle, who helped John move into the lucrative vending machine union in the 1950s. Nardi claims, "He got the job by merely asking William Presser. However, police believed Nardi was placed as a principal liaison between organized crime and the Teamsters.

By the mid-1940s, Nardi became a member of the Vending Machine Service Employees Local 410, part of the Teamsters Union. He soon became Secretary-Treasurer of the Local. Nardi also formed strong ties with Aladino "Jimmy the Weasel" Fratianno, a future boss with the Los Angeles family with whom he also ran a bookmaking operation in Cleveland's Little Italy. By this time, Nardi's brother Nick was the Secretary-Treasurer of Teamsters Local 416. John's other brother Robert was now the Secretary-Treasurer of the Teamsters Production Maintenance & Allied Workers Union Local 415.

John Nardi soon built various street rackets connections, which included drug trafficking and extortion. John diligently worked to kept his drug business away from his uncle's ears.

Sometimes during the late 1940s, Nardi and William Presser became founders of the Youngstown-based Triangle Music Company, which owned and operated vending machines. Also, they collaborated with the Windsor Distribution Company, a coin-operated machine firm.

Nardi could have enjoyed a bright future with the Cleveland family, but he was too dame stubborn, bull-headed, independent, and ambitious to accept its stable structure. Frustrated and not content to wait years to become a made man, or a full member, of the organization.

1959

It was in March, as the McClellan Senate Rackets Committee hearings were interested in questioning several members of the 1940 West Triangle Music Company. Most importantly was their connection with the Teamsters Local 410, Vending Machine Service Employees Union. The union was heavily involved with Jukeboxes, and coin-operated vending machines. Mentioned to be subpoena is Teamsters Union President, William Presser along with John DeMarco, Joseph Fontana, President of Local 410, John Nardi Secretary-Treasurer, and Tony Sara a union representative. Subpoena, were also issued for Frank Embrescia, a partner with John Scalish in the Buckeye Vending Machine Company. Years later, in 1975, it would be revealed how Fontana and Nardi both earn $17,400 in salaries (equal to $82,214 in today's money.) John Nardi Jr, aka Jack, was an agent for Teamsters Union Local 507 and making $15,500 a year

By the late 1960s, the Cleveland family was losing patience with Nardi's stubbornness and independent nature, along with his arrogant attitude and lack of respect toward them.

John's brother Nick succeeded Nicholas Francis and became president after the disappearance of Patrick Catalano in 1968. Many police officials believed Catalano was murder when his new Cadillac was found burnt beyond any recognition on a deserted dirt road in Stark County, his disappearance has-never-been solved.

Another brother of John's is William, who became the secretary of the Italian newspaper, L'Araldo Publishing Company when it was in business from 1938 until the 1960s.

Sometime between the late 1960s and March of 1970, Nardi Sr. borrowed an estimated $20,000 from the Caesars Palace in Las Vegas to help him pay off some gambling debts. John only paid back $10,000 and was sued for the remainder.

1970

It was now December as the FBI raided 25-business in Cleveland, Warren, Niles, and Youngstown areas. Lead by Special Agent Charles Cusick. The attacks were based on the ongoing investigation into illegal gambling and organized crime. One building was labeled as the headquarters of Local 410, Vending Machine Service Employees Union, located on 22nd Street in Downtown Cleveland. The search focused on the office of John Nardi Secretary-Treasurer of the union, along with his home on Colony Road in South Euclid. Their detailed investigation includes records obtained at the Teamsters Joint Council 410 office, which is located in the same building. Other men involved in the raid was, Joseph Lanese, aka "Joe the Hat" and known as a significant Bookmaker in Cleveland, John Calandra, owner of Royal Machine and Tool Company. The charges against the three men were later dropped in 1975 for lack of evidence.

During their investigation, the FBI gathered evidence from the Royal Machine Company, which included playing cards. They also found an assortment of paper receipts, which alleges that loans were given to many individuals since it included their names and address. Armed with a search warrant, they entered Calandra's home in University Heights. Agents found brass knuckles, a rifle with a high-powered scope, and a shotgun along with 3,800 shares of some type of stock certificates. The names of the shareowners were listed as Calandra, Mrs. Anthony Delsanter, Leo Moceri, and

James Licavoli.

1975

On November 21, John Nardi was arrested at his home in University Heights, on a warrant from Miami, Florida. The arrest warrant charged him with Racketeering and for conspiracy to import large quantities, which included 2-tons of marijuana. Nardi was released on a $50,000 bond and a court date of December 18, was scheduled in Miami. During the extensive trial, evidence-informed the court how Nardi spent over $150,000 to buy 5-tons of marijuana and to bring it into Florida from Columbia in several separate shipments.

During the trial, it was revealed that on August 22, US Drug Enforcement agency had videotaped and listened in on a conversation between Nardi and an undercover investigator discussing the 5-ton marijuana deal on Pier 66 in Fort Lauderdale, Florida. For some unknown reason, this secret meeting was never disclosed. Nardi was later acquitted of these charges even with the damaging videotape discussion. Allegations spread that it was possible Nardi became a Federal Informant to avoid a lengthy prison sentence.

Sometime during August, John Nardi was quoted saying, "It's so easy to rob a bank but… Getting away from the bank with the money is the hardest part of the whole deal! You know, it's the same with anything you do."

Nardi's personal problems have multiple over the last few years. He became a heavy gambler and drinker who continued to lose, resulting in owing large sums of money to a Vegas casino, along with an assortment of local bookmakers in Cleveland. This in itself made it difficult for Nardi to be viewed in high respect and defiantly not as a Mob boss and leader that he believes he was.

1976

It was May 26, as the news of the death of John Scalish destroyed the stable empire of the Cleveland Mafia. Scalish had died expectantly on the operating table for a heart ailment. This led Cleveland almost overnight to rise from #7 in the nation in the criminal bombing world to the #1 spot. This is because there were 21-bombings throughout the city, giving a grand total of 37, in Cuyahoga County alone. These bombings alone brought in the Alcohol, Tobacco, and Firearms Unit of the U.S. Treasury Department. The ATF designated northeastern Ohio as the new district headquarters and doubled the size of its staff.

During the summer, Nardi returned from Florida, where he successfully defended himself against federal narcotics and gun-running charges. Charged with Nardi were a Beachwood businessman, Morton Franklin, and two other men. Their names were never disclosed but mentioned as an international gun runner from Power Springs, Georgia, and a former CIA officer who now lives in Deerfield Beach, Florida. Later the man was named Mitchell Werbell, who was a known weapon dealer to anti-communist regimes in South America. Somehow at the end of the trial, all four men were acquitted of the charges pending against them. Nardi informed the investigators that the only way he knows Franklin is that he purchased a life insurance policy from him.

Meanwhile, his uncle, Anthony Milano, was hoping to have his son, Peter, return from the West Coast to work with Nardi to re-establish control of Cleveland, and then to rebuild it to the glory days of peace and harmony. Nardi had a different view of his future upon his return to Cleveland; Nardi approached Danny Greene. His goal was to form a stable alliance between the two. The Cleveland crime family had already made several attempts on Nardi's life, and Nardi needed to find powerful allies. The two men wanted to control the city, grow their personal fortunes, and formed an alliance to fight James Licavoli for control of the Cleveland Empire.

At the end of the 1976 Feast of the Assumption festival, Nardi claimed that the Cleveland family owed him a share of the illegal gambling profits from the event. James Licavoli was hoping he and Nardi could calm down, put their differences behind. At this time, Tony (Dope) Delsanter was running the Youngstown rackets and encouraged Licavoli to go after both Nardi and Greene.

The disagreement escalated as Loe Moceri publicly denied Nardi's claim to share in the take from the games. Shortly after this altercation, the last anyone had seen Moceri was at the Feast on August 22, 1976. Moceri disappeared, as his Mercedes-Benz sports car was found in the parking lot of an Akron Motel. The Police concluded that the trunk was soaked with blood, yet nobody was discovered in the vehicle. Federal authorities speculated the bombing of Nardi may be in retaliation for Moceri's disappearance and presumed death.

James Licavoli was livid and was now looking for revenge. Soon, Delsanter suggested Jimmy "The Weasel" Fratianno to do the job and to bring him back to Cleveland to help with the problem of Green and Nardi.

At this time, it is believed that Greene and Nardi went after Eugene "the Animal" Ciasullo, the family's most feared enforcer. Ciasullo has been severely injured by a bomb placed on the front porch of his home. This action convinced Ciasullo to leave Cleveland and change his wicked ways, as he headed for a peaceful and quiet life in Florida.

It was on September 10, as Nardi exited the Italian American Brotherhood Club on Mayfield Road. He walked across the street, where he parked his car. It so happened to be in front of the Holy Rosary Church in the heart of Little Italy. John reached for the door handle when a window exploded from a rifle shot, which just missed his head. Two speeding cars were seen leaving the area; each car had two people inside. Nardi barely escaped with his life, but firmly believes Licavoli order the hit on him. Nardi looked at a few of Licavoli's underlings as the possible assassin; Butchy

Cisternino, Joe Iacobacci, Glenn Pauley, Allie Calabrese, or Joe Bonariggo.

In 1976, after Moceri's disappearance, his cousin James Licavoli and his new underboss Angelo Lonardo went to New York to seek advice and to talk to Anthony (Fat Tony) Salerno.

There were two assassination attempts on Nardi's life by Butchy Cisternino and Allie Calabrese. The first was with the rifle. The second attempt was made a few days later when a shotgun blast fired at Nardi from a moving car. In a harsh response to these murder attempts, Nardi threatened revenge against everyone responsible for taking shots at him; and they would be killed!

Just weeks before his death, Nardi granted an interview to a *Plain Dealer* reporter inquiring about a rumor that he and Licavoli were feuding. During the engaging conversation, Nardi stated that he and Licavoli were lifelong friends and denied the allegations. He also refused the statement that Danny Greene worked with him, saying that they were just friends.

1977

It was now May; when Greene was, informed by a street source, that Licavoli was planning Nardi's murder. Greene was looking after his new close friend and sent two of his trusted men to watch over him. One man was Brian O'Donnell and the other Keith Ritson, an ex-fighter and Golden Gloves champion. Nardi thanked the two men. However, he felt he was in no danger from Licavoli and told them, "Don't worry boys, I have known Jack all my life, he is my friend."

On the same day, May 17, 1977, Nardi parked his car in the rear parking lot of the Teamster Joint Council 41. Unknown to Nardi, a bomb car was placed in a vehicle in the rear of the lot, across from the Musician's Union building. When the 61-year old Nardi left his office at 3 PM, he entered his vehicle. Soon the bomb was detonated by remote control. The enormous impact of the explosion had blown away both of Nardi's legs. The FBI investigation led to a hitman hired by Licavoli to be John "Curly" Montana.

Police informed the media that, "A red 1975 Pontiac was wired with a high-grade explosive. This explosion was equivalent to fifteen sticks of dynamite.

Police think someone watched as Nardi walked through an alley behind the building and approached his car, then detonated the explosive by remote control as he stood between the vehicles. Nardi's body was found moments later by two people. John was lying across the front seat with most of his clothing blown off his body, with his legs lying behind him.

Several men worked diligently to pull Nardi through the shattered window and start CPR. Moments later, Nardi's brother, Nick, quickly joined them until an Emergency Medical Service ambulance arrived. Nardi was immediately taken to St. Vincent Charity Hospital, where he was pronounced dead: at 3:27 p.m.

According to the book *To Kill the Irishman* by Rick Porrello, as Nardi was being pulled away from the wreckage, Nardi whispered, "It didn't hurt" in a final act of defiance.

Investigators called it one of the most sophisticated gangland slayings. They believe the car bomb contained a combination of several pounds of nuts and bolts that acted as shrapnel. The left side of Nardi's Oldsmobile was found perforated by the metal fragments.

A story was told how the incredible force of the explosion blew a vinyl roof of the Pontiac parked a few spots away from Nardi. It was then swept over the two-story, yellow brick Teamsters building, about 200 feet away.

JOHN NARDI'S OLDSMOBILE

(Courtesy of the Cleveland Plain Dealer Archives at Cleveland State University)

Although investigators are confident, it was a rackets-related slaying and an act of retaliation. The police and federal agents have maintained that Nardi was among the most powerful men in organized crime in Cleveland.

One investigator dubbed him, "the caretaker capo." Throughout Nardi's life, he always denied involvement with organized crime, saying he was nothing but a legitimate labor leader. "'They're trying to make a big man out of me," he said. "I'm not involved in any illegal things."

After their investigation of 6 months, the Cleveland Police and local FBI agents believed that Licavoli, Carabbia, Ray Ferritto, and Butchy Cisternino were behind the killing. In an FBI affidavit, it disclosed that Ferritto was promised membership in the Detroit Mob and a portion of the Youngstown area gambling rackets if he kills Greene and Nardi. Ferritto stated, "I asked Cisternino, who killed Nardi? The response he received was. "I did not have the contract and had nothing to do with it."

Attending John's wake at DiCicco's Funeral home in Mayfield Heights was estimated to be over 100 known mobsters. Sadly, John's wife Lillian and his uncle Anthony Milano now 91, were too distraught to attend.

Nardi and his wife, Lillian, lived in a modest $65,000 condominium at 2626 S. Green Rd., University Heights.

46

PART V

ANGELO ANTHONY LONARDO

We all have heard how fathers have driven their sons to take over the family business or follow in their footsteps. Whether it is as a mason, carpenter, Doctor, barber, or lawyer. However, for a "Mafia Boss," it was seen to be ironclad and destiny. "This Sicilian Thing" all started in Sicily. Fathers had dreamed about passing on the incredible wealth, power, and control to their son's. That is one reason why so many Sicilian men were delighted to have a son (seen as a privileged child) to continue their family legacy.

Angelo Lonardo was big, reliable, and born to take the leadership role in the Cleveland Mafia. Just as his father Joe had done. Angelo was born in 1909 in Warren, Ohio to Joseph and Concetta Lonardo, as they soon moved to Cleveland. His godfather was Cleveland's powerful underboss Anthony Milano. Joe Lonardo had three brothers John, Frank, and Dominic. Angelo's first wife was Margret Yacalo, who would divorce him in 1945, after one year of marriage and just as he was being released from prison. This second wife and sweetheart were Mary Elizabeth Scalish, the sister of his criminal friend, John Scalish. Mary's other sister would marry another close friend Maishe "Milton" Rockman. Mary sadly passed away in March of 1985.

Later in life, Angelo became known as "Big Ange" like his father, who was "Big Joe." Angelo's legitimate business in life was as a bar and restaurant owner.

1927

Unknown to Angelo Lonardo, his experience in crime would start within a year at the young age of sixteen soon after his father and uncle were ambushed and murdered in cold blood.

It was on October 13 when Joseph "Big Joe" and John Lonardo both became influential as "underworld criminals." Many believe that "Big Joe" was the "Boss" in Cleveland as they found themselves in a trap they did not expect. They were killed inside a barbershop owned by Angelo Porrello on 110th and Woodland Avenue. Police believe the bitter feud between the rival family gangs finally reached a pinnacle for the fight to control "Corn Sugar" in Cleveland.

At the time, Safety Director Edwin Barry announced he has several commanding leads, which led the police to arrest one or two men who committed the murder. Police have received first-hand information stating the main reason the brothers where killed was that five of the Porrello Brothers had paid Joe Lonardo a large sum of money to get yet another brother Raymond released from prison. The story goes Lonardo was either unable to do this, or just took the money. The Porrello's retaliated after Lonardo blatantly refused to return the money back to the Porrello family.

The other possible or principal reason for the murder was the Lonardo clan was working feverishly to take over the illegal whiskey brewing business from the Porrello's. Lonardo's crew then hit several homes that would not change suppliers to his company.

1928

It was mid-January when young Angelo Lonardo found himself in front of Juvenile Judge Harry Eastman for his first arrest. He was arrested and plead guilty to carrying a concealed weapon back in mid- December. Lonardo's defense to the Judge was a simple one. He was bringing a deposit to the bank for his widowed mother from a few of the rental properties she owned and was carrying the weapon for protection from being robbed.

1929

It was now June as both Joe and John Lonardo's families found themselves in a dangerous financial situation they have not felt since they arrived in America from Sicily. The families were dead broke, no food or rent money. Many had speculated that it was from the miss handling of their fortune by John when Joe was away vacationing in Sicily. Soon another sad event took place. Their expensive car was repossessed. Subsequently, Concetta Lonardo, "Big Joe's" wife, lost her twenty-room home to the bank. It was estimated to be a $70,000 home on Larchmere Boulevard, In Shaker Heights. (Note, this is equal to over $1,040,000 in today's money)

To add insult to her now grieving heart and life, Mrs. Concietta Lonardo had just learned that her late husband Joe was married to another woman, Mrs. Fannie Lanzone Lonardo. Fannie claims the couple was married in Sandusky, Ohio in 1925, and has filed a lawsuit against the family's supposedly great wealthy fortune. The estate was estimated to be worth 1 Million dollars. The suit will be heard in the courtroom of Probate Judge George Addams. Meanwhile, the judge decided both women will get a small settlement monthly until the case can be solved.

It was now June 11, as "Black Sam" Todaro, a man who enjoyed his family and loved his wife and three young children, was speaking with his brother-in-law's, Angelo Sciria and Angelo Porrello. A man came up to him and said, "Sam, a man, and women want to talk to you. They say it's important?"Later, Sciria came forward and told the police he heard gunshots, and when he got to 110th Street, a large car was driving off as fast as it could down the street. He then told the police he noticed a male driver and a woman in the front seat and a man sitting in the back seat but did not know who they were.

Police found five bullets in Todaro's short, stocky frame. In the evening paper, *The Cleveland News* posted, "Near the body of Todaro's was a calling card of death, the Ace of Spades."

Lead by Detective Inspector Cody, within two days, twenty police officers and detectives questioned witness and pick-up known suspicious persons in the city. Their quest was to find the shooters of "Black Sam: Todaro. Police soon had three leads to the identity of the criminal.

Concetta Lonardo, the common-law wife of "Big Joe," was arrested for either being the shooter or partaking in the brutal daytime murder. Neither, Angelo Lonardo or Dominic Sospirato, the other two suspects have been found living in the city. It was rumored, they fled for the sun along with the peace and quiet of San Francisco, California.

Scared, nervous, and worried about going to jail, Mrs. Lonardo told her story of how she was in the car, with her son Angelo now 20-years old, who was driving the vehicle with her nephew Dominic Sospirato in the back seat. They went to the local grocery store to pick up a few items, and then he drove by the 110th and Woodland business, and near the barbershop where her late husband had been killed, but she has no idea who fired the fatal shots. Ms. Lonardo then said the boys dropped her off in Angelo's Lincoln at her Larchmere home and drove away.

TODARO'S MURDER SCENE

(Courtesy of Dennis Sutcliffe)

By July 2, Lonardo's coupe was found at Cedar and East 105th Street. Meanwhile, Mrs. Lonardo has been held under indictment for the murder of Todaro. Police believe that Lonardo used a Lincoln for the criminal act.

YOUNG ANGELO ON TRIAL FOR MURDER

(Courtesy of Cleveland State University)

In November, Concetta Lonardo was found not guilty of the death of Sam Todaro. The announcement came from Common Pleas Judge Fred Wolf. Soon it became evident that this was a ploy by the Cleveland County Prosecutor Ray Miller. " That if the city allowed Mrs. Lonardo to go free, her son Angelo and nephew Dominic Sospirato would willingly turn themselves in." Many of the citizens knew Angelo for his short and boiling temper. The city also believed they had substantial evidence that Angelo, in fact, pulled the trigger and shot Sam Todaro in cold blood while his mother held Todaro's hand so he could not getaway.

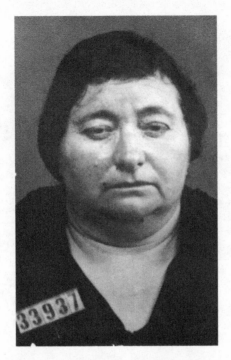

MRS. CONCETTA LONARDO

(Courtesy of the Cleveland Police Museum)

1930

It was now February as twenty-one-year-old Angelo Lonardo turned himself in sitting quietly in his cell. Police Detective Captain James Hogan wanted to question him about the murder of Salvatore Todaro. After several hours of grueling, exhausting questioning, the exhausted Angelo finally admitted, "that he killed him." He stated, "It was a deep-rooted desire for revenge, a Vendetta." One of the primary witnesses and trapped in the middle of the feud was "Little Angelo" Sciria, who had left the country so he could not be brought in for questioning. As a strange twist of fate, Sciria was Todaro's brother-in-law and a cousin to Lonardo.

By June, with the abundance of evidence against them, both Lonardo and Saspirato were tried and found guilty of second-degree murder of Salvatore, "Black Sam" Todaro. The two men were sentenced to "Life in Prison," and sent to the Ohio State Penitentiary. Attorneys for both men soon filed multiple petitions in 1931 and asked for a second trial, which was later granted. Whether it was from pure luck or the grace of God-feeling sorry for the young men, the accused men won their second trial and were acquitted of all murder charges.

In the summer of 1932, Lonardo was soon arrested along with George Angersola in a police raid. John and George Angersola were identified by the Florida Organized Crime Council as being a member of a nationally recognized organized crime family.

1933

The first evidence to link the organized crime to "The Mayfield Road Gang" was revealed as four men were arrested for running an illegal "Policy Racket" in the basement, in a Woodland Avenue home.

Little Angelo Sciria, who had returned to Cleveland and suspected to have been in Sicily, met up with young Angelo. The two men discussed the possibility of moving into a new lucrative avenue, the "policy and clearinghouse games." They planned that a few of their men or just Little Angelo, would visit a game or home. Their guns were drawn as they fired a few warning shots, just to get their undivided attention. They would then take all the gaming equipment in the room. Lonardo or Sciria told them in a few short words. "he wanted a piece of their lucrative action for himself. Then they would receive their equipment back undamaged, and they would now have him to protect them from any unsavory characters. At first, most of the men were shocked at his crazy scheme. They were already paying off the police, so why did they need him to protect them? Angelo gave them some settle reminders along the way, and soon many gave in to his intimidation.

47

1942

It has been almost three long years as the twenty-five men have been waiting for their trial in operating a Policy Racket, and a blackmail scheme against other operators. Lonardo anxiously claims he has never been a member of a gang of policy managers.

By the end of July, Judge Day announced that Angelo Lonardo, Joseph Artwell, and William Richardson were found guilty of the charge of blackmail while Thomas Boyce was found not guilty. Seven other men are now facing a sentencing hearing.

1949

It was in September as the year-old case came before the Court of Appeals, in the blackmail and with bombing the home of racketeer Joe Allen, killing him. The three men accused our, Angelo Lonardo, Charles Amato, and Joseph Artwell. The men are all sitting in jail for the last nine days since they are not able to meet their extreme bail of $75,000. (This is equal to $801,424 in today's money.) Soon Shondor Birns and Nick Satulla will be arrested and join them in jail for the crime. The men and their attorneys have requested their bail to be lowered to only $15,000. Judge Joy Seth Hurd accepted the amount on September 27. By the middle of November, the trial has not even started, since the defense and prosecution debated one the exact charges. One man who came to his defense and testified for the men was the owner of the Cleveland Indians, Bill Veeck, who was a frequent visitor to one of Birns taverns.

In a brave attempt to end the trial quickly in Judge Blythin Court, Attorneys Louis Ferneber, Edwin Stanton, Neil McGill, William Corrigan, and Fred Garmone, plot their vigorous defense for Angelo Lonardo, Shonder Birns, Charles Amata, Nick Satulla,

Joseph Artwell. Lonardo, who stood five feet nine inches tall and weighed over 220 pounds, testified in his own defense and stated, "He had nothing to do with the killing of Allen." Lonardo then said, "I was on Kinsman Road at the time, and going to sell his Cadillac to a dealer. I can always be seen at the Stage Door Club at 915 Chester every evening from 9-midnight." The state's star witness is William Billingslea, who says he was an aid for Birns and currently a guard at the Warrensville Workhouse. He stood proudly and testified that Lonardo and Birns were both in jail at the time. Both were pulling strings and organized the now-famous bomb, blackmail, extortion plot against Joseph Allen.

It has been firmly believed that the National Crime Commission decided to have all the primary five family's, slow down, and stop all their activates. Their goal was to help cool down the pressure and the graft in the U.S. Senate.

1950

During a cumbersome investigation, Lonardo was accused of being involved in three different taverns in the Cleveland area. One of them was a favorite evening hot-spot named Frolics in downtown Cleveland. Later on, in his career, he owned the very popular Highlander Motor Inn located in Warrensville Heights in the community of North Randle. The motel was suspected of having been purchased from an insurance claim on an old tavern or was given the money from the former Seaway Acceptance Company.

This trial for the murder of Joseph Allen. was dubbed, one that the city of Cleveland has been waiting for. It was scheduled to begin in April.

By May 17, the case was coming to a close with plenty of accusations, debates, and motions, asking to not allow statements from several witnesses. However, the trial and the state rested their case, and the jury was sent to their room for what could be a long deliberation.

Common Pleas Judge Joseph Silbert was notified the jury has reached a verdict. The jury and the court were in session by 9:45 PM. After reading the conclusion himself, in a stunning look of disbelief, the shocked judge requested in a soft but firm voice for the Jury Forman to state their decision. It was short and sweet, Not Guilty, as the seven-week trial ended. Every person in the packed courtroom, including County Prosecutor Frank Cullitan and the twelve deputy sheriffs, were stunned.

1951

It was interesting to find that Angelo Lonardo was not among the twenty known Cleveland criminals summoned to appear before the Kefauver Hearings in Cleveland.

1957

It was June 15, as Angelo A. Lonardo married the girl of his dreams, Mary Elizabeth Scalish, at Saint Cecilia's Church. Mary Elizabeth is the daughter of Frank Scalish Sr. and the sister of John T Scalish. The elegant reception was held at the Hotel Statler in beautiful downtown Cleveland.

By this time, Angelo, with his brother Dominick and Frank, became interested in the lucrative bail bond business in Ohio. Soon they all united alongside and aligned themselves with the Trans-American Corporation. By the end of 1959, Trans-American had written thousands of Bonds and growing stronger every year.

Angelo's health suffered a significant setback; in 1958. On April 10, he needed back surgery for his discs to relieve the excessive pain. It helped to a small degree. However, Lonardo still suffered from back pain for the rest of his life.

THE ELEGANT DINING ROOM OF THE STATLER

(Courtesy of the Cleveland State University Memory Project)

1960

Lonardo soon found himself being investigated once again, along with Dominic Bartone, who had been convicted of arms smuggling and fraud of the Northern Ohio Bank. Both Lonardo and Bartone were exposed as being the head of a 23-state bail bonds syndicate using an insurance company in Indianapolis.

1963

Lonardo had control of the favorite Frolic and Sonny's Bar in the heart of downtown Cleveland on St. Vincent Street and managed the Tasty BBQ. At this time, the new Highlander Inn and Lounge opened up at 4353 Northfield Road, opposite of Thistledown Race Track and walking distance to the favorite Musicarnival.

By 1968, the Highlander Inn was well known as just "Angelo's Place." The Highlander became as famous as Morris

Wexler's The Theatrical Grillor Birns Alhambra club.

THEATRICAL THEATER ON ST VINCENT STREET

(Courtesy of Cleveland State University Memory Project)

Different popular nightspots sprang up around the city, which included the Post and Paddock, Saints, and Sinners located in the Eastgate Shopping Center in Mayfield Heights, Leo's Casino on Euclid Avenue, The exciting Blue Grass in North Randle. The Blue Fox on the westside and then in 1974 came the amazing heater in the round in Highland Heights on Wilson Mills Road named, "The Front Row Theater."

48

1972

The timeline is cloudy as to when Lonardo met some of the critical players inside his Highlander Inn to discuss the next murder plot to assassinate Danny Greene. One-man Tommy Sinito, who worked for Lonardo as a friendly bartender, and Joe Gallo, whose sister was one of Lonardo's bookkeepers. Under Lonardo's guidance, both Sinito and Gallo became a lieutenant in the Cleveland family.

Brother Frank Lonardo, a well-known Bails Bondsmen at this time, operated the AAA Bail Bond Service and was convicted in 1973 of Federal Income Tax Evasion.

1976

Working quietly behind the scenes, in January, Ohio Attorney General William J. Brown filed a civil lawsuit against a few men who have defrauded over three-hundred Ohioans. The crime was a simple one. These men would solicit $200 from the naive citizens who owned land out-of-state. Their scam was to list their property in a unique approach to ensure their property was appealing to respectable estate developers living in Europe and Japan.

It was now May as the city soon heard about the fifty-two-year-old Angelo Lonardo once again. In Pittsburgh PA, a Federal Grand Jury has indicted Lonardo, and five others of a mystifying land fraud scheme valued up to $800,000.

The other men include David Davis, Sanford Levin, Joseph Lonardo, David Wheatley, and D.R McLean from Pittsburgh. The men never obtained a license to publish this so-called promised to sell their home. Their adventurous crime was swindling money from unsuspected citizens in a phony land deal in Florida, Arizona, New Mexico, and Texas.

The city of Cleveland's gang war was soon going to erupt beyond anyone's wildest dreams. The death of John Scalish unleashed a criminal scrimmage for power and to rule over Cleveland.

Lonardo strongly felt he was to have been the correct choice and successor and secretly had Rockman in his corner to take over the reins of power in Cleveland. It was not meant to be. At a secret meeting, Rockman informed the Cleveland boys that he and John often spoke about this. John truly believed Licavoli would be best suited to control the family in Cleveland. Who knew at this time that this one simple statement from a trusted member of the family would lead to the devastation and demise of the Cleveland mob within a few years?

On one side of the coin was James Licavoli, who later had Angelo Lonardo as his underboss, and then there was Danny Greene, the thick head Irishman who thought he and John Nardi, should be ruling the city with their iron fists. It has been documented that this rival consisted of 35 bombings between the two factions.

1977

By December, after the death of the Irishman back on October 6, the hearings in Cleveland have indicated nine people in his death that rocked the Midwest. Listed with James Licavoli, the "Boss" was Angelo Lonardo, Ron Carabbia, Raymond Ferritto, Pasquale "Butchy" Cisternino, Allie Calabrese, James Fratianno and Tommy Sinito. Inside the courtroom of Common Pleas Judge Leo Spellacey, three men Licavoli, Lonardo, and Sinito filed pleas of "Not Guilty" in the ordering of Greens death.

1978

At this time, fifteen people have been singled out for taking part in Greene's murder. The outcome of this critical and well-organized prosecution of the Cleveland Mobsters led by John T. Corrigan proved to be devastating. It is rare in a gangland slaying like this, as the top men in Cleveland Organized crime were brought in for murder. Even though many of the men were freed, this trial sent a great shock wave across America.

An informant who had given the FBI over one hundred reliable tips over ten years told them that, "at first, Licavoli did not want the job as Cleveland's crime czar." The informant went on and said, "Licavoli took the role because of the fact he feared trouble could erupt due to Scalish's untimely death."

Later it was learned that back in October 1976, after Scalish's dearth Chicago's "Boss," Joe Aiuppa warned his top men to avoid any contact with the Cleveland people saying, "it was too unstable, unsafe and a dangerous situation."

It would not be until spring when Lonardo, Licavoli, and Sinito would be found innocent of ordering the murder of Danny Greene.

Angelo Lonardo and his brother Dominic were still in the bail bond business and being accused by the Federal Law Enforcement agencies of being the power behind the United Public Insurance Company of Indianapolis. A company that had written over 8 Million dollars in bonds, which brought about the collapse of Trans-American Corporation.

The elderly, sly like a fox, old man Lonardo enjoyed the little things in life. Driving and visiting friends, going to Corky and Lenny's, a favorite neighborhood Jewish Deli on Chardon Road in the Village Square Shopping Center located in Woodmere, Ohio. He would often meet Sinito and Gallo there to discuss business in private, in a secluded rear booth. Ignoring the frank warnings from Licavoli, Lonardo plotted and focused around allying with Carmen Zagaria. Zagaria lived on the west side of town and a known drug dealer. Understanding the traditional Sicilian lore of not dealing in drugs. Lonardo's taste for the extraordinary life and idealistic wealth was more significant than his good sense. In deciding his future fate, he could only see the vast amount of money that could be made. He chose to back Zagaria extended enterprise and go against the "old-timers" warning. In this world of crime, there was no code of silence and no loyalty among drug dealers and thieves. In multiple conversations, Sinito never referred to Lonardo by his name, just using the name "The old man or the old guy" in case the phone was being taped by the police or FBI.

1980

The eighties became a difficult time for the Lonardo family.

By March, the FBI was well aware of Lonardo's operation with a drug lord Carmen Zagaria and began what they named "Operation Bismark." This code name was the original investigation into Zagaria's drug trafficking operation. During the next two years, the FBI carefully watched the day-to-day movements of Lonardo, Zagaria, and their associates.

The FBI released a staggering statistic. It was between the years of 1977 and 1982 the cities of Youngstown and Cleveland enjoyed their highest arrest record. Many, if not most of all, the men arrested for racketeering have been successfully convicted. The FBI claims that it was because of the RICO act.

Finally, since John Scalish's untimely death, more than 30 mob members have been assassinated in the last five years, as the war on organized crime and control of both cities

49

1982

It was now July and, in a surprise, the U.S Government; Organized crime leader Angelo Lonardo now 71, was arrested in his luxurious Pepper Pike home on a sealed Federal Grand Jury Indictment, on Federal Racketeering Charges. The warrant consisted of an astounding 92 pages. This was due to an extensive investigation into a 15 million dollar a year drug trafficking business. This charge was 74 different counts of racketeering. Lonardo's defense attorney was his nephew, Angelo F. Lonardo. Also arrested was Carmen Zagaria. Both men were facing astonishing charges and allegations of murder, tax evasion, and dealing drugs. Ironically, on the same day, James Licavoli and other mob members were convicted on similar racketeering charges coming from the murder trial of Danny Greene.

Throughout the challenging and lengthy trial, John Congeni was subjected to several personal and obscene insults, along with specific threats on his life from various defendants and their attorneys. One of the most damaging audio tapes heard during the trial was played for the Grand Jury. Joey Gallo, a member of the Lonardo family, was talking with Joe Triscaro, the brother of the late Babe Triscaro, in December of 1980. He said, "Lonardo is probably one of the most respected and connected guys in the whole country. This guy commands a lot of respect from just about everyone."

The Grand Jury heard testimony and charged that the six men were engaged in a conspiracy to control organized crime activities throughout Ohio. Accomplishes listed of the same offense are John Calandra, another top crime associate. Joey Gallo, and Thomas Sinito. Also charged with 72 counts of this indictment is Carmen Zagaria, who is currently in hiding and has been placed on the FBI's "Most Wanted" list as number 11. Then we have Hans

Graewe, who is a German citizen and an associate with Zagaria and is charged with 70 counts. Fritz Graewe, Hans's younger brother, is accused of 71 counts as well. These men have all filed "Not Guilty" pleas with the court. Last on the list is Kevin McTaggart, who is facing 70 counts and is a murder suspect and listed as missing.

U.S District Judge Donna Manos refused all bond proposals by the attorneys for any of the indicted men.

By August, all the people remained in the city jail waiting for their Bond Hearing, except for Angelo Lonardo. The gingerly old man was taken to Shaker Medical Center under a special heavy guard and is still under arrest. However, he was in terrible pain. Lonardo was found to have a gallbladder problem with stomach ulcers, including a heart problem as surgery would be needed to save his life.

In September, a bond hearing was finally underway as Lonardo's new Attorney, Leonard Yelsky, pleaded for his client's reasonable bond request. He used testimony from doctor Victor Ippolito who stated, "Lonardo is seriously ill and cannot stay in prison if he is to survive his current illness."

Judge Manos listened carefully to the reasons for this unique bond appeal and decided since Lonardo was a resident in Cleveland most of his life and his current severe medical condition, she would set his bond at $250,000. The other men would not be as lucky.

By November, an unexpected turn of events transpired as Carmen Zagaria trying desperately to save himself from a life spent in an eight by eight-prison cell with no chance of parole. He considered the alternatives and has agreed to become a Government witness. His only hope was to gain some type of leniency, as he agreed to testify against Lonardo.

During one of his interviews, Zagaria stated, "Hans Graewe continued to push me to join and become a member of the Cleveland Mob and said, "Once you know where all the money is hidden and coming from along with the in's and out's I'll blast both Licavoli and Lonardo, then we will be in control the city."

1983

By the end of January, the crucial federal criminal case against the Cleveland criminals begin. Lonardo, who had once ruled with overall intimidation, fear, terror, now saw his case reduced to 54 counts of drug trafficking.

On January 24, the Federal Government won one of the most significant cases of drug trafficking in Ohio. Lonardo, Joe Gallo, Hans Graewe, and Kevin McTaggart were all found guilty of being drug kingpins.

On April 7, Judge Manos clearly stated the four men would pay for their immoral acts of drug trafficking, as she gave the maximum allowed by law, a lifetime in prison with no chance of parole.

An appeal would be filed by the lawyers for all the men and would go on deaf ears, as Judge Manos refused to allow Lonardo a release from his prison sentence, no matter what his health concerns were.

F.B.I. Agents have been placing settle thoughts in Lonardo's ears since he was arrested, and are now offering an attractive deal since his conviction. Sentenced to life without parole in the Federal Prison in Springfield Mo. Was not what he wishes for the rest of his life. The Feds promised to get him out of prison on an appeals bond. His sickly old body deteriorating with age would be free from the cold, lonely damp cell where he would surely die in. No doubt, it was a tough decision to break his Omerta obligation. However, in August of 1985, Lonardo agreed to help the Feds and was brought to Kansas City to testify before the U.S. Grand Jury investigating the large skimming case involving several Las Vegas casinos.

On August 18, Lonardo refused to testify under a grant of immunity before U.S. District Judge Elmo Hunter. He declined to speak about his role in delivering the skim money from Las Vegas to Chicago and Cleveland in the late 1960s. Also, Lonardo refused to discuss his extensive business relationship with the Kansas City, Nick Civella, who was arrested at the Apalachin Summit in 1957. The Federal Government became enraged as they could not pressure him with more jail time since he is already serving life without parole. However, they could offer him his precious freedom. Soon the Feds came to him with an offer he could not refuse. If he decided to help them and testify, he could move on with his life. Lonardo would be living free under a new name and residing in a new state, and possibly in a warm climate. Federal officials had stopped by the Federal prison in Springfield Mo to speak with Lonardo once again and dangle the freedom carrot in his face.

It was now October, as Lonardo told the agents in a secure room, "Perhaps he might be willing to talk." The government used Lonardo to give condemning evidence in Kansas City, Milwaukee, Chicago, and Cleveland. FBI agent Richard Hoke spent over ten days interviewing and recording the intense conversations between themselves, learning all the colorful details of his life in organized crime.

Lonardo told the story of how they convince Allen Glick a Case Western Reserve University graduate to help them purchase the Stardust and Fremont Hotels in Las Vegas. Lonardo explained how the crime families of Cleveland, Chicago, and Milwaukee shared a third of the weekly skim money. Different men would deliver the cash from Las Vegas, and often, Pete Tamburello would fly from Kansas City to Vegas and leave to visit the other friends in various cities to spread the wealth among friends.

ALLEN GLICK

(Courtesy of the Author collection)

1985

It was in Kansas City in August, as the federal prosecutors, became frustrated and unhindered by Lonardo's refusal to tell his exciting tales. For some unknown reason, Lonardo seemed to have a change of heart once again as he continued to avoid answering their direct and specific questions.

If he stayed in prison, it would undoubtedly cut his life short. It is not known how long it took Lonardo to decide, but it must have been some time and a lot of soul searching to make the hardest decision of his life... To testify and become a Federal Witness and break his Sicilian Code of Omerta!

Lonardo soon gave in to the massive presser as the government returned indictments in what was being called; "The Historical Strawman" skimming trial. The five-year-long investigation by the FBI, IRS, and U. S. Attorney's office, which has brought about this unprecedented trial. Among the defendants was Angelo's once dear and close friend, and brother-in-law Maishe (Milton) Rockman, who was his lifelong companion and believed to be the financial advisor to the Cleveland, crime family. However, while his mind was twirling at what must have been 100 miles per hour, Lonardo was now 78 years old, his loving wife Mary was a faithful part of his life, and now with multiple health problems of her own, as her life was coming to an end.

David Helfrey, who led the Organized Crime Strike Force in Kansas City, stated, "The Cleveland bureau needs to have all the credit for turning Lonardo and making him a protected witness."

Joseph Griffin, the FBI special agent in charge in Cleveland, proclaimed, "Lonardo is the highest-ranking La Cosa Nostra figure to become a government witness. With his help, he will be able to fill in the many blanks we have about their extraordinary activities throughout the country." Griffin went on to say, "James Fratianno was critical to our complete federal investigations of the mob. However, he was only a Capo. We now have an actual "Underboss." When asked if he plans on using Lonardo in the Cleveland hearings, he said, "You bet we are."

50

Lonardo finally testified about his long and dark past and disclose several of the Mafia's most shocking secrets in court throughout the country in exchange for a general dismissal of his 1983 conviction of managing a criminal drug enterprise.

A letter to Cleveland Judge Manos, who proceeded over Lonardo's 1983 case, informed her of the current situation. David Helfrey stated, "Lonardo is viewed by me as an important witness in a current federal case in Kansas City. Furthermore, it is my considered opinion the government subjects him, his wife, and son to be in grave danger and risk of physical harm."

The Kansas City FBI, suspecting unparalleled mob involvement at the Tropicana Casino in Las Vegas and set up an extensive investigation, known as *"Operation Strawman,"* which involved their lead witness Angelo Lonardo and multiple wiretaps on phones of reputed mobsters and their associates in Kansas City. From the substantial evidence collected by the various wiretaps and eavesdropping equipment in the late 1970s, the FBI discovered the conspiracy of skim money from the Tropicana Casino.

"Operation Strawman" learned how Joe Agosto controlled the famous Tropicana's Folies Bergere show and controlled the spirited skimming of the Tropicana. Agosto was secretly sending cash from the casino to Kansas City organized crime chief Nick Civella and Joe Aiuppa of Chicago, as well as to John Scalish in Cleveland and Milwaukee mobsters.

Back in 1981, a grand jury in Kansas City indicted Agosto, Kansas City mob boss Nick Civella, Civella's brother Carl Cievlla, along with fellow mobsters Carl DeLuna, and Carl Thomas, who had directed the illegal skimming of cash at the Tropicana.

These defendants were all convicted in 1983.

Lonardo is one of the 400 witnesses on the astonishing list of people to testify. This will include five other protected witnesses, which included former Teamster Union President Roy Williams, who is serving a ten-year sentence, along with James Fratianno, who has already testified in organized crime cases in Los Angeles, New York, and Chicago.

Roy Williams becomes a critical federal witness since the Teamsters Central States Union pension funds have been alleged to have been used to help the Mafia to purchase the Stardust, Fremont, Hacienda, and Marina Hotels, during the 1970s. Williams also testified he earned $1,500 a month for seven years for his favorable vote to approved the excessive $87 million-dollar pension loans.

Walking into the jam-packed federal courtroom for the first time with several guards around him, the nervous and frightened and frail 74-year old Lonardo looked scared of testifying in front of his ex-friends, goombahs, and fellow mobsters. During Lonardo's intensive testimony in Kansas City, he stated, "Rockman told the men in Kansas City, that he felt that Cleveland controlled Jackie Presser, who was the Teamsters International Vice President." Lonardo said, "Jackie Presser was getting $1,500 a month for his help in the Las Vegas operation."

Lonardo also informed the government that after John Scalish died in 1976, Rockman became one of the men who picked up the "skim money" in Las Vegas and would deliver it to Kansas City and on occasion to Chicago. Lonardo stated that when he became "Underboss," his portion of the skim money quickly increased from $1,000 to $10,000 per month, along with the earlier death of DeMarco and Brancato. Rockman also told Lonardo that Licavoli would be "easier for them to control" as the "Boss" than anyone else around, especially John Nardi.

For an old man, Lonardo's incredible memory was excellent. According to Lonardo, who testified that Rockman told him, "The Chicago family was very hesitant in allowing Roy Williams to the presidency of the International Teamsters Union. Then in 1980, Rockman explained how, as a group, we would control the immense power within the teamsters union. Later, when Jackie Presser became a trustee, they could have total control of the Teamsters Central States Pension Fund.

It was October 1985, while in the courtroom of Judge Alvin Krenzler, Angelo Lonardo made news once again. At this point, Lonardo was discussing the information he had regarding a link between organized crime figure John "Curly" Montana and a contract killing of a 1981 Cleveland nightclub owner, Stanley Lentza's, who operated the *Artmis Club* on W 6th Street. Lentzas; was killed by a shotgun blast and allegedly involved as a pornographer in Cleveland. Lonardo calmly revealed how Montana was hired by James Licavoli to kill John Nardi. Montana then offered Lonardo (out of respect) some of the money he received for killing Lentzas. Montana, who is 66 and lives in Orange Village, is free on a $150,000 bond from a March 1984 conviction in a federal court case. Which was dealing with a scheme to defraud Chicago businessman Henry Podborny? Podgorny was slain in a strategic plan to get a significant share of his 17 million dollars in assets. Montana is one of the men charged with Podborny's murder.

Christopher Stanley, the attorney for Montana, submitted affidavits to remove his client from the Nardi murder. Stanley stated he had specific documents that Montana was on the phone with Anthony Hughes, a former $53,000 a year Teamster Recording Secretary that afternoon when Nardi was killed. The reports will show how Montana was in Buffalo, and Hughes was in Cleveland, as they discussed a real estate investment.

In November, one of Lonardo's many testimonies became headline news. Lonardo informed them about the differences between Cleveland and Chicago. Presser was Cleveland's person, while Chicago did not like Jackie Presser as a Union boss. Chicago mobster John Cerone said he had received reliable information that "Presser was no good." Rockman needed to calm the icy stress and tension between the two great cities and do it fast. He said, "Don't believe what you hear, Presser is ok, I can control and handle him."

Lonardo testified that in the early 1950s, Rockman had to use his remarkable influence and place pressure to persuaded William Presser to help back a Teamsters Pension Fund loan to Allen Glick. Rockman was supposed to have told Scalish. "Johnny let's do this, we could make a significant amount of money, come on buy it." Lonardo said, "Scalish was against the idea at the time."

Lonardo went on to say, at one-time, Youngstown was operated and controlled by Cleveland, then in the 1950s, they gave Youngstown to Joe (The Wolf) DiCarlo so he could make a good living. Lonardo went on to say that the Pittsburgh family sought and received permission to take over Youngstown, and we told them to go ahead, 'just give us our cut and a piece of the action." Another source has revealed that the Pittsburgh mob went in to take over Youngstown, as a feud with Cleveland began in the mid-sixties. Then the dispute was settled. Lonardo foolishly stated, "Between the skim money and Youngstown, I was making about $16,000 a month."

According to author Rick Porrello   Seated in the witness chair, the seventy-four-year-old Angelo Lonardo looked tanned, aged and weary. However, his testimony became very useful. In addition to Rockman, now 73 who received a prison term of 24-years and ordered to pay $80,000 penalty. Other numerous mobsters were convicted of skimming more than $2 million from two Las Vegas casinos they were partners in. They included:

- *Joseph Aiuppa, 78, boss of the Chicago Mafia*

- *John "Jackie" Cerone, 71, Chicago underboss*

- *Joseph Lombardo, 57, Chicago capo*

- *Angelo "The Hook" LaPietra, 60 a Chicago capo*

- *Frank Balistrieri, Milwaukee mob boss (plead guilty)*

• *Carl DeLuna, Kansas City underboss (plead guilty)*

The former Teamster President Roy Williams testified and became the first person in such a high position to admit he took orders and was paid off by Kansas City Mafia Boss Nick Civella.

Other witnesses in the ironclad case where Carl Thomas, a Las Vegas casino manager who testified, and provided expert evidence on how the skim was performed at the casinos. Mob associate turned witness Jimmy "The Weasel" Fratianno was yet another primary witness during the sensational trial and filled in many gaps for the committee.

51

1986

It was now January 21 and after the long sixty-one days of testimony by Angelo Lonardo, during the seven-and-a-half-year in-depth investigation, and trial came to an end.

It was now September 23 as the fall cold weather became a reality in New York City as the attention across the country was now on them. An old, frail, and weak looking 75-year old man Angelo A. Lonardo was about to testify once again in a federal court. He was to tell his thrilling life story along with other activities of many criminals. Lonardo calmly and efficiently informed the attentive jury, how his father Joseph was the first recognized "Boss" in Cleveland, Ohio, in the early 1920s, and then he became involved by the late 1920s at the age of sixteen.

Then in the 1930s, "The Commission" was formed and starting with the "Five Families" of organized crime. "The Commission had other members outside the New York five-families, men like Al Polizzi, and Frank Milano from Cleveland, and Angelo Bruno from Philadelphia.

Several cities in the Midwest had their own form of the mighty commission in the cities of Chicago, Kansas City, Milwaukee, which would settle any personal disputes. Lonardo stated, "Cleveland would often visit and sit in on these meetings."

Lonardo then related that when John Scalish died in 1976, he personally spoke with James Licavoli and mentioned how important it would be that he and Licavoli went to New York to talk with Anthony Salerno the Genovese, family leader. Realizing this vital importance, Licavoli left within a few days and reported to Salerno that he was now considered the "Boss" in Cleveland. According to Lonardo, Salerno was Cleveland's connection to New York and link to the Commission

It was now late September, as Angelo Lonardo (whose new

federal code name became "Top Notch.) On the witness stand, Lonardo slowly clears his throat and speaks softly. Now, ready to testify about his vast knowledge of the activities of the New York crime families.

Lonardo's first explosive remarked to the jury was how Anthony (Fat Tony) Salerno, was the man who Cleveland had to report to. Lonardo went on to relate how he met with Salerno on several occasions at his East Harlem hang out, known as the *"Palma Boys Social Club."*

Lonardo recalled one particular meeting, which took place four years ago, and how he met with Salerno to gain his approval for a necessary move to help engineer the election of Clevelander Jackie Presser as the Teamsters Union President.

Lonardo stated that one year after Scalish death, he and James Licavoli drove up to New York to meet with Anthony Salerno. Lonardo needed to come up with a solid story that would alien Salerno with their problem. The main reason Lonardo gave Salerno for wanting Nardi and Greene killed, where they were responsible for the death of Leo (Lips) Moceri, the former "Underboss" in Cleveland. Lonardo went on to inform the packed courthouse how Nardi and Greene both died later that same year in a car bombing.

At yet another meeting with Salerno back in 1977, Licavoli and Lonardo asked for Salerno's permission to "Make a few more members" because the family was getting into a dangerous situation and low on real mob members to depend on. Salerno deliberated for a few short moments and gave his permission to "Make" ten new members. Lonardo seemed proud that he and Licavoli agreed to made Anthony Liberatore, John Calandra, along with Philip Testa, Frank Sindone, and John Simone, all members of the Philadelphia family.

In one of his testimony in New York, Lonardo described in detail how, in 1930, he was denied membership since the New York five families put a hold on making new members. He waited patiently until the late 1940s. Then inside a hotel room in the Statler Hotel, he was finally granted the highest honor, to become a

"Made man" in the La Cosa Nostra. However, Lonardo told a whitewashed version of the "rules."

- You cannot sell narcotics {even though this was the best way to make money for the gangsters. The code was, just don't get caught, or tell the boss}
- You cannot have girls working on the streets and be a pimp
- Before you do anything, you need to get permission from your Capo
- No matter what you are doing nor what time of day it is, that when we call you, you come, even if a family member is sick or dying, you have to get up and leave and do what you are told to do

In 1985, the Cleveland FBI agent in charge was Joseph E. Griffin. He stated to the public, "Lonardo is a tremendously important witness for the government. This should have a tremendous impact nationally because of who this man is."

Several Mafia Historians have wondered or even believed that Angelo Lonardo was ever actually "Made." Their reason being, that if in fact he was actually "Made," why did he not name the men who brought his name up for membership to the commission, and who was the "Boss" who had vouched for him? Why did he not mention the people who attended this secret ritual? Surely these men would have been apparently dead by now and could not come up to depute his long, lavish tails or move against him after all these years. However, no one can deny the murders and the crime he has committed over his lifetime and the influence he has had in the organized crime business across the country.

Many of the top men in law enforcement firmly believe that Lonardo's robust and relentless testimony helped them. Lonardo was praised for having an incredible memory and immeasurable facts about key organized controlled cities that make-up the mob in America. His statement supported prosecutor Rudy Giuliani and his fight against the earlier untouchable, "Five Families in New

York."

The complex Mafia Commission Trial has been well documented and started, "on February 25, 1985, and ended on November 19, 1986. This major criminal trial was set in New York City. Using the elaborate evidence obtained by the FBI, eleven organized crime figures, including the heads of New York's "Five Families," were indicted by U.S. Attorney Rudy Giuliani under the old 1970 (RICO act) on 'charges including, extortion, labor racketeering, and murder for hire. "

The men from the Commission who were found guilty included, from the Genovese Family Anthony "Fat Tony" Salerno. From the Gambino family was Paul Castellano. From the Lucchese family was Anthony "Ducks" Corallo. From the Colombo, family the boss Carmine "Junior" Persico and from the Bonanno family was Phillip "Rusty" Rastelli. Included in the indictment was Aniello "The Lamb" Dellacrose underboss in the Gambino family. Gennaro "Gerry Lang" Langella underboss in the Colombo family. Salvatore "Tom Mix" Santoro underboss and Christopher "Christy Tick" Consigliere, both from the Lucchese family. Ralph "Ralphy" Scopio, a Colombo soldier and finally Anthony "Bruno" Indelicato, a Bonanno soldier.

The remaining eight-defendants had been found guilty on all 151 counts on November 19, 1986. The men were then sentenced on January 13, 1987.

Giuliani's stated his personal intention: "Our approach... is to wipe out the five families and we have succeeded.

1987

During one of Lonardo's long and intense fifteen private conferences with Federal agents and the Justice Department, Lonardo confirmed the violent threats and intimidation of many police and political leaders. He went on to establish all the gambling activities and the ease to operate without interference so the mob could reap huge profits. With Lonardo as the government star performer on the witness stand, he has now led the prosecution to the doorstep of Teamster boss Jackie Presser, and two close associates tried to Cleveland, Ohio.

In August, Lonardo sated, "Presser illegal took more than $700,000 over ten years from the Teamsters and Bakers Union. The excessive money came from a payroll padding scheme that he controlled. Even with this public trial and pending indictment hanging over his head, Presser was re-elected by an overwhelming margin and remain the President by the Teamster delegates at the Nation convention in Las Vegas.

In Lonardo's New York testimony, author Rick Porrello states; Six years of the intense investigation were capped by indictments of numerous high-ranking mobsters, including the bosses who make up the elite Mafia ruling commission. The case was dubbed "*Star Chamber*" by the investigators. In all, there were 37 counts of loansharking, labor payoffs, extortion, and racketeering. It has become better known as the "Commission Case."

All of the commission case defendants were convicted and sentenced as follows;

Anthony "Fat Tony" Salerno (Genovese family boss) 100 years; $240,000 fine

Aniello "Neil" Dellacroce (Gambino family underboss) 100 years; $240,000 fine

Carmine "Junior the Snake" Persico (Colombo family boss) 100 years; $240,000 fine

Gennaro "Gerry Lang" Langella (Colombo family underboss) 100 years; $240,000

Ralph Scopo (Colombo soldier) 100 years; $240,000 fine

Anthony "Tony Ducks" Corallo (Lucchese family boss) 100 years; $250,000 fine

Salvatore "Tommy Mix" Santoro (Lucchese family underboss) 100 years; $250,000 fine

Christopher "Christy Tick" Furnari (Lucchese family consigliere) 100 years; $240,000 fine

Gambino family boss Paul Castellano was killed in the streets of New York as a plot led by his cocky lieutenant, John Gotti.

SOME OF THE MANY HEADLINES FROM THE CLEVELAND PLAIN DEALER DESCRIBED ANGELO LONARDO'S UNPRECEDENTED FEDERAL TESTIMONY!

> "Mafia chief to testify in casino scam."
> Cleveland FBI turned mobster into an informant."
> Mafia life bared in spite of vow."
> Lonardo tells of mob killing since the 1920s."
> "Mob skimming case now in the hands of the jury."
> Lonardo tells of Mafia's history in New York."
> Feds want Lonardo testimony to show the vital Teamsters-Mafia link."
> Mafia rigged Presser's election; U.S. Jury is told."
> "Mob figure says mafia helped Presser get to post."

Lonardo's opens up and gives accurate and sincere testimony of his personal knowledge of sixty years in the organized crime world. These secret meetings lead to much discussion with the Attorney General to dismiss and dismantle many of the significant crime cities Strike Force on Organized Crime. Besides Cleveland, other federal offices included Buffalo, Los Angeles, Chicago, Boston, Brooklyn, Las Vegas, San Francisco, New Orleans, Miami, and Philadelphia played a crucial role in the success of Leonardo's testimony.

Lonardo died quietly and silently in his sleep on April 1, 2006, at the ripe old age of 95.

He is buried in Crown Hill Cemetery in Vienna, Ohio.

ANGELO LONARDO AT THE AGE OF 50

(Courtesy of Cleveland State University Archives)

52

"THE IRISHMAN" DANIEL J. GREENE

Danny was born on November 9, 1933, to John Greene and Irene Fallon. Seven short days later, Irene was in Saint Ann Hospital with severe health complications. On the same day, she silently passed away. The official cause being an enlarged heart. John Greene was heartbroken as he began to drink heavily. He quickly lost his job as a Fuller Brush salesman. John soon was unable and unwilling to provide for his young son, as he turned him over to the Parmadale home for children without a home.

By 1939, Danny's father put his life together, remarried, and Danny left the orphan home and started to live with his father and stepmother. Unhappy with this new situation, Danny ran away several times as he went on the path to become a troubled young boy.

Raised a good Irish Catholic boy, Danny went to school at Saint Jerome's Church located on Lakeshore Boulevard in Collinwood. As he got older, Danny struggled in school, lost his interest in religion, and was considered to be a weak student but enjoyed a splendid athletic ability. Danny placed all his attention into sports and flourished in baseball, basketball and found a love for boxing. Getting into trouble during middle school, Danny found himself going to Saint Ignatius High School. Since he would often cut class and soon found himself being expelled. Danny then went to Collinwood High School to finish his last few years.

Danny always had wild and carefree dreams of being a man respected and had ambitious plans for himself. He seemed to see himself as a leader of men. Then in 1951, he dropped out of school, and for some unknown reason, he joined the Marine Corps. Weeks later, Danny found himself stationed at Camp LeJeune, North Carolina. By 1953 after several transfers for not getting along with the other recruits, Danny was honorably discharged.

After his discharge, the handsome Irishman who enjoyed being with the ladies went to live in New York, where he met and fell in love with June Thomas Tears. The couple soon moved to Cleveland, where they were married, while Danny worked as a brakeman in the Collinwood railroad yards, unfortunately by 1956 they were divorced. Earlier in 1955, Danny had met a beautiful young woman named Nancy, who took over his lost heart and soul. She had the most stunning blue eyes and enjoyed his warm charm. However, she did not know about his earlier marriage, and soon Danny won her heart over. The couple was then married in 1960. They had two daughters together. A few years later, Nancy had had enough of Danny's late evenings and dishonest bullshit and filed for divorce accusing Danny of gross neglect of duty.

A few years later, Danny found yet another beauty he played around with until he was tired of her. Danny was working at the dock at the Cleveland Harbor, where he gained recognition as a member of Local 1317, The International Association of Longshoremen.

In his spare time, Danny found the love of reading. He chooses books about his proud Irish heritage. The books began to speak to him and telling the folk lord stories of the Celtic and Irish life. Like the mighty Celtic warriors before him, Danny gained the inner strength and success of inspiring people with his profound words of wisdom, his gift of gab, and his skills as a fighter.

During the early 1960s, Danny's popularity within the union grew strong as he ran to manage Local 1317 and quickly won the presidency. It was about this same time that Danny began working a sideline job in the evenings and alongside Frank Brancato and then young Tony Liberatore. His position was a simple one, to help organize many of the private rubbish haulers and have them join the newly founded Cleveland Trade Solid Waste Guild.

To many people, Greene was like royalty in the Eastside community of Collinwood. He became a member of the Collinwood Mob, known as the "Young Turks." Greene reigned as king over his followers, who admired his bravery and his negotiation skills. The Collinwood crew had several members, Phil Christopher, who became known as "The Supertheif," Allie Calabrese, Joe Iacobacci, and Butchy Cisternino, who would later work together to kill Greene.

Unknown to his faithful friends, at some point in time, Greene became arranged with the FBI to become an informant. They allowed him to work freely to obtain enough reliable information on mob activities in Cleveland. Greene was given the code name, "Mr. Patrick."

During this stage of his life, in the early 1970s, Danny became close friends with Mike Frato, an independent waste hauler. Frato would not give up and pay Danny a tribute or join the new corrupt waste hauling union. Once close friends, the two now were brutal enemies as Danny plotted to make an example of Frato to the other haulers. It was on Halloween night, October 31, 1971, when Danny made a move and tried to blow up Frito's car parked on Coventry Road. One of Greene men, Arthur Sneperger, was sent to wire the truck. Danny had just found out weeks earlier that Sneperger was giving information to the Cleveland Police. Danny knew he was in trouble, so Danny did what Danny had to do. While Sneperger was under Frato's car to set the bomb to kill Frato in the morning, Danny calmly stood, just a short block away and detonated the weapon himself, watching the explosion and death of his old friend.

Less than a month later, and with little remorse in his cold, cold heart, Greene shot and killed Frato at White City Beach. A judge had ruled the shooting self-defense, and Greene; was free to go. This could have been a spot where the Feds stepped in to protect Danny?

Danny thrived on achieving more power as his notoriety grew. Danny often visited all the "Hot Spots" in town, Captain Frank's Seafood House, The Frolics Bar, and the Theatrical Grills on Short Vincent, where he met mobsters like John DeMarco, Shondor Birns, and John Scalish. Many called the Theatrical the "Switzerland of Cleveland." Operated by the connected gambler Morris Wexler. Many local citizens frequented the restaurant in the slim chance that they would see and then meet a mobster, politicians, judges, or a visiting celebrity.

Over the next several years, Danny's fight and disrespect of the Cleveland Italian crime family grew stronger and stronger. Only one Italian, John Nardi, became a trusted friend. Then we have Alex "Shondor" Birns, once a friend of Danny's who help him secure a loan from his friends in New York and later became an enemy over a debt of $70,000. Which Greene owed to the Gambino crime family. Green seems to have a unique ability to make enemies of just about all the Italians.

The feud and hatred for one another grew over time, and by the fall of 1974, Birns had paid an associate $25,000 to kill Greene. This was after a failed attempt to kill Birns and a girlfriend as they walk down the street.

It was about this same time, Danny, moved into a new home on 147 Street and Waterloo Road in Collinwood near Interstate 90. As Greene became famous in the neighborhood, he also grew wearier of the Cleveland Syndicate. Greene soon brought another woman into his life, a young lady named Denise Schmidt.

As his enchanting life and pride grew stronger, revenge grew inside Danny. It was now the spring of March 1975, the Blessed Easter Holy Saturday in the city of Cleveland. Birns left one of his hangouts, known as a Go-Go Club, Christy's Lounge. It was around eight PM, just as the High Mass at St Malachi's Church was letting out. Birns reached for the door handle, as all hell broke loose. The explosion rocked the quiet neighborhood.

By 1976, and sound asleep with Denise by his side, Danny heard a noise, and quickly the silence was gone. A window broke downstairs on the quiet street of Waterloo Road. Several seconds later, the first bomb exploded, throwing Danny and Denise off their bed. As Greene carried Denise down the stairs, a second bomb exploded. With the luck of the Irish on his side, Greene and Denise somehow made it out of the house and into his car, where they quickly drove off to safety. During their investigation, the Cleveland Bomb Squad found a large chunk of C-4 attached to a five-gallon container of gasoline that did not explode.

Greene was confident that a mob enforcer, Eugene Ciasullo, aka "The Animal," was the man who placed the bomb at his home. Danny wasted little time, and in retaliation, Greene sent a message back to Ciasullo. He had a bomb put in a flower pot located near the front door to his home. The weapon was full of lethal C-4 as the blast hurled Ciasullo into his home. Rumors around the city were that Greene hired two Hells Angel thugs to do the job.

AFTER THE BOMBING OF GREENE HOME

(Courtesy of Cleveland State University Archive Department)

Once in the hospital, Ciasullo, was in critical condition, as nails had devastated his stomach, intestines, and Gall Bladder. Doctors were not sure if he would survive until the morning. Standing guard by his side were his friends, Butchy Cisternino, and close friend Jimmy Martino.

Danny did not take any chances as he started to hang around several of his close friends from the Celtic Club, 28-year-old Keith Ritson, 19-year-old Keven McTaggart, and Brian O'Donnell. Greene's son Danny would ride along with him during the day. Greene used another old friend Billy McDuffy as a bodyguard.

A defiant Italian, John Nardi, soon approached Greene to team up against his new rival James LIcvoli and the Italians who denounce Nardi his right and role as "The Boss" in Cleveland. Since Greene and Nardi had many of the same enemies, it was easy for the two men to join forces.

EUGENE CIASULLO

(Courtesy of Cleveland State University Archive Department)

1976

Then we have James Licavoli, "The new Boss" of the Cleveland Mob, who made a choice to get rid of "His pain in the ass, the Irishman" for the last time.

Thanks to the mob wars and trying their hardest to kill the stubborn Irishman, Cleveland became known as the number 1 city in America in car bombings.

It did not take long before Greene's long list of enemies tried once again to blow him up. This time it would be his Celtic Social Club where they had hoped to kill Greene and several of his friends and their enemies. Just like the past bombing, this one failed once again.

Greene wasted little time and looked into another opportunity to gain control of his future empire. With John Scalish dead, the question now became, who would be interested in taking over Buckeye Cigarette Service Company. Greene decided to move in on them and take it over. Cleveland Police was currently investigating Greene for the murder of a rival Lake Vending Company, Salesman John B. Conte, who was bludgeoned to death and found in an empty field.

Licavoli was under extreme stress and the incredible embarrassment, from his fellow Mob Bosses across the country because he could not kill one man. At the funeral of Youngstown "Boss" Tony Delsanter, who died expectantly, Licavoli decided to talk to a few of his old friends, who had helped and worked with James Fratianno. "Jimmy the Weasel" had come to town to pay his last respects to Delsanter. Other men came to pay their respects, as well. Raymond Ferritto was a known hitman and burglar who had worked on the west coast and in the Pennsylvania area for many years. Butchy Cisternino and Licavoli went as well. Licavoli informed Ferritto that if he needed any help to call John Calandra, another of Licavoli associates. Unknown to the men at the time of the meeting, Fratianno had been a Federal informant for about a decade now.

THE CELTIC SOCIAL CLUB

(Courtesy of Cleveland State University Archives Department)

1977

The long and drawn-out battle between Greene and his multiple enemies continued on, as Greene came up with a sure thing! He had convinced Nardi to go into the cattle business with him, the company was named Maverick Meat Processing. This was a failing cattle ranch in Texas owned by Richard Harper that they could buy. They planned to sell the beef through their extensive connections in the labor unions across the country. John Nardi asked his uncle, Tony Milano, to set up a meeting with Paul Castellano, the boss of the Gambino family, for the seed money.

Butchy Cisternino, with Allie Calabrese, watched the two men and heard about their plan to meet up with Castellano. When Nardi and Greene arrived at Cleveland Hopkins Airport, Cisternino and Calabrese were there watching every move. The two knew Greene and Nardi would be gone for two days. On March 14, both Cisternino and Calabrese were looking for Greene and Nardi to walk towards their car. Butchy pressed the red detonator buttons several times, sadly nothing happened. He then shouted they were too far away as he ran from the hotel towards the airport. Greene and Nardi silently left the airport, not knowing they had almost been blown to pieces.

The long list of men interested in killing the Irishman was Ray Ferritto, Butchy Cisternino, and Ronnie Carabbia and John Calandra. Then we have Greene's old friend turned enemy Tony Liberatore who was now a union official, who then gathered a few of his own men to kill him. They had a simple plan, to just sit in an old police car dressed as uniformed officers and wait for Greene to drive by, and then shoot him on the spot.

A date that will live in Cleveland's criminal history came to be. On October 1, Greene's girlfriend Denise made a phone call to a dentist, Dr. Candoli's whose practice was located on the third floor at Brianard Place in Lyndhurst, Ohio. She informed the receptionist that she was calling for her boyfriend Danny Greene and that he had a loose filling that was causing him great pain. After a few minutes of silence and reviewing her appointment book, she told the women they could fit him in on Thursday, October 6, at 3 PM.

The wire tape that Ferritto placed on Greene's home phone paid off in the most significant way. The Cleveland Mob now had a perfect way to get rid of a rodent. This became the happiest day in recent times for the Cleveland mob as James Licavoli, Angelo Lonardo, Ray Ferritto, and Butchy Cisternino all celebrated and planned for the October 6 deadline.

Over the next several days, which consisted of getting a setup car to place the bomb in. Cisternino gathered the parts for the weapon. Carabbia drove the setup car, a Chevy Nova, into the lot with Ferritto. Within twenty minutes, Liberatore's men arrived with the old worn-out police vehicle armed with rifles just in case they had an opportunity to shoot the Irish bastard in the head before he got into his car.

53

Shortly after 3:15, with severe pain in his mouth, Greene arrived at the six-story grayish brick building, located on the busy northeast corner of Cedar Rd, which runs east to west and Brainard Road situated in the Eastside suburb of Lyndhurst. He drove in with his green Lincoln and parked. As Danny got out of his car, he cautiously looked around to see if the area was clear. The newer building and medical complex could be easily accessed from miles around. Dr. Candoli worked on a loss tooth fitting that was giving Greene such intense pain for over two weeks. The skilled dentist worked for nearly 25 minutes, before relieving his pain and wishing him a good day.

After Greene was inside the building, the ordinary everyday beat-up blue Nova with the bomb hidden inside the passenger's door panel drove around the lot and soon found a space next to a green Lincoln. As luck would have it, the parking space was on the driver's side of Greene's car. The men could not have asked for a better placement. Cisternino ordered Liberatore's people to leave and that he and Ray would finish the job when he came out.

As Greene slowly walked out of the building and towards his car, he opened the driver's door and slowly looked around once again to see if anyone was near, the coast was clear, so he climbed in. In an instant, the bomb was triggered as a giant fireball filled the thin afternoon air around the vehicle. The noise could be heard for at least a mile in all directions. The bomb tore the once arrogant Greene's back apart as it ripped off all of his clothes, along with his left arm. The separated limb astonishingly still maintained the large five green stone ring that Greene cherished. His right wrist held his gold bracelet with raised letters, "DJPG" During the intense search of the devastated area, the police were unable to find his Gold Celtic cross neckless he proudly wore daily. However, they did find a duffle bag with a 9-mm pistol in it.

THE DEATH OF "THE IRISHMAN."

(Courtesy of Cleveland State University Archives Department)

Several days after the bombing, the FBI, and the Lyndhurst police obtained critical evidence. The FBI had a secret conversation from the wire tape of two men, one being John Calandra and an unidentified man. Both men complained about Greene's arrogance and blamed Brancato and Nardi for his relentless rise to power, and how great it was that Greene, was finally dead.

Meanwhile, the Lyndhurst Police received a vital piece of information on their own. It seems while Ferritto and Cisternino got onto the highway, known as Interstate 271 going north, a young couple noticed their suspicious behavior. It seems the young woman, Debbie Spoth, was an accomplished artist and drew a detailed sketch of the man driving the blue Plymouth, along with the license plate number of the car they were driving. Both were turned over to the Cleveland police department as possible evidence of the significant crime. Soon the police placed the sketch of the man and matched it up to an Erie, PA mobster Ray Ferritto.

Initially indicted for the murder of Greene included, Ron Carabbia, James Licavoli, Angelo Lonardo, Ray Ferritto, James Fratianno, Allie Calabrese, Butchie Cisternino, Thomas Sinito, John Calandra, Tony Liberatore, Louis Aratari, Vic Guiles, Thomas Lanci, Kenneth Ciarcia and Carmen Marconi. Soon Ferritto's picture was all over the local news.

After Ferritto heard the incredible news which now changed the future picture of the rest of his life with his devoted wife, Susan. The cheap old man, Licavoli, refused to pay Ferritto for the agreed hit on Greene. Licavoli's irresponsible behavior forced Ray to protect himself; he had no choice and decided to work with the FBI. Ferritto soon turned himself into the Pittsburg police. While in custody, Ferritto told the agents everything, he knew about the plan to kill the Irishman. As part of his agreement with the government, Ferritto had to plead guilty to killing Clevelander Julies Petro in Los Angeles, several years earlier.

With the credible testimony of a certified mob member Ray Ferritto, the prosecution indicated James Licavoli, Angelo Lonardo, Ronnie Carabbia, James Fratianno, Allie Calabrese, Butchy Cisternino, Thomas Sinito, John Calandra, Tony Liberatore, Louis Aratic, Vic Giles, Tom Lanci, Kenneth Ciarcia and Carmen Marconi. Ferritto, Aratari, Guiles, and Fratianno became protected government witnesses in an agreement to testify against the others, as Licavoli, Lonardo, Carabbia, Cisternino went on trial.

In the long and exhausting trial, which captured the nation's interest for 79 days, only Cisternino and Carabbia were convicted of killing Greene. Licavoli, Lonardo, and Sinito were cleared of all charges just because there was not enough evidence connecting them to the murder and only Ferritto's testimony against them.

Some criminal historians firmly believe that in one way, the Demise of the Cleveland Mafia may be contributed to this one man.

With all of Danny Greene's robust and forceful ways, his diligence to achieve his dreams and the goals he set for himself along with his Celtic pride and heritage, which gave him the strength to fight a war he could not win but gave his enemies one "Hell of a battle."

A VIEW OF THE DEATH OF DANNY GREENE

(Courtesy of Cleveland State University Archives)

54

RAYMOND W. FERRITTO

Ray's birth name was Remo Ferretti, and he was born on April 8, 1929. His friends nicknamed him "Knuckles" because of his toughness as he grew up in Erie, Pennsylvania.

In 1958, at age twenty-nine, Ferritto was arrested for burglary. He pled guilty and served three years of a three to five-year sentence. Once out, Ferritto spent some time in Cleveland, Ohio. He committed several burglaries, jewelry, and grocery store safe jobs with his childhood friends, Allie Calabrese, Pasquale "Butchie" Cisternino, Tony Delanster, Julius Petro, and Ronnie, the Crab, they decided their name would be "The Infamous Cleveland Crew."

By the late sixties, Ferritto had moved to Los Angeles, where he met up with and associated with a group of Cleveland mobsters, including Julius Petro. In the 1940s, Petro wriggled free from a death sentence on a retrial in a murder case. Ferritto and Petro were associates with Jimmy "The Weasel" Fratianno, who was closely associated with the Los Angeles family. Likewise, Ray Ferritto was working diligently to make a name for himself in the Mafia.

In 1969, Ferritto booked a flight from Los Angeles to Erie. He was driven to the airport by another burglar friend from Cleveland. Ray had accepted the hit request from Sparky Monica, who lived in L.A. and offered Ray $20,000 for this one job. Accompanying the two, just for the ride, was Julius Petro. The accomplice drove the car into an airport parking garage and parked away from other vehicles. Telling everyone he was not ready to leave, Ferritto waited for a plane to take off. He suddenly thrust a .22 gun to the back of Julius Petro's head and pulled the trigger. The roar of the jet muffled the fatal shot. The murder of Petro resulted from a conflict with a well-known bookmaker in Los Angeles who used Petro as muscle. Nevertheless, they were likely candidates for the contract since they both disliked Petro. To Ray's dismay, he was stiffed on obtaining the $20,000 he was promised.

A few years later, this event in Ferritto's life brought him closer to his ultimate destiny and endured him with the boys in Cleveland.

In 1974, Ferritto was soon released from a Chino prison and returned to Erie. Regional police and the Pennsylvania Crime Commission reported Ferritto was a member of the Buffalo crime syndicate and sought by the FBI for questioning. Ray now 48 started booking again and worked for a local vending company that was owned by a cousin.

1975

On one of his visits to Cleveland, James Fratianno informed James Licavoli that Ray was a stand-up guy and could be trusted to do the job on Danny Greene. Ray was eager for the work, and had been disappointed and passed up repeatedly to become a Made- Man.

At this time, Ferritto was 49 and had an active life. His

nervousness gave him plenty of ulcers, and to ease them, he chewed antacids like candy and often smoked marijuana. To keep his agitation controlled, half of his stomach was removed in surgery to give him some relief. Ray worked different odd jobs to make a living outside the law. He worked as a repairman for a vending machine company during the day, a bookmaker, and a nightclub operator at night. Ray was tall and thin, wore large glasses that covered half of his small shaped face with salt-pepper hair. Ray was well known to have a violent temper when provoked.

In May of 1976, to show his great respect to the fallen "Cleveland Don" John Scalish, Ray, and his partner Bolo Dovishaw made the two-hour drive from Erie to the funeral home. The Cleveland underworld was in turmoil, as Lonardo, Licavoli, John Calandra, and Tony Liberatore all current ranking mob lieutenants were clashing heads to kill Danny Greene. Ronnie Carabbia, the believed underboss in Youngstown, had already failed eight times to kill the "Irishman."

Early in 1977, Ray meets up with Licavoli as he offered Ray the contract to kill Greene. Ray was an outsider and unknown to Greene. Ray firmly believed this was his last and only chance to become made. Ferritto made several trips from his home in Erie, PA to Cleveland to meet with Cisternino as little help and support came from Licavoli.

Frustrated, Ray kept in contact with Fratianno, who kept him informed with the Cleveland situation. Both Butchy Cisternino and Allie Calabrese had taken potshots at Greene with high-power rifles. They even tried a drive-by shooting, which missed Greene. Cleveland was viewed to be "a wild west town" and out of control and becoming the focal point for federal investigators, and looked like a bunch of vaudeville clowns, who could not shoot straight.

As their plan developed, Cisternino and Calabrese decided to get two cars for Ray. A 1973 blue Plymouth, which served as the get-a-way car and a Chevy Nova, which became the Joe blow car. Ray had the vehicles registered in PA, as he and his trusted friend Bolo drove the two vehicles to Cleveland from Erie. Bolo, placed himself in a phone booth as a backup to shoot Greene as Ray and Carabbia drove the beat-up Nova into the lot.

After the death of Danny Greene on October 6, 1977, Ray felt betrayed by Licavoli and the men he worked with, as the deal he made; was no deal at all. Ray was troubled and angered and told by a source that Licavoli and Lonardo agreed to make him a Made-Man. Ray later learned from a close and trusted friend, that Licavoli and Lonardo were going to kill him when he showed up for the special ceremony he had been waiting for, for many years. At the last minute, Licavoli decided not to kill him, but let the climate in Cleveland cool off. Once this was completed, then Ferritto would die.

After his conviction in the Greene murder; Ray turned state's evidence and confessed to other crimes he had committed over the years and took responsibility for the 1969 killing hoodlum Julius Anthony Petro. Petro's murder was unsolved until Ferritto's testimony. Ferritto served a total of four years in prison for both killings.

Ray testified that at one meeting with James Licavoli, aka, Jack White, "White gave him permission, the go-ahead to kill either man, Nardi or Greene.

Ferritto testified that during a meeting he had with Calandra, he informed him how many men across the country were concerned about the death of Leo Moceri. Calandra went on and told Ray how men from other cities offered help to White. White needed to get the problematic situation in Cleveland under controlled, and fast, or they would have to take care of it themselves. With his, White refused the offer and informed them it was his problem, and he would take care of it, his way. It would have been too embarrassing for the boss of Cleveland to ask his criminal friends to take care of a problem like that.

On Sunday, May 9, 2004, at his home in Sarasota, Florida, Ray suffered a major heart attack and died. Ray was survived by his beautiful and loving wife, Susan. Ray survived a plot by the Cleveland Mob to kill him, and he was now laughing in their face.

55

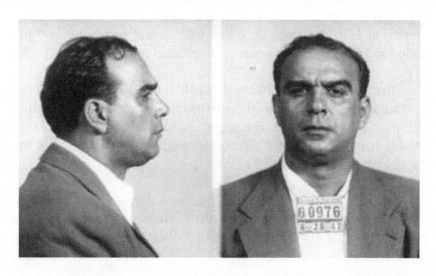

JAMES (AKA JACK) T. LICAVOLI

James T. "Blackie" Licavoli was born on August 18, 1904, in Sicily and became better known as "Jack Wright or White." And died on November 23, 1985. The accomplished mobster did what he needed to do as he rose to the rank of "Boss" of the Cleveland Mafia after the sudden death of John Scalish. White became one of the earliest organized crime figures to be convicted under the 1970 RICO Act.

His humble parents Dominic and Girolama, immigrated to the United States and eventually settled in the St. Louis area for several years along with other members of their family. James Licavoli was one of four children.

The nickname "White" became a play on his dark complexion and southern Italian heritage. Several of his cousins in St. Louis, diligently worked the tough and rugged streets and became known as the infamous Licavoli family, which controlled various rackets in St. Louis, Detroit, and Toledo. One of his cousins was Thomas

(Yonnie) Licavoli. Yonnie was considered to be the leader.

Jack White left school in the spring after the fourth grade and for a short time working at his father's vegetable stand. By the time he left St. Louis for the big city of Detroit in 1926, he had been arrested at least 15 times on minor crimes and had been shot and wounded by a policeman while fleeing an attempted robbery.

Then on October 6, 1926, Licavoli found himself shot in the leg and arrested after a wild hair rising auto chase and shootout with the St. Louis Police. The happy go lucky Licavoli now found himself being charged with carrying a concealed weapon, as the charges were later dropped.

Between 1926 and 1938, White was arrested another two-dozen time in the Detroit and Toledo areas on charges ranging from carrying a concealed weapon to robbery and bootlegging. By this time, he also was questioned as a suspect in at least one murder.

1927

On August 9, 1927, on the outskirts of Chicago, Licavoli was lucky once again as he survived a deadly "one-way ride" that claimed the lives of his trusted friends, Anthony "Shorty" Russo, and Vincent Spicuzza. Scared for his life, Licavoli then started to work with his brother Pete and cousin Yonnie. Together they began a new phase of their criminal careers as part of the Detroit Mafia. Over several battles with other would-be gangsters, the cousins fought for control of the city's rackets from the self-destructing arrogant members of the old Purple Gang, who previously dominated Detroit. Soon White was convicted of bootlegging and served a minor stint at Leavenworth prison. Upon his early release, he joined his cousins once again and was now living in the Toledo area.

By 1929, James Licavoli found that his experience with the "Purple Gang" from Detroit gave him some influence and power, as he viewed Ohio to be a new frontier. Later in 1951 during the

Kefauver Hearings, Licavoli would perjure himself, as he denied that he ever met Moe Dalitz and Sam Tucker. Although he did admit meeting Louie Rothkoph and had met Morris Kleinman once or twice.

The Licavoli's and their cousin, Leo "Lips" Moceri, did not remain in Ohio for very long. Five members of the gang, including his brother Yonnie, were arrested for the murder of a famous Toledo bootlegger.

Peter Licavoli decided to return to Detroit and regrouped his strength and popularity with several faithful underworld friends as he forced himself into power and retaining the original Purple Gang title. Subsequently, at the same time, James Licavoli went into hiding and found himself living in the Pittsburgh area, where he stayed with the up-and-coming mob associate John LaRocca, who would eventually become the "Boss" in Pittsburgh.

Now hiding out in Toledo, Ohio, on December 24, 1931, Licavoli was wanted in Detroit for questioning and possible imprisonment for a gangland slaying. Ohio Governor George White refused the extradition papers because Licavoli was being held in Toledo for an indictment for the slaying of Henry Tupancey. The controversial refusal was based on Licavoli's sworn statement that he was not in Michigan at the time of the murder.

By July 1932, substantial charges of blackmail have emerged in Michigan by Assistant Prosecutor Duncan C. McCres. He states that the estimated amount of $30,000 (In today's money it would be $505,700) was given to S. P. Dunkle, the executive secretary, to present to Governor George White. The gift was a simple "thank you" from an associate of Licavoli's for his assistance in not allowing Licavoli to return to Michigan, where he was wanted for a murder trial.

McCres stated, "A clerk in Governor White's office passed on the suitcase and ordered Licavoli freed, and that was when the

Governor learned of this corrupt action as he fired his once trusted secretary."

Dunkle mentioned that after hearing this outrageous allegation, he remitted that Licavoli was, in fact, at Cedar Point beachfront relaxing on the day of the murder. Dunkle then went to Toledo, and in the presence of Michigan authorities, he was interviewed by Assistant Director Howard. During the interview, Dunkle aggressively added, "There was never any money offered to me at any time."

1933

By February 15, the murder trial of James Licavoli started for the slaying of a rival bootlegger Henry Tupancy back on July 14, 1930. In a surprise announcement after the hearing, Judge John A. Boyne announced that Licavoli is not guilty of the crime. The Judge then admonished the prosecutor for attempting to put a man with a similar name who has been convicted of the murder over one-year ago. At this time, Peter Licavoli, the brother of James, is now serving a life sentence for the killing of Tupancy.

1934

By early March, the long and hard battle in Lucas County, Ohio, came to a halt. The principal underworld activities of the notorious Thomas "Yonnie" Licavoli gang finally reached a climax. The grand jury indicted Yonnie, and twelve accomplishes in four-gangland murders. The men were charged with killing Jack Kennedy, a nightclub promoter, and presume beer baron in Toledo back on July 7, 1933. Then they added the murder of Louise Bell, Kennedy's girlfriend, who was hit with a barrage of stray machine gun bullets intended for Kennedy on November 30, in 1932. The other two murders consisted of Abet Lubltsky and Norman Blatt back on October 6, 1931.

Besides Peter Licavoli, the other men indicted include Joseph English, who has already been convicted of the murder and under a death sentence in the Ohio Penitentiary. Then we add in, Licavoli's cousin Leo "Lips" Moceri, Jacob Sulkin, John Miravella, Ernest LaSalie, Russell Syracuse, Ralph Carsello, and Harry Leonard, his cousin James Licavoli, John Rai, Anthony Beasase and Sebastian Lupica.

The trial for Thomas Licavoli was over just after midnight on November 9. The Toledo gangster was found guilty of first-degree murder and assisting in the four other slayings. However, in a strange twist of fate, the jury recommended mercy instead of the death penalty. Nevertheless, the panel of five women and seven men decided to make the life sentence mandatory. Still missing, and in hiding, somewhere was James Licavoli and his cousin Leo Moceri, the other men were found not guilty.

1938

By this time, James Licavoli was living in the Cleveland area, and soon became good friends with Jimmy "the Weasel" Fratianno and Tony "Dope" Delsanter.

1940

Among their active exploits at this time, the gang teamed up to rob several of the smaller northeast Ohio gambling halls. Sometime during the 1940s, Licavoli was made into the Cleveland Mafia Family and quickly established control over the illegal gambling and the vending machine industry in the neighboring cities of Youngstown and Warren, Ohio. During this period, Licavoli was a suspect in the murders of Jim Mancini, Mancini was a gambling slot czar associated with Nate Weisenberg.

1945

It was early in the year as the police tried to tie a close net around twenty-three people suspects in the shotgun killing of the "Ohio Slot Czar" The sixty-year-old, Nate Weisenberg, was killed while sitting in his car on February 23, on Silsby Road, in Cleveland

Heights.

Arrest warrants have been issued for the two men missing and in hiding. They are James Licavoli and Morris Haas, who was an associate of the late Weisenberg. The men are believed to be hiding in Phoenix, Arizona. Another man sought for questioning in the murder is Charles Gerak, a known pinball machine operator. Weisenberg told the police that someone stole 40 of his machines from his warehouse.

Gerak found himself in jail because of his twisted tails of his slot machine brokerage company. A bond of $25,000 was set. (In today's money, it is worth $319,455.) Gerak insisted to the police that he was not having problems with Weisenberg and knows nothing about the missing 40-slot machines. With this present information in hand, Detective Lieutenant Martin P. Cooney sent out a statewide radio call to have James Licavoli located, stopped, and arrested for further questioning. Several witnesses have told stories of how the forty-slot machine was taken out of state and distributed to California, Washington State, Arizona, and even to North Carolina.

Because of the recent turmoil, Weisenberg had lost almost 75 percent of his once very profitable and lucrative slot machine business to Licavoli and Charles Polizzi, who was now working for Buckeye Services in Cuyahoga, Lake and Geauga Counties. It was now mid-June as the long wait to arrest the forty-one-year-old James Licavoli for questioning about the murder of Nate Wesenberg.

Licavoli was spotted at the North Randel Racetrack on the fifteenth. Police quickly sent Deputy Sheriff Mason Nichols and Dave Yetra to the track to follow up on the hot tip. Licavoli was then spotted with several other men, who the deputies could not identify, as they took him into custody.

Licavoli gave his home address as 2483 Kingston Road in Cleveland Heights, which is the actual home of Vincent (Doc)

Mangine, who is a member of the Buckeye Services along with Louis Carriere. Licavoli told the story of how he has been living in the Warren and Youngstown area, as well as Cleveland, and has used the name of James Wright.

By June 20, Detective Lieutenant Martin Conney ordered that James Licavoli, to be arrested and held for an inquest hearing. Cooney then checked with Toledo Police and found that Licavoli is wanted on an old warrant from 1931 for his part in a murder of a rival gang member Abe Lubitsky. Licavoli was soon released into the custody of the Michigan police.

James Licavoli temporarily returned to Toledo in 1945, where he was arrested for blackmail. He pleaded guilty to a lesser charge and served a year in prison. But other than a small stretch in Leavenworth for bootlegging in the Twenties, his next significant encounter with the law would not come until 1977.

Licavoli was paroled in 1946 through the faithful intercession of a Catholic priest, and ironically, an Irish one. Licavoli also found enthusiastic support from a businessman who owned a construction company with Al Polizzi. Licavoli subsequently went to work as a bartender in an East Side restaurant owned by Vincent (Doc) Mangine, who 30 years ago controlled slot machines in northern Ohio. However, Licavoli's primary interest was in the profitable gambling casinos, notably the Jungle Inn in Warren. This venture added to help him become a very wealthy man.

By the late Forties, Governor Frank Lausche closed the lavish gambling clubs that catered to wealthy high-society patrons. By now, Licavoli was considered to be a millionaire. Years later, with the casinos shut down, Licavoli became a wise investor and was content to place his earnings in legitimate securities purchased through other names. He spent very little of his money and conserved it by living a low-keyed lifestyle until his death of natural causes.

56

1951

This year, became known as the year of the Kefauver crime hearings, led by Senator Estes Kefauver. More trouble began for Licavoli during his interview. He would later have additional federal charges to deal with.

The Cleveland newspaper caricatured the mob men as high profile, influential, well-known, and often well-liked. They usually control politics, businesses, and public officials. However, they were sharp dressers with diamond rings and fancy suits and drove Cadillac's and Lincoln's. Despite warnings from Kefauver and his committee, James Licavoli and Joseph DiCarlo both faced contempt of court charges as they refused to answer any questions asked of them. Licavolis Attorney was D.J. LaPolla of Warren, Ohio. The only testimony Licavoli gave to the court was his current address being, 1953 East 121st. After a brief discussion between Kefauver and LaPoll, about possible questions asked in regards to his involvement in a crime. Licavoli stood and said, "Excuse me, Senator; I refuse to answer all questions posed to me today."

In contrast, Licavoli declined to respond to questions about if he knew Jerry Milano and Vincent Mangine. He continued and stated, he has never heard of the "Purple Gang," however he did admit he was arrested some two dozen times over the past years.

It was early February in Detroit; Mich. as the Senate Racket hearings came to focus on all aspects of criminal activity throughout the country. For today's session, there was considerably interested in Peter and James Licavoli. Pete, now 48-years old, is known for his well-established and very popular Gross Point Mansion and the Grace Ranch, located in Tucson, Arizona, which is a known mob hangout for many of the top political leaders and crime figures in the country.

Pete is believed to have many connections with Cleveland and other major cities across the country, as he refused to testify to most of their questions. However, he did admit before the crime hearing members that he stays in touch with Morris "Mushy" Wexler from Cleveland, Al Polizzi, of Cleveland, Joe Di Carlo from Youngstown, Ohio, Mike De Angelo (his cousin) of Columbus and James Brink who once lived in Cleveland. The crime hearing was interested in asking about Licavoli's support to get some friendly congressional help to stall or stop the current deportation hearings against his brother-in-law Frank Cammerata, another infamous gangster from the Warren area.

On March 28, *the Cleveland Plain Dealer* headlines read, "Licavoli, and two other indicted here," the article was written by Ted Princiotto.

Federal Judge Charles J. McNamee and United States Attorney Don C. Miller have signed the paperwork to issue an arrest warrant for James Licavoli, Joe Di Carlo, and Joe Aluppa, from Chicago for refusing to answer thirty-one "pertinent" questions during their testimony.

Some of the eleven counts Licavoli is being charged with dealing with his refusal to respond to questions. 1. What Business are you currently involved in? 2. Did you know Mike Farrah, one of the owners of the Jungle Inn, in Trumbull County? 3. How do you now earn your living? 4. Have you ever been in gambling ventures with others?

The defendant's lawyers apparently are concerned with their client's Fifth Amendment rights, since answers and testimony could incriminate them in Federal Crimes. The trio is currently out on a $3,000 bail.

Licavoli would later be acquitted of these charges under his Fifth-Amendment rights of incrimination.

57

1952

It was now October as the much older looking, short and stocky James Licavoli found himself in deep, intense hot water once again. This time it was with the IRS. Charges by the Bureau claimed that Licavoli was looking at a Federal Tax lien worth an astonishing $164,273.74. His meager income for 1948 claimed he had an income of $45,075 (worth $429,752 in today's money) for 1949 $47,687 and for 1949 it was $71,510. These figures included his proper taxes, income, and penalties, papers have been filed to seize any and all of his known assets.

By November Leo Lips) Moceri, 45, is a cousin to Peter and James Licavoli and has even used the alias of Leo Licavoli was in jail. This time it was in Los Angeles where he was arrested in an embarrassing situation. It seems the wealthy Moceri while driving his expensive new Cadillac, was arrested for using a "two-bit slug" in a phone booth. For some unknown reason, he was trying to call Las Vegas. At the time when he was searched, the police found over $1,800 in cash in his pockets with an assortment of actual change. Moceri was a known criminal and arrested over 28-times for grand larceny, assault, and armed robbery, as well as a narcotics violation.

Los Angeles Police Captain J. E. Hamilton of the intelligence unit has stated Moceri is currently under indictment for four-gangland style murders in and around the Toledo area from 1931 until 1933. Hamilton mentioned how Moceri is considered to be one of "the nation's most-wanted trigger man" and was even a possible suspect in the murder of Bugsy Siegal back in 1947, and other Hollywood slayings.

1970

By 1970, his friendly familiar manner gained James Licavoli to be known as "The king of the hill" on Murray Hill, in Cleveland's Little Italy. He never married nor had any children and remained a lifelong bachelor. "The Old Man" lived with a 70-year-old roommate Paul Ciricillo (aka) Paul Lish, who was also a bachelor and worked as a carpenter. His small home was on Fairview Court, which was located behind the ever-popular Golden Bowl Restaurant. Since Licavoli's income was never declared yet somehow, he was able to draw a monthly social security check. "The old man of the hill" started using a plain-looking cane most days to help steady his aging knees and legs as he walks.

Despite his immense unknown wealth, he had a candid reputation for being cheap and occasionally foolish to the point of unbelievable embarrassment. Once, while he was shopping by himself at a local strip mall, known as Severance Center on the corner of Mayfield Road and Taylor Road, not far from where he lived. Licavoli was detained by store detectives for switching the price tags on a pair of ugly colored pants. After hearing about his background, the department store manager declined to prosecute the old man. Another time, he was caught red-handed using slugs on a vending machine. It was also alleged that he even would use stolen credit cards while on vacations just so the expenses could not be traced back to him.

With the newly acclaimed RICO Act in place, the once assortment of mob tuff guys, killers, and enforcers went crawling on their hands and knees to the Fed's for protection and saving their own ass instead of rotting out in the cold, dark and lonely prison, or a death penalty.

1976

It has been the most troubling, turbulent and explosive time in the Cleveland Mafia history, and it was about to get even worse.

Longtime Cleveland family boss John Scalish unexpectedly died while having open-heart surgery. James Licavoli was older and yet wiser as Scalish's logical successor, although John Nardi believed, he should be the boss.

Many of the more thoughtful men in organized crime initially thought that Scalish's old and trusted friend and brother-in-law Milton Rockman would have been a perfect choice. However, the problem was, Rockman was of Jewish descent, and not Italian or Sicilian.

Licavoli was seen as the last of the old-time mobsters who adhered to the old codes of conduct. Jack believed in the code of Omerta, personal honor, and viewed cooperating with the feds as a "betrayal" of the family and his secrete oath.

During this turbulent time, Licavoli had to deal with the powerful Irish gangster Danny Greene and an active friend of John Nardi, who sided with Greene and switched his alliance with his Italian family, strengthening Greene's criminal empire and giving him an advantage over the Cleveland family. This single action erupted into an all-out war across the city, leaving many of Licavoli's supporters being killed in the process. As both sides started planting car bombs in mobsters' cars, to kill whoever got in their way.

The tremendous tension and growing warfare escalated with the assassination of Cleveland underboss, Leo Moceri.

During the early phases of the growing war, Licavoli was on the defense at all times. Although no direct attempts were made on his life, many of Licavoli's men and associates were killed in this unique power struggle. The embarrassment of the war would cause an overwhelming reaction from across the country.

The wooden cane Licavoli used made him seem weak and more like a great-grandfather than a mob boss in the eyes of many of his neighbors in Little Italy. He was always known to tap his cane on the floor when he was giving a direct order, he never spoke the words, just tapped his cane on the floor, which gave his individual approval. His cane was said to have a thin eighteen-inch knife hidden inside.

The FBI released to the newspapers in Cleveland that they had a secured FBI informant, who related the alarming information that his life would be in danger if anyone found out his true identity. The man then went on to tell them how Licavoli personally said to him back in October of 1976 that Greene must be killed, and how he has already given the order to his men. According to the FBI and police investigators, Licavoli, at the age of 73, is the most powerful crime figure in Cleveland and has significant influence.

With the deaths of Nardi and Greene, Licavoli assumed complete control of criminal activities in Cleveland. Under Licavoli's insistence, the Cleveland syndicate took on a bold new agenda as they successfully infiltrated the FBI branch in Cleveland. This was accomplished by the good old fashion use of money and bribing an intelligent female clerk, with riches that she desired. Her job was a simple one, to update them on present organized crime investigations and provide them with the essential critical identities of government informants.

In a later conversation with his trusted lifelong friend turned FBI informant Jimmy Fratianno now 64, Licavoli ironically commented, "Jimmy, sometimes, you know, I think this fucking outfit of ours is like the old Communist Party in this country. It's getting so that there are more fucking spies in it than actual members."

On Saturday, November 23, 1985, James Licavoli, aka "Jack White," aka "Blackie," died of a fatal heart attack while serving his seventeen-year sentence at the Oxford Federal Prison in Oxford, Wisconsin.

58

DENNIS KUCINICH

(Courtesy of the Cleveland Plain Dealer)

1977

The young, flamboyant, and decisive new mayor, Dennis Kucinich, took the city by storm, which has been in turmoil from the weak Ralph Perk, just as the gangland bombing violence was reaching its climax. Kucinich related, "The mob had their greedy hooks into city hall, our banks, and institutional activities and became in control of many aspects of our daily lives."

During his mayoral career, Kucinich proclaimed he could not be bought. However, he was outspoken and enjoyed a no-nonsense approach, which enraged many of the everyday citizens and his political enemies as well. At the young age of 31, he was the youngest mayor of a major city, earning him the nickname "The Boy Mayor of Cleveland." After Kucinich refused to sell Muni Light, Cleveland's publicly owned electric utility. Newspapers dumbed Kucinich's tenure as mayor, "as one of the most tumultuous in Cleveland's history."

Kucinich started to interfere with the day to day operation of the Cleveland mob. This action resulted in them offering a hit on Kucinich. The story goes that a hitman from Maryland planned to shoot him in the head during the 1978 traditional Columbus Day Parade, which ran through the heart of the Little Italy district. The order was for payback on his multiple attempts to crack down on numerous organized crime members and their controls on the industry in Cleveland. Allegedly, the hit on Kucinich was organized by Tommy "The Chinaman" Sinito. The plot fell apart when Kucinich was unexpectedly hospitalized with a stomach ulcer and missed the big event. Amazingly, the city fell into default shortly after that. This resulted in the mafia leaders to call off the contract on him.

59

THE INVESTIGATION

1978

By January 18, the climate in Cleveland became the critical turning point in the study of the assassination of Danny Greene. This caused James Fratianno to become more nervous than at any other time in his criminal life, and soon became alarmed that Licavoli would discover he was in-fact the informant against him and his Cleveland boys. Fratianno knew damn well that Licavoli would not hesitate to have him killed. The agreement to save his life was a simple one, he had to enter into the Witness Protection Program.

Fratianno did not appear at the opening hearing in Cleveland's Common Pleas Court on February 21. Six people were scheduled to start the celebrated trial for their involvement and participation in Greene's death. To everyone's surprise, the Assistant County Prosecutor Carmen M. Marino announced to the courtroom that an agreement with James Fratianno was complete. The Federal Government offered him protection for his family for his full discourse of events in Greens murder.

With the depth of Fratianno's criminal information, the FBI closed the slight leak in their Cleveland Office. Prosecutors now targeted Licavoli for prosecution under the RICO Act.

As the trial was set to begin on February 23. The long and grueling three-day to select a jury who had not read the hundreds of newspaper articles and had very little knowledge about Greene's long life of crime, and his exclusive long list of enemies. Many of the jurors told the court it would be impossible for them to be sequestered for up to three months. After long deliberation, Judge Carroll instructed the prosecutors and witnesses in the trial that they needed to move swiftly, and it could possibly last a month or longer.

The defense requested a significant consideration in the case. Judge Carroll needed to address this in a clear-cut fashion. His next comment was seen as his most crucial ruling up to this time. It was that a single keyword, **"Mafia"** can be used by anyone during the trial. The judge decisively proclaimed, "I cannot restrict a single word that is a part of our everyday language." Judge Carroll goes on and states, "This ruling is based on the multitude of sworn affidavits, testimonies, and statements from a witness, and police documents that would become unintelligible if the references to the word "Mafia" were removed from them.

The defendants included James Licavoli, Pasquale Cisternino, Alfred Calabrese, Ronald Carabbia, Angelo Lonardo, and Thomas Sinito. They were all charged with aggravated murder.

YOUNG JAMES FRATIANNO

(Courtesy of Cleveland State University Archives)

It was on April 13, as *The Cleveland Palin Dealer* had an article written by W. James Van Vliet, which told the happening of the day's trial.

The calm and confessed James Fratianno, related his own life story to the pack fill courtroom on how he and his friends staked out Danny Greene's at his Lake Shore apartment between 25 to 30 times in 1976 after he was given the hit order from Licavoli. "I was watching him closely." Fratianno told them, "If I had seen him, and had the chance I would have killed him, right then and there." However, the circumstance and opportunity did not become good until October 5 when the bomb car was placed in the parking lot next to Greene's car at the dentist's office of Brainard Place Medical Building parking lot.

Ray Ferritto has already pleaded guilty to his role in the elaborate murder. Ferritto has testified that Fratianno contacted him in May last year at his Erie PA home and informed him that he wanted to meet with him in Warren, Ohio. At the meeting, Fratianno told Ferritto, "they are having problems in Cleveland...that somebody was trying to muscle in and that Tony Delsanter might have some "work" for me." By "work," Fratianno explained that Delsanter wanted someone taken care of...Someone killed.

Underneath heighten security, the trial of the accused men continued until May 25, it has now been seventy-nine long grueling days of hearing testimony, defense motions, and many witnesses. This case became the most extensive murder trial in Cleveland history. The city of Cleveland and most of the country waited after the thirty-three long hours of intense discussions and heated deliberation. The exhausted jury finally agreed on a decision.

Two men, Thomas Lanci and Kenneth Ciarcia were given a life sentence for their role in Greene's death. However, they are currently free on an appeals bond. The eight men and four women decided and convicted two men, Pasquale "Butchy" Cisternino and Ron Carabbia. Both were found guilty of the aggravated murder of Danny Greene and sentence them to life in prison. For James "Jack White:" Licavoli, Angelo "Big Ange" Lonardo and Thomas Sinito, all were cleared of being involved in the bombing plot.

1979

It was now May 17, as the trial of the men the police believed were responsible for the bombing murder of John Nardi was back in court after two long years. Seven men have been charged. All plead not guilty in U.S. District Court. U.S. Magistrate Charles R. Laurie.

Bond for Thomas Lanci, now 36, was set at $400,000, James Licavoli, 74 was established at the same amount. The other men, Anthony D. Liberatore 57, was set at $350,000. He could not make the 10% bond and was held until he reached his bail. The other defendant John Calandra 63; his bond was set at $200,000. He put up his $20,000 and was released. Kenneth Ciarcia bond was set at $50,000 and was being held.

1980

In January, seven men were indicted for bribing an FBI Clerk, Geraldine Rabinowitz. She was charged with gathering critical, confidential, FBI information about James Licavoli's criminal life. The secret records were found during a search by agents. Curiously it was hidden in a cereal box inside the Lincoln car dealership Ciarcia worked for. The nervous and stressed Rabinowitz admitted on the stand after intense questioning how she and her husband Jeffrey were paid $15,900 for the secret records of Licavoli.

At this time, Fratianno informed the jam-packed courtroom that Rabinowitz did, in fact, give vital information to Tony Liberatore, along with secret code numbers used by the FBI. However, to his knowledge, she did not get the names of the confidential informants.

By April, the FBI had two affidavits declaring the city of Youngstown; Ohio was under control by both the Cleveland and the Pittsburgh Mafia. To confuse the matter, even more, Angelo Lonardo and Ron Carabbia seem to be involved in some of the Youngstown area crime wave. It seems a significant disagreement started last year as the FBI reported that Lonardo went to Youngstown to obtain a cut of their action, what he calls his fair share of the illegal activities in Mahoning County.

In yet another embarrassing moment for the Cleveland Mob Syndicate: Fratianno explained to the court how he was asked to perform the mysterious "Mafia Oath" to Anthony Liberatore and John Calandra to become a "Made Member." Crazy as it seems, the current men in Cleveland did not know the exact words to use or the proper pronunciation in Italian, including Lonardo and Licavoli. The secret ceremony was held in the basement of the Roman Gardens restaurant on Mayfield Road in Murray Hill in May 1977. Fratianno testified he told both men in a watered-down version of the oath, "Not to fool with narcotics (which everyone was involved in at this time, just do not get caught.) Do not talk to the FBI or mess around with other members' wives." He then pricked their finger with a knife until blood ran out.

1982

Revealed in court, a surprise witness discussed how it took several stakeouts, to develop a plan to take control of all Cleveland mob. The man was Louis J. Aratari, another Clevelander in the protected federal witness program.

The six men were once again on trial, which includes Licavoli, Liberatore, Calandra, Carabbia, Cisternino, and Ciarcia.

Aratari told the chilling story of his involvement and what he understood about the murder plots of Danny Greene and John Nardi. Aratari responded how he was offered $5,000 to kill Greene and Nardi. He openly discussed how he was told by Liberatore that Greene was a pretty tough guy and that Licavoli wanted him out of the way!

Another principal witness for the prosecution case was Thomas Lanci, who stated, "Sometime after the death of Nardi, the plot to kill Green began to be formed." That is when Liberatore told me, "the rest of them have to go." The targets in questioned where Kevin McTaggart, Keith Ritson, and Brian O'Donnell. Later, both Liberatore and Lanci agreed, "They have to be taken out." Aratari was assigned to make the killing as Liberatore, informed him he would supply the gun and pay him $5,000 for each man.

Lanci then testified that after Greene's death, Aratari asked Lanci and Liberatore if he should still "get rid" of Greene's men? This murder plot never developed.

It was now July 8, as the jury announced their courageous verdict for the six men accused of taking part in the racketeering and murder plots.

Licavoli and the five other men were convicted on federal RICO charges and sentenced to seventeen years imprisonment.

The full circle of crime and racketeering has come to a close in Cleveland after its beginning in the early 1910s as *The Cleveland Plain Dealer* states "Mob here is crippled by death and prison says the FBI" written by Mairy Jayn Woge

> *Joseph E. Griffin, the special agent in charge of the FBI in the northeastern, Ohio, reported last week on how the upper levels of the criminal organization have been paralyzed, and the day-to-day operation was being conducted by sub-par underlings. Griffin's announcement was a result of the convictions in the $15 Million-dollar Mafia-controlled drug ring in Ohio.*
>
> *The current "Boss" James Licavoli now 77 will be living in a Federal Correctional Institute in Oxford, Wisconsin. Angelo*

Lonardo 72, the "Underboss," is fighting for his life as the head of the drug ring. John Calandra 67, along with Anthony Liberatore 60, were both convicted of the murder of Danny Greene. Ronald Carabbia 53, who was to be supervising the gambling operation in Mahoning Valley and Trumbull County, is serving a life term for Greene's murder. Joseph Gallo, 44, and Thomas Sinito 43, both Captains under Licavoli, are in prison on racketeering charges, loan sharking, and tax evasion. Other Mafia soldiers include Cisternino, Ciarcia, Lanci, and all our serving time for Greene's death.

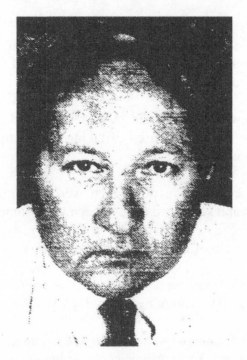

FBI AGENT JOSEPH GRIFFIN

(Courtesy of the Cleveland Plain Dealer)

60

PART VI

EARLY TEAMSTER

Back in the 1930s, Anthony Milano took credit and great pride in helping his Jewish friend William Presser to obtain his first union position. For a long time, it was alleged for many years that Presser got his daily instructions and orders from Anthony Milano. Years later, in 1973, the tide of change began. Milano opposed the younger Jackie Presser for a higher union position. Milano stated, "He is a brat, unruly and can't be trusted." Milano refused to endorse him for advancement in the Teamster union and would talk about his weaknesses with his fellow criminal friends.

In 1952, Jackie Presser, now 26, was hired as an organizer by the International Teamsters Union and held a series of low-level jobs for the next twelve years. Presser's big break came in 1964 when he and his father brokered a substantial real estate deal in Cleveland for a group of local investors, including himself. The plan was to build an upscale sports club and restaurant on the property secured by a $1.1 million loan from the Teamsters' Central States Pension Fund. Later, the project went bankrupt. No one was surprised as the pension fund lost more than $265,000.

In October 1954, Dave Beck, the current International President of the Teamsters Union, along with William Presser, was on the hot seat once again, dealing with the corruption of the unions. The case was heard inside a downtown Cleveland Federal Building. The select committee was led by Congressman George Bender, of Cleveland. One questioned ask of Beck was, "did he know the background information on both Presser and Louis "Babe" Triscaro before their rise in power in the Teamsters, and if so, what are you going to do to clean up this terrible situation of eminence distrust among your union members?" Triscaro and his brother Joe have been accused of extorting, between $15,000 and

$20,000 from a contractor Richard Finley. It was a simple business deal for Triscaro. Findley was eager to avoid a bombing, a work stoppage, or a sledgehammer job, which would vandalism some of his pricey construction equipment.

Beck's only comment to Bender was, "The current union activities would be investigated in depth. And any of the information discovered during the investigation will be disclosed, and the board of directors will take swift and appropriate actions at that time if any is needed.

Bender closed the afternoon hearing by saying, "The city of Cleveland is the center of multiple conspiracies. The citizens are in great despair and in the restraint of wanting a fair-trade agreement for all. There has been no sincere effort to investigate or solve some of the forty-bombing in the city. More racketeering information has been discovered and brought to light through these colorful hearings than what was produced by the city investigators in over a dozen years."

By November, Jackie Presser and six other local union officials of the Hotel and the Restaurant Employee Union, Local 274, were accused of misusing funds and issuing personal threats to International Union officers and defying specific orders ousting them from the union. Presser was charged with giving himself, and a few of his close business agents lavish new and expensive automobiles valued at $12,000 when his fund only had a balance of $5,000. (Note, this is equal to over $113,300 in today's money)

One crazy incident involved Marcel Kennedy, the International Vice President of the AFL-CIO Hotel and Restaurant Workers Local. He refused to turn over all the union records. Presser warned Kennedy, "to leave or be thrown out" of his union office on East 17th Street. Kennedy testified that his salary of $1,000 a month, (or $9,404 at today's income) came from a sixty-cent tax or assessment on each of the 406,000 International Union members to pay for the union official's salaries.

SENATOR GEORGE BENDER

(Courtesy of the Cleveland Memory Project)

In January 1959, Max Goldschein, a lawyer for the Criminal Division of the Department of Justice, arrived in Cleveland from Washington D.C. Goldschein would not comment on any upcoming indictments in his monumental probe inside the powerful labor unions in Cleveland. Goldschein noted that "The grand jury has the authority to investigate any and all violations of federal statutes that may come to their attention."

Later in the day on January 19, it was learned that William Presser, President of the Teamster Joint Council 41 had been served a subpoena. Other indictments included 23 different union funds along with other Cleveland union members. Some listed at this time was John Nardi, a business agent for the Vending Machine Service Employees Local 41. Louis "Babe" Triscaro, President of Local 436, and John "Skip" Felice, President of Teamsters Local 293. Also mentioned in this subpoena was to review their personal financial records from 1953 until 1957. Additional men listed were, Frank Visconti, the owner of Captain Frank's Seafood House on East 9th Street pier; mob "Boss" John Scalish, and his brother Sam, who are both to bring their personal and financial records from Buckeye Cigarette Vending Machine business along with mobsters Frank Brancato and John DeMarco.

It was on Wednesday, January 20, as the Grand Jury gathered in Judge James Connell's court. The primary focus would be hearing on whether serious charges should be cited on four men. The people were facing contempt of court charges for pleading and taking their fifth amendment right not to answer questions asked of them by Max Goldschein from the Department of Justice. The men included John and Sam Scalish, John DeMarco, and Frank Brancato. Judge Connell informed them, "To leave the court and given a day to consult with their attorneys and then return tomorrow to answer the specific and direct questions asked of them earlier or face contempt of court charges."

In a separate closed-door investigation into the slot and coin machines racket, Senator John F. Kennedy mentioned how William Presser, who is involved in the Jukebox investigation. Kennedy said how their in-depth inquiry would include Cleveland, Youngstown, Akron, Cincinnati, areas. They will be focusing on two union locals, Local 377 from Youngstown and Local 100 in Cincinnati. Both unions have asked for our help while fighting a battle against the fierce lieutenants sent by Jimmy Hoffa and William Presser.

It was now March of 1959, as Senator John McClellan headed up a subcommittee to investigate the vending machine and jukebox industry. Ohio was considered to be a focal point for McClellan. From Cleveland came Frank Embressia, an owner in the Buckeye Vending Machine Company. Louis Perlman, an officer in the L. &

N. Music Company, Joseph Fontana President of the Vending Machine Local 410, which is a part of the Teamsters Union, Anthony Sara, a business agent of the union. Also included is John Nardi, a member of 410, John DeMarco, Joseph Nemesh, head of the Music System Inc. From Youngstown came Leo Dixon, who is a well-known Jukebox magnate. William Presser, the current chairman of the Ohio Conference of Teamsters, was also issued a subpoena.

61

THE MARRIAGE OF THE UNION

AND THE MOB

In Cleveland, the TEAMSTERS UNION is officially known as the International Brotherhood of Teamsters, Chauffeurs, Stablemen, & Helpers, and is considered to be one of the largest and most influential labor unions. Organized locally back in 1912, when Local 407 was chartered for the sole purpose of unionizing the hardworking men as day workers and drivers for hauling and delivery services. In its first few decades, Edward Murphy and John Rohrich guided the bold union, as they worked desperately to kept it free of the racketeering.

After Murphy died in 1950, the union was taken over by William E. Presser, who was born in 1907. William went on to married Faye, the daughter of notorious Cleveland bootlegger Louis Friedman, who was a close friend of policy racketeer Max Diamond. Earlier in the 1920s, Presser had saved Friedman from a kidnapping attempt by rival gangsters. This bold action sealed Pressers' loyalty to the up and coming Cleveland Four.

It was in September 1953, when Clare Hoffman declared his in-depth investigations into racketeers and organized crime. A resident of Michigan, Hoffman, shown a link of substantial evidence of "labor racketeering" and extortion in at least eight major cities across America. He found that the governors in these cities have been bribed, intimidated, and scared by the local racketeers. The cities listed in this document included Chicago, New York, Detroit, Cleveland, St Louis, Los Angeles, Minneapolis, and Indianapolis. In Hoffman's opinion, "the governors and the state law enforcement agencies are afraid of the gangsters and their incredible power."

WILLIAM PRESSER

(Courtesy of the Cleveland State University Archives)

By January 1954, Cleveland Congressman George Bender, who is the Chairmen of the House Operations Committee, requested that the government freed up $100,000 out of the annual budget to help investigate irregularities in the national labor field and associated labor racketeering. Bender claims he would like to start in Cleveland and then move to Kansas City, Minneapolis, Detroit, New York, Indianapolis, and then to Los Angeles.

During his investigation, Bender received valid information of extreme intimidation and threats. He said, "They are afraid to attend organized union meetings, while many others are scared to ask a simple question or speak up if they disagree with a statement. If you do complain, you will soon be out of work, and no other company or foreman will hire you. These men are afraid of what would happen to their families." Additional information came forward to the committee from business people, who claimed they felt compelled to pay substantial sums of money to prevent a work stoppage, damage to their building or equipment, or even threatened labor dispute by the mobsters.

By the end of May, Bender was running out of money to continue with the probe, which became more extensive than he first thought. Bender informed Congress that they needed more funds to continue the investigation into labor racketeering. That it was critical to the safety and stability of the country. Bender has found "unsavory" actions throughout Ohio, and this dangerous situation may never be exposed if the committee is silent at this critical point of the investigation. Bender explained how he has found positive links between New York, New Jersey, and Cleveland racketeers who operate vending machines industry throughout the neighboring states, which implications of Ohio members of the notorious Mafia have infiltrated and taken part in labor violence."

By June, Bender was still battling with Congress for an additional $75,000.

It was by the end of August when William Presser gave in to the massive attacks made by Congressmen Bender and Hoffman of the House and Racketeering Subcommittee. The men finally convinced Presser that he needed to bring all his financial records in for the court to review. Of course, this only happened after they filed a subpoena for the documents. Presser brought in just one set of books for the Vending Machine Service Employees Union Local 410 for the committee to review.

In a surprise developed during the next round of inquiries, Benders committee learned that out of town truckers are used to unload trucks. When this happens, the drivers are forced by union labor leaders to hire other unneeded union workers known as "gypsy-chasers" and pay them the sum of up to $16 an hour for eight hours; and they do NO work at all. (Note, the average rate of pay at this time was as high as $10.00 an hour)

After hearing these disturbing comments, Benders and his committee have asked Governor Frank Lausche for his help to secure safe working environments for these workers. Lausche has ordered State Safety Director U.C. Feity to have the state highway police protect any future witness in the investigation as well as any trucker who seeks their help to safely unload their trucks.

An unknown man who has been staying in the Warrensville Workhouse revealed to the congressional racket committee how he has personally bribed several police officers over the last twenty years to look the other way and not to investigate an incident. He said, "Police don't bother you if you have money in this town." The man continued and claims he was paid between $15,000 to $20,000 for fifteen different bombings and for five "sledgehammer attacks. Against his rivals." This did not include three other incidents where he poured sand into the crankcase of the expensive machinery on a job site. This testimony helped to convince business operators to work alongside unions.

By November, Ohio A.F.L. Teamster Union boss William Presser was in court once again to explain his recent activities to the Labor Racketeering Committee. Presser needs to answer several tough questions on how and why he authorized three or four unsecured loans, worth more than $500,000 from several Cleveland Banks. During the court proceedings, Presser refused to answer every question about the union funds or his personal net worth an estimated $223,000. (Note, this sum is equal to $2,107,827 in today's money)

Records have shown that Presser's income is only $14,000 a year plus another $2,000 for his expenses. Leading the subcommittee's charge against Presser is Congressmen Clare Hoffman from Michigan. Others have been subpoenaed to testify. First is Presser's wife Faye, Louis "Babe" Triscaro head of the Teamsters Local 436, and his brother Joseph who operates several trucking companies. Then there is Milton Rockman from the Buckeye Cigarette Vending Machine Company, John Nordie of the Vending News organization, and John Cohen President of Photographers Merchants Association.

Later Louis (Babe) Triscaro, who started his career as a young and powerful boxer, found his God-given skills could be used to make some money. Now, as a leading union organizer. his talent was accompanied by several attempts of violence and personal threats.

In 1957 corruption and reported ties with the underworld characters resulted in a federal probe for twenty Teamster Cleveland Union leaders. Subsequently, the Teamsters and its 40,000 proud members found themselves expelled from the newly formed AFL-CIO. Cleveland Teamster where lead by William Presser and his son Jackie Presser. Both men held an office in the Teamster Union Joint Council 41 and the Central States Conference of Teamsters, organized in 1953.

THE YOUNG BOXER LOUIS "BABE" TRISCARO

(Courtesy of the Author collection)

Allen Friedman was a labor organizer in the early years and became Vice President of Teamster Local 507. Allen grew up in the Glenville area, attending school through the 7th grade. By 1939, he was acting as a guard and enforcer for William Presser, who was in charge of union organizing activities. Friedman was a man dedicated to his cause, which was to organize Local 274, The Hotel and Restaurant Workers for young Jackie Presser in the mid-1950s. Beginning in 1966, Friedman began recruiting warehouse workers for Teamster Local 507 and served as the union's Vice President. After he suffered a heart attack in 1969, he lowered his position with Local 507 and started his own independent warehouse workers named Local 752.

During the 1940s, William Presser gained a stronger control of the Cleveland area's jukebox and vending machine operations. He did this by organizing its distributors into regions. Presser then began to apply exclusive territories, which were then allocated to the members. This eliminated any and all competition and built a stronghold against rival vendors. Presser completed his monopoly by establishing a new union for the workers who serviced the jukeboxes and vending machines. He soon gained more approval, as he negotiated their yearly wage increases. Membership fees and union dues, which often ranged from $15 to 30 dollars a month, gave Presser a sizeable personal income, which increased as his extensive operations expanded. Presser then joined the growing Teamsters Union in 1951, bringing his unions with him. Two years later, with the support of James Hoffa, who was currently the President of the Ohio Conference of Teamsters and Joint Council 41. Under William Presser's leadership, its membership grew from 23,000 to 100,000. Presser soon became the subject of several federal investigations for labor racketeering. Presser served a brief term in prison in 1961 for destroying critical evidence and fined $12,000 in 1971. Presser's influence continued to grow in the Teamsters Union with his election as Vice President for the International Union in 1967, a position he held for the rest of his life.

William Presser, however, was still viewed as a protégé of Jimmy Hoffa. Presser was then elected President of the Ohio

Conference of Teamsters and eventually became the Vice President of the International Union. At this point in time, Bill Presser was intimately connected with the Cleveland mob.

Jackie Presser was born in Cleveland, Ohio, in 1926. The son of William and Faye (Friedman) Presser. Jackie's grandfather was a Jewish immigrant from Austria, who went on to become a garment worker, and was active in and participated in several strikes led by various garment makers' unions in New York's Garment District. The Presser family was destitute for many years. Bill Presser often told others how he used to stuff newspapers into his shoes to block holes in the uppers and strengthen the soles.

Young Jackie's childhood, by his own account, was a happy one. However, he omitted it was greatly influenced by his family's poverty. Jackie dropped out of school in the middle of the eighth grade. Using his father's connections, he got a job delivering jukeboxes to local restaurants and bars. In 1943 and just 17, Jackie enlisted in the Navy and served in WW II. After the war, Presser returned to Cleveland and got a job once again as a truck driver for a vending machine company.

After one year as a truck driver, Jackie; was hired to be a union organizer for Local 10, a Cleveland affiliate of the Hotel Employees and Restaurant Employees Union. In 1948, Jackie was elected President of Local 10. He united this local with four other local unions to improve and expand the workers' collective bargaining position. Jackie Presser soon began receiving a substantial salary and spending significant amounts of money on travel and luxury automobiles. He wore impressive pinky rings and diamond bracelets and became notorious for wearing brightly colored sports jackets. Over time he began to gain substantial amounts of weight, a health problem he would fight for the rest of his life.

The 1970s

By the end of July, William Presser: who has always been a strong supporter of International President James Hoffa, even after Hoffa went to jail on jury tampering charges. Presser has obtained an impressive 44-year career as a union leader and organizer. Presser raised an astonishing $125,000 to help retarded school children. Two years later, he led the fight to raise money from 1,500 of his close friends and union officials. William was leading a passionate drive and aid for Israel. Presser successfully raised 1.5 million dollars.

By October, William Presser and Louis Triscaro decided to fight the severe charges against them. Both men were acclaimed organizers and ran their unions with a stern hand, as they controlled the 75,000 plus membership and planned to keep their union healthy and vibrant. Presser was now 63 as he told the union members that if for some reason he cannot fulfill the full four-year term as President, then Louis Triscaro would take over as president, not his son Jackie. This may have seemed strange to many members, but not to the mob.

Bill and Jackie Presser soon where some of the most influential men in the Teamsters Union. By 1972, the father-son team led the Ohio Conference of Teamsters. In addition, both Pressers were trustees of the Teamster's Central States Pension Fund, one of the wealthiest and most influential pension plans in the nation.

By 1971, Local 507 had grown to 4,430 members across northern Ohio and included 121 different bargaining units. Jackie Presser acquired more salaried positions, including President and General Manager of Teamster Local 10, Hotel and Restaurant Employees; Financial Secretary of Local 19, Bakery and Confectionery Workers and Vice President of Joint Council 41.

In 1976, Jackie was elected as the International Vice President of union communications. Jackie planned to innovative program for Teamsters. His goal was to attract positive media attention that he desperately needed? Official Federal Court records years later would show Jackie Presser and his father becoming informants for the FBI in the late 1970s.

Secret federal transcripts of wiretaps linked both men to several significant organized crime figures across the country. Even with the incredible heat on Jackie, he was elected President of the International Union in April 1983.

Jackie soon became the dominant leader of the giant 1.6 million-member Teamster Union. To add to his eminence popularity, Presser was then appointed to yet another essential position as the labor advisor to President Ronald Reagan in return for the tremendous influential union's support of his presidential campaign.

62

INVOLVEMENT WITH THE MAFIA

By the time 1970 came around, William Presser was under investigation once again, this time with the Labor Department and the Justice Department Organized Crime Strike Task Force. This time William was facing 23 counts and accused of shaking down several trucking companies to advertise in his *Ohio Teamsters Journal* that was published twice in four years. With the help of a friendly U.S. District Judge, William pleaded guilty to a misdemeanor and fined $12,000. However, he accepted over $500,000 from several trucking companies for this magazine.

It was now 1973, as the heavy-set 46-year old Jackie Presser emerged as a powerhouse in the Teamster Union. Pressers' newest role in the union is officially noted to be the Executive Assistant and Personal Representative of the President of Teamsters Joint Council 41. Presser informed his friends, "that his father is currently in ill health. However, he is not retiring, he just needs some time off to rest and regain his strength. I will be taking over more of the day-to-day operations of the union." Presser then stated, "His father has been falsely accused of co-operating with several Mafia figures from across the country. However, look at me, how does a Jew like me, get to become a member of the Mafia?" The jubilant Presser somehow failed to mention that a powerful Jewish Clevelander, was a member of the modern-day Cleveland Syndicate. A gangster named Moe Dalitz and Milton Rockman, who both have joined forces with the Italians, Frank, and Anthony Milano.

According to court records, in 1974, Jackie Presser became deeply involved in many mafia affairs. He allegedly told the leaders of the Chicago Mafia, that he was willing to do favors in exchange for money and their assistance. Later in 1981 James Fratianno, testified that the Chicago crime boss Joseph Aiuppa told him in 1974 that, "if you ever need anything from Jackie Presser, he said he'll do it for you." Fratianno also testified that he worked together with Presser to set up a union dental program whose profits were skimmed into Presser's and the Mafia's bank accounts.

After several meetings with the FBI Presser was concerned for his life, Presser went on to hire muscular bodyguards from his union business agents who accompanied him everywhere he went, which including Teamster meetings. One man was a former boxer, Tony Hughes. Despite being surrounded by guards.

By 1979, Presser was making an estimated $231,676 a year. He drew a salary as both Secretary-Treasurer of Local 507 and as an International Vice President of the union. (Note in today's money, this is equal to $809,000.)

Jackie Presser, along with his father and Teamsters President Frank Fitzsimmons, allegedly became secret informers for the federal government as early as 1972. The reason became very apparent when Bill Presser was indicted by the government on bribery, embezzlement, and a variety of other charges, which could land him in prison for the rest of his life.

Meanwhile, Jimmy Hoffa had been released from federal prison and was seeking to regain the presidency of the Teamsters. The three men gladly offered the Internal Revenue Service damning and compelling financial evidence about Hoffa and other rivals in the Teamsters Union. The Pressers agreed to freely supply their conclusive evidence if the Department of Justice would decide to drop its indictment against the senior Presser.

To add to Presser's wealth, it has been documented that he began receiving $2,500 a month salary from the FBI for providing his unique insider information. Presser was considered-to-be a "top-echelon informant." His vast knowledge of labor unions and the mob activity was marking him one of the Bureau's most prized sources of information on organized crime.

Shortly after this, Presser allegedly received permission from two local FBI agents to pad the Local 507 payrolls with fake employees. The story was he would hire people as "ghost employees" of Cleveland's Bakers Union Local 19. They would not be required to do any work at all. Nevertheless, the four men received substantial weekly paychecks. The four paychecks were then used to funnel payments to other Teamsters officials, or members of the Cleveland mob for their continual support and cooperation.

It would not be for several years until the four men were named. They were Anthony Hughes, an x-boxer and close associate of Jackie Presser. George Argie, a close friend of Mafia Boss James Licavoli. Jack Nardi., the son of Teamsters leader John Nardi. Finally, Allen Friedman, the uncle of Jackie Presser and no relation to Teamsters President Harold Friedman.

JACKIE PRESSER

(Courtesy of Cleveland Memory Project)

63

By March 1958, Jackie Presser found himself in a familiar situation. He was facing contempt of court charges by Chief Justice of Common Pleas Court Judge Samuel Silbert. The action against Presser arose when an attorney for the AFL-CIO, Hotel and Restaurant Workers Union informed Judge Silbert of a dangerous situation. Judge Silbert's concern came when he learned that Presser had violated an earlier agreement to stay away from any union affairs, after Presser had lost his job as President of Local 274 back on March 7.

In the earlier 1960s, Jackie Presser invested in another grand venture, this time it was in the Eastgate Shopping Center on the corner of Mayfield Road and Som Center Road in Mayfield Heights. Set way back about two hundred yards from Som Center Road. The Eastgate Coliseum was a large state of the art venue for the Eastside community to spend their money and leisure time. Thousands of weekly visitors enjoyed the state of the art bowling alley, billiard room, restaurant, lounge, swimming pool, and exercise room. This added to the mesquite of the large venue along with the possibility to see the man himself, Jackie, when he visited the club.

By 1964, Presser asked Common Pleas Court to dissolve the five companies involved in the sport's complex of the Eastgate Coliseum. Presser's petition to the court requested the dissolution and receivership necessary to protect the creditors and the corporation. The Coliseum continued to serve the community and stayed open until the end of the 1970s.

It has been alleged that another of Jackie Presser's personal investments in Cleveland during the early 1970s was the operation of a theater in the round located in the quiet city of Highland Heights, Ohio, known as "The Front Row Theater." Located on Wilson Mills Road, just west of Interstate 271. The marvelous music theater thrived and became the social elite location for many of the top entertainers in the country. The Front Row lasted until the early 1990s, where many high schools even held their graduation ceremonies. Some of the most influential entertainment acts in the country came to Cleveland, from comedians like George Carlin, to special speakers with high caliber appeal, such as Oprah Winfrey, and Oliver North. Music legends included The O'Jay's, Sammy Davis, Danny Thomas, Diana Ross, Air Supply, Tony Bennett, and many… many more.

The Front Row Theater became an obsession for the federal government as they investigated Presser's extensive holdings in the late 1980s. Teamster President Presser was now alleged to have a significant role in the $300,000 kickback scheme with the theater operation, which involved many of the local mobsters. The federal lawsuits stated, "Presser embezzled $300,000 from 1972 until 1976 under the disguise of two contracts between the union and Hoover-Gorin and Associates, a Las Vegas public relations firm. The lawsuit claims Presser received more than a 1 million-dollar payoff for his help in connection with the Central States Pension Fund. The 1 million dollars was seen as a shell for the transfer of ownership of the Front Row Theater.

In 1973 and making an astonishing $160,000 a year salary, the young 46- year old Jackie Presser is emerging as a dominant force in the Teamsters Union. Presser's new title and role as an Executive Assistant and personal representative of the President of the Teamsters Joint Council 41, or should we say to his father, William. Jackie's new role will be to promote the union in community projects like the United Torch, which provides kidney dialysis programs and the Cleveland Labor Management program.

Jackie soon found his roles in the union expanding. Presser is now the International General Organizer, Recording Secretary, Director of the Ohio Conference of Teamsters, and President of the Ohio "Drive" (Democratic, Republican, and International Voter Education," known as the political arm of the union.

The demise of the theater in the round known as The Front Row Theater continued, and by 1989, the city of Highland Heights city council reported the theater was behind in their city taxes by $75,000. Builder Larry Dolin President of the Front Row declined to make a statement to the press except that the town owes the theater an apology for the untrue remarks in the paper.

Although mobsters and others had accused Jackie Presser of being a government informant, the first official confirmation did not come out until August 22, 1981. In its August 31 issue, *Time* magazine reported that union president Fitzsimmons stated how William E. Presser and Jackie Presser had served as government informants, staring in the early 1970s. The reason was a simple one, to avoid prosecution on multiple federal charges. The comprehensive information was revealed in declassified reports filed by IRS agents. Presser confirmed that he, his father and Fitzsimmons had met with federal officials, but declared that there had been only one meeting back in 1972. This was later disclosed to be false.

Soon after, however, editors at the *Plain Dealer* retracted the revealing story despite protests from several reporters. The Mafia had long doubted claims that Presser was an informant, and the later retraction helped renew the mob confidence in Presser. The Mob's faith in Presser reaffirmed a year later when the Justice Department publicly ended their investigation into the alleged kickback scheme. In February 1983, Presser was re-elected to the international union's policy committee.

Just two months later, Roy Williams was convicted of conspiring to bribe U.S Senator Howard Cannon. Williams announced he would resign as Teamsters President while appealing his conviction. Williams' conviction was no surprise to Jackie Presser. Beginning in 1979, Presser, turned over the critical evidence, which showed how Williams arranged to give Senator Cannon a parcel of land as a bribe to defeat trucking deregulation legislation.

The Cleveland Press reported that a violent disagreement erupted over who Williams' successor would be. William's surprise resignation came just fifteen days before the Teamster annual convention. Presser and other candidates were reported to be, M.E. Anderson, President of the Statewide Teamsters organization in California, Joseph Morgan, President of the Teamsters Union in Florida. Don Peters, President of the large Teamsters local in Chicago, and Ray Schoessling, Secretary-Treasurer of the International Teamsters Union. *The Press* reported that Presser had formed a strong alliance with Anderson, which gave him enough votes to help him win the presidency.

The 1980s

During the 1980s, Jackie forged a strong partnership with Presidential hopeful Ronald Reagan. After the election in November, Presser served as one of President Regan's union advisors, even though he had links with organized crime. With the help of the Cleveland family, Presser enjoyed contact with the DeCavalcante crime family in New Jersey and the Patricarca family in Boston. Presser maintained his friendship with Reagan and even went against the dominant AFL-CIO when they announced they would be supporting Walter Mondale in 1983. Presser soon announced the active multi-million union members of his Teamsters were going to help and support Ronald Reagan for a second term as President of the United States.

Initially, organized crime figures did not prefer Presser. However, mob leaders Angelo Lonardo and Milton Rockman from Cleveland and New York's Anthony "Fat Tony" Salerno met with several mafia officials throughout the country to build support for a Presser presidency. The final decision was then made at a meeting in a Chicago hotel attended by Jackie Cerone, Joe Aiuppa, Lonardo, and Rockman. Presser himself informed the FBI shortly after the mob meeting that he "had the support of all the East Coast families" and that he would be the next Teamsters President.

Jackie Presser was officially elected President of the Teamsters on April 21, 1983. He pledged to reinvigorate the union, and organize new members, and end trucking deregulation. He also said he had no opinion as to whether the Teamsters should rejoin the AFL-CIO

Presser's most prominent opponent within the Teamsters had been William McCarthy, President of Joint Council 10 (which covered all Teamster locals in the New England area). In an attempt to discredit McCarthy, Presser informed the FBI that McCarthy had sought the support of organized crime in an unsuccessful effort to persuade Presser to appoint him as secretary-treasurer in 1983.

Reports later surfaced that Presser was paid more than a half-million dollars in salary in 1983 (the year of his election to the presidency). He received an additional $216,000 as Secretary-Treasurer and Executive Officer of Local 507. Then you add in a $42,500 salary as Vice Chairman of the Ohio Conference of Teamsters; and $59,500 as President of Teamsters Joint Council 41 in Ohio. By the end of 1983, Presser was making $755,474 a year. (note this is worth $1,927,988 in today's money.)

64

By April 1985, the President's Commission on Organized Crime held hearings in Chicago as they focused on the extensive involvement and cooperation between the labor unions and organized crime. During his spotted testimony in front of the committee, Presser invoked his Fifth Amendment rights a total of fifteen times.

By early September, a Federal Grand Jury was meeting in secret to review Jackie Presser's case. The driving force behind the investigation was Paul Coffey, the Deputy Chief of the Justice Departments Organized Crime Task Force. Coffey led the charge against Presser, who now lives in Washington DC. His prime focus was on Pressers, "Ghost Employees" inside the Teamsters Union Local 507.

Former Teamster President Roy Williams then testified in Kansas City federal court in regards to the Las Vegas skimming trials of nine organized crime figures. He swore he became friends with Jackie Presser, whose nickname was "Plug" since he was short and round, like a fire hydrant.

Roy Williams was facing charges of "kickbacks" for helping a few of his friends in organized crime. The investigators focused on his close ties and friendship with Nick Civella, the Kansas City crime boss, and how he became named as a trustee of the Teamsters Pension Fund in 1974 with William Presser. It was also revealed that he knew Jimmy Hoffa and crime figure Allen Dorfman, who was slain in 1982 after Hoffa was convicted of conspiring to bribe a U.S. Senator. To help save himself some jail time, Roy Williams agreed to testify against Milton Rockman of Cleveland, along with several gangsters from Kansas City, Milwaukee, and Chicago.

During their detailed investigation of Presser's relationship with the FBI, the probe found that as far back as 1968, Jackie

Presser and Anthony Hughes of Local 507 were FBI informants against associates in Organized Crime. Jack Nardi, the son of John, was also going to be a key witness and testify that he was a "Ghost Employee" and that he, along with Anthony Hughes, George Argie, and Allen Friedman. The men were assigned to keep an eye on organized crime activates in Ohio and report their findings directly to Presser. The men focused on gambling, loan-sharking, and labor racketeering. Hughes owned the popular Eastside mob hangs out with Presser's wife Carmen named the "Forge Restaurant" Inside a massive four-building high-rise apartment complex during this time located on Mayfield Road in Gates Mills, Ohio. This just so happened to be behind the Eastgate Shopping Center, where Pressers Collisum was located.

Ghost employee George Argie a childhood friend of Hughes, testified that he was paid $400 a week as a so-called business agent and did whatever Presser asked him to do.

If a conviction came to Harold Friedman, Presser would lose his reign as President of Teamsters Local 507, his position as the International Vice- President, and his position as President of the Ohio Conference of Teamsters.

It was now September 1985 in Kansas City, as Cleveland's "Underboss" Angelo Lonardo was seated inside a jam-packed courtroom once again. It was his turn to take the stand and testify in court as a Federal witness. Lonardo gave critical and concrete evidence about the Mafia families in Cleveland, Kansas City, Chicago, and of course, New York and the significant roles they all played, as they helped Jackie Presser rise to power in the Teamsters Union.

In a 48-page statement to the FBI, Lonardo described a detailed and historical account of the astonishing criminal influences the Italian Mafia organization had over the Teamsters across the country and the incredible funding they held.

Lonardo gave particular testimony on how Rockman attended a meeting in Kansas City with Nick Civella. Civella, along with his underboss Carl DeLuna who is the brother-in-law of Nick's brother, Anthony. The Kansas City men wanted Roy Williams as the next Teamsters President. However, Williams needed the support from many other Teamsters delicates throughout the country. Rockman told Civella that Cleveland controlled Jackie Presser, who was then the current Teamsters International Vice-President. Through Presser, they would manage and secure the thousands of delegate votes. Rockman suggested to Civella that if Williams is elected: he steps down from his post as the head of the Central States Pension Fund and allows Jackie Presser to become the chairman of the influential fund.

Later in his sworn testimony, Lonardo told the story of how there was another meeting in Chicago with Joseph Aiuppa "the Boss" and John Cerone "the Underboss." The two men quickly objected to Presser becoming the head of the pension fund and wanted another man in his place. Once again, Lonardo said, Rockman told the men, "not to worry, he would control Presser."

Rockman then informed Aiuppa and Cerone, that Cleveland would support Roy Williams if it came to that. The people ultimately trusted Civella, and that was good enough for them. Before their trip to Chicago, Rockman told Lonardo that he already mentioned to Presser about their plans to help elect Williams for President, and his new post would be as the head of the massive pension fund. Presser told Rockman that he could produce enough delegates from across the country to support and ensure Williams's election.

Roy Williams went on to win the election for President of the powerful Teamsters Union, which proudly held 1.9 million members. Williams failed to co-operate with the original agreement and broke his promise with the Kansas City and Cleveland families by not making Presser the head of the pension fund. Then in 1982, Williams was convicted in Chicago of conspiring to bribe a US Senator Howard Cannon; Williams was forced to step down.

According to FBI documents, Rockman told Lonardo that Roy Williams and Jackie Presser met with President Ronal Ragan back in 1983 at a Washington gathering. "When the President met Williams, he was cordial and polite to him. When the President greeted Jackie Presser, both Jackie and the first lady hugged Presser and showed a great deal of personal attachment to him. The first lady even kidded with Presser that he needed to lose some weight. Williams was offended by their friendly actions and was visibly hurt.

65

November 1985

According to the documents, the FBI has obtained since 1983, Jackie Presser, the Teamster President, was heading for the deepest trouble in his life. A Federal Grand Jury in New York is investigating specific, concise allegations of his connection with the mafia and their control of Teamster's pension fund from 1.7 million members. The FBI received additional critical wire-tapes from Angelo Lonardo operations. They openly stated that Presser had considerable help from the Genovese crime family and Anthony "Fat Tony" Salerno.

Leading the charge against organized crime in the U.S. was New York Attorney General Rudolph Giuliani. Giuliani is requesting the grand jury to take enthusiastic action against Presser. Presser soon found himself added to the criminal list consisting of Salerno and 14 other top Mafia associates in the wide-spread construction bid-rigging, extortion, gambling, multiple murders, and widespread labor racketeering. Lonardo then testified that Rockman and Salerno met in a card shop in Harlem on W 116 St. where Rockman told him, "He wanted Presser for president because it was someone they all knew."

At this time, the FBI has John (Peanuts) Tronolone, as the man heading up the Cleveland crime organization, although he was also indicted in this pending New York case.

It was in July 1986, inside a closed Cleveland Federal courtroom, Jackie Presser and his associate, former fighter Anthony Hughes waived their right to file appeals based on conflict-of-interest claims of federal racketeering and embezzling charges. The allegations of embezzlement are stemming from the payroll padding scheme at the Teamsters Local 507. A third man accused in this acclaimed plot is Allen Freidman from the Bakers Union Local 19.

Over the years, Jackie Presser gave the FBI valuable information on over 69 organized crime figures across the country involving eleven states. If you can believe the FBI, who claims Jackie Presser freely gave them this information based on his patriotism. Some critics of the government say, "it was because he exchanged viable information for their support in getting rid of his enemies and helping his rise up the mighty Teamster ladder."

Tony Hughes, a ghost employee in Pressers Baker's Union Local 19, has hired attorneys Michael and his brother John Climaco. The brothers are general counsel for the local Teamsters. It is unknown the exact date, sometime in the late 1980s, when Tony Hughes turned state's evidence and became an FBI informant. Later in 1989, Tony Hughes and Allen Friedman, both officials in Teamsters Local 507, were found guilty on charges of racketeering and embezzling over $700,000 of union funds.

By the end of 1986, the President's Commission on Organized Crime claimed Jackie Presser admitted that the Front Row Theaters made him a cool million dollars. The lawsuit also alleged Presser offered to fix trials for his friends, and former Teamster President Roy Williams, for $10,000. FBI Director William Webster quickly ordered an extensive internal investigation into this alleged FBI misconduct with the Teamster boss.

1987

A man who had testified back in 1981 came forward to tell his spellbinding story on what he knows about the racketeering charges against Jackie Presser. James Fratianno decisively explained how Presser re-laid to him back in 1977 how he had a close relationship with James Licavoli. Prosecutor Alan Cohen asked Fratianno, "What was the real relationship between La Cosa Nostra and the Teamsters?" Fratianno replied, "It is easy. They run the Teamsters. Presser was handled by Licavoli and Milton Rockman." Rockman is a defendant in this trial, along with Jackie Presser. These charges include fixing the Teamsters elections of Jackie Presser and Roy Williams in the early 1980s.

March 1988

Presser's life was marked by contradictions. Earlier back in 1980, he was the only union leader to endorse Ronald Reagan for President. Now, the mob was out to get him. Presser fooled them all, as he died of a heart attack on July 9, 1988, before the mob and cancer could kill him.

Before Jackie died, he provided enough damaging information to indict over 69-people in 11 different cities in his secret role as a government informant.

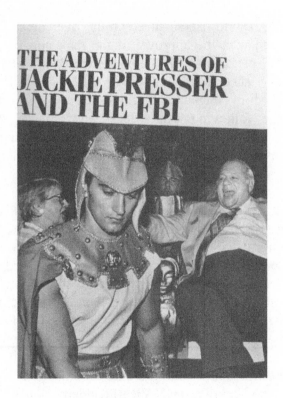

JACKIE PRESSER WAS OFFICIALLY ELECTED PRESIDENT
OF THE TEAMSTERS ON APRIL 21, 1983, LAS VEGAS

(Courtesy of Cleveland Magazine)

66

THE CORRUPTION OF

AMERICAN UNIONS

Throughout many industries during the post-war period of the countries acclaimed growth, union leaders have boosted their political power and helped the elected leadership of the unions to participate in many power struggles

In 1946, David Beck successfully overcame Dan Tobin's opposition and won the approval of the rank and file. Beck then won the 1947 election to fill the new Vice President position. In 1947, Beck successfully opposed the new Tobin-backed membership dues increase to fund several new organization projects. The following year, Beck was able to demand the removal of the editor of *International Teamster* magazine and install his own man in the job. This action helped him to gain additional power and support.

Then in 1948, in a change of heart, Beck allied himself with his long-time rival Jimmy Hoffa and seized control of the union. Beck had more than enough support from his new-found allies Hoffa and other top members of the executive board, soon force Tobin to back down. Five months later, Beck won a critical battle and approval of a plan to dissolve the union's current four main divisions. His new format consisted of a sixteen-unit organization based on the major job categories in the union's membership. By 1949, the union's membership topped the one-million-member mark. To the little surprise to the union members, Dave Beck was elected as the International Vice-President in 1950 and was increasingly influential in the international union.

On September 4, 1952, Tobin announced he would step down as President of the Teamsters at the end of his term. At the union's 1952 convention, Dave Beck was elected General President and pushed through some changes intended to make it harder for him to be challenged in the future.

THE INFLUENCE OF ORGANIZED CRIME

On August 13, 1953, Dave Beck was elected to the Executive Council of the American Federation of Labor (AFL) However, he soon found himself in a political battle with the current AFL Union President, George Meany. Rumors ran through the union that Beck was corrupt and should not be in this position. Beck became the first Teamster President to negotiate a national master contract.

In 1956, Jimmy Hoffa began challenging Beck on various union decisions and policies to unseat him as General President in the regularly scheduled elections in 1957.

Throughout the turbulent 1950s, organized crime dominated the agendas of the Teamsters. The Teamsters suffered from massive corruption scandals. Their rich history began back in 1929, as the Teamsters and unions in Chicago. Evidence of widespread corruption within the Teamsters began emerging shortly after Tobin was paid to retire. Soon, a major battle broke out within the Teamsters as unrest of the members led to inquiries by the U.S. Department of Justice.

Senator John McClellan, the chairman, hired Robert Kennedy as the subcommittee's chief counsel and principal investigator. Together, the Select Committee exposed widespread corruption in the Teamsters union. Dave Beck fled the country for a month to avoid its subpoenas. Dave Beck appeared before the select committee for the first time on March 25, 1957, and invoked his Fifth Amendment rights 117 times during his intense questioning. The McClellan Committee soon turned its focus on Hoffa and other Teamsters officials and presented significant testimony and evidence of widespread corruption in Hoffa-controlled Teamster units.

David Beck died at the age of 99 in 1993.

DAVE BECK ON THE RIGHT WITH HIS ATTORNEY
ANSWERING ROBERT KENNEDYS QUESTIONS

(Courtesy of Cleveland State Memory Project)

67

THE CLEVELAND UNIONS

In January 1931, the Cleveland Athletic Club sponsored the upcoming Golden Gloves event against a rival team from Detroit. Featured in the nine-bout ticket was Cleveland's own champion Nunzio Louis "Babe" Triscaro. A 112 pounder has dominated his opponents over the last few years and considered to be an up and coming boxing star, and possibly the Flyweight champ. Triscaro won his bout that evening. "Babe" found his fame and, of course, his fortune in the National Teamsters Union. Triscaro; was labeled a "strikebreaker" by many of the people who feared him. Triscaro suddenly died of a heart attack while in his Presidential office at the Excavating and Building Materials Drivers Local 436 in late August 1974.

According to the city records, the unions in Cleveland began in 1919, and then with the second birth of the Bakers Union in Cleveland, which started around December of 1933 with only 49 members. Later in 1938, the Master Bakers of Cleveland Union Local 19 became the most powerful union in Cleveland's history with Arthur Wethered as President and Harvey Friedman as Secretary and Business Agent. By 1939 the Bakers Union became a part of the National A.F. of L. Council with membership listed at 1,590.

1947

It was on May 31, the House Labor Committee announced it has accumulated over 250 cases involving physical abuse, death threats, and racketeering from Union members. The dangerous situation across the country has become overwhelming. Chairman Hartley from New Jersey said, "We intend to get into every phase of this massive contempt operation and consider this as a severe matter. Chairman Harley plans on taking his investigation into every major city in America if necessary

Then in June 1949, Harvey Friedman was embarrassed when his son Harold was arrested, along with his brother Harry and cousin Allen Friedman. The trio was charged with stealing a 1948 Pontiac sedan from the town of New Castle, PA.

By December 1949, Judge Emerich Freed placed a bail of $33,000 for the 37-year old Harry E Freidman, (equal to $352,643 in today's money.) Then a $50,000 bail for 26-year old Harold Friedman and a whopping $90,000 bond was set for the 27-year old Allen Friedman, believed to be the ringleader of over fourteen-auto thefts.

In January 1950, it only took eighteen minutes for Judge Freed to find Harold Friedman guilty on just one charge in the auto theft charges. He was given only a two-year sentence. At this time, Harold had a respectable job as the Financial Secretary for the Baker and Confectionery Workers Union Local 19.

The FBI proudly announced they smashed a seven-state car theft ring that operated inside Cleveland. Harold Friedman testified he did not know anything about stealing a car on that evening. Friedman claims he was under the understanding that he was just going to New Castle with the other men for a ride. During the trial, one of the other men testified they had a large set of 64 car keys. This keychain helped to unlock all makes of cars manufactured by the General Motors Corporation from 1943 to 1949. Allen Friedman is looking to serve 1-5 years in prison for his four counts of auto theft.

1953

Congressman Clare Hoffman announced he has undercovered damaging evidence of labor racketeering and believes it starts in eight major cities across the country. Hoffman promises a completed investigation and indictment against several AFL officials of the Teamster Union. The men could be charged with extortion, embezzling, and taking illegal gifts. Hoffman enthusiastically declares, "The men in the rackets are collecting millions of dollars, and not only from private businesses but from honest members of the unions. .."

1954

George Bender from Cleveland explains how new legislation is needed to bring this corruption to a stop. Bender continued and stated, "It is evident to me from the evidence uncovered that many businessmen felt compelled to pay a substantial sum of money to prevent construction setbacks."

Bender declares he has specific links between "Ohio, New York, and New Jersey racketeers and the Cleveland operators of the vending machine business throughout Ohio where John Scalish and Tony Milano operate and control." This even includes unsolved bombings and several other acts of violence, which we know to be directly linked to union-management relationships. Further testimony has implications of several notorious "Mafia figures" in control of the labor organizations and specific violence.

It was now late August as Congressman George Bender of Ohio has threatened Ohio President William Presser with a contempt charge. William Presser has finally agreed to allow some union records released to the House subcommittee investigating alleged labor racketeering in Cleveland and throughout Ohio. These papers will be from the Vending Machine Service Employees Union Local 410 in which Presser is listed as President and Chief Officer.

Bender is convinced these records will show without a doubt the increased levels of illegal irregularities and provide concrete proof that the Cleveland and Ohio crime syndicate is controlling the wealth inside these unions' funds.

Other men listed are Milton Rockman, who has agreed to provide his records of the Buckeye Cigarette Service. Another man listed in Bender's study in the improper action of the President of the Excavation Drivers, Louis "Babe" Triscaro, who has denied any interaction with racketeers.

William Presser has denied any involvement and has claimed even the FBI and The Interstate Commerce Committee has found nothing of interest and no interaction into these funds.

Just before Labor Day, the committee met once again as Congressman Clare Hoffman confirms. Racketeering by local union members has some elements of reaching an "Epidemic proportion" in Ohio. Many of the victims haven't the nerve or heart to come straight-out to testify.

It was now the end of September as George Bender opens up his fourth-day of sub-committees hearings. Desperate appeals for help go unheard, they are stuck paying ridicules high wages, or they may receive unwanted "picketing by the union, and continual threats of personal violence, and worst of all, the destruction of their property or equipment."

Witness after witness went on and claimed that two men have gained the most from receiving the money. They named Joseph Triscaro Jr. and Sebastian Morabito; both are officials in the Shaker Trucking Company. Triscaro is the brother of AFL Teamsters Joint Council Boss Babe Triscaro.

68

The American Federation of Labor, AFL, was holding its yearly convention in Los Angles to resolve more concerns of corruption. They are looking to ask the Federal Government to help to clean up the mess from several mishandled union funds across the country. George Meany, the National President, requested the delegation to conduct a "housecleaning of sorts," on their own and stated that Cleveland is an excellent place to start.

Continuing the ongoing investigation in the racket probe into the Teamster funds, Chairmen George Bender announced five surprise subpoenas were issued by the subcommittee. One being for Inspector James McArthur, the head of Cleveland Detectives. Other listed on the warrants were William Finegan, the Secretary of the Cleveland Federation of Labor, Anthony Civetta, the Chairman of the Taxi Drivers' Union, and Detective James Foley, Chief Inspector of the Cleveland police department labor unit.

A photograph merchant Sam Abrams who is the President of the Ohio Advertising Agency. Abrams stated he has personally paid Presser $650 a month on behalf of his association for a half-page ad, which actually came out to be only a little 2x3 inch ad, in the union's monthly four-page pamphlet with circulation on a mere 1,000 copies. All Presser could say was that he did sign the checks, but his secretary deposited them into the union account, not his.

While testifying at one of Bender and Hoffman's investigation, William Presser skirted many unkindly questions. Stating his Fifth Amendment rights several times on every issue dealing with his personal net worth of over $223,000 in 1946. Presser also denied answering the question about the eight companies he may be a part-owner in or a silent partner, dealing with the jukebox factories and distributors.

William Presser's presence and involvement with John Scalish and his Buckeye Cigarette Service Company; was nonexistent until after 1951 when Presser helped them to grow to over a chain of

400 cigarette vending locations. Partners with Scalish and Presser included Frank Embressia, Louis Carriere, Milton Rockman, and Sam Scalish, John's brother. According to inconsistent testimony, Frank Embressia from Buckeye purchased over 200 vending machines from Louis Golden and his failing Ace Cigarette Service. Then it was Buckeye who took over an additional 140 vending machines, which came from an unknown business at several locations in Lake County.

Committee member Congressman Clare Hoffman added, "The court records have shown that William Presser rose up the ladder from an ordinary hoodlum status to become the "Topman" in Ohio and the Teamsters Union. "His pattern is clear, you cannot own a vending machine in Ohio unless you buy it with Presser and his group of happy go lucky partners."

Bender declared, "This is not a headline investigation, we have barely scratched the surface, and who knows how far the long arms of extortions, blatant intimidation, and unlawful mishandling of the massive welfare union funds will go, which have extorted money from law-abiding citizens." Bender continued, "Cleveland is at the center of this enormous conspiracy, and it goes across our country. In my opinion, there has not been a sincere effort made by the Cleveland Police to solve the over forty mysterious-bombings in the construction industry as more racketeering information is discovered through our in-depth investigation."

Bender and Hoffman asked William Presser, "what happened to the $75,000 you received back in 1951 from the treasury fund of a union you headed?" The investigation showed the funds were never transferred directly into Pressers personal account, nor was it transferred into a union account either

During their intense research, Bender found an active link between William Presser and the Bank of Ohio, where Presser had mysterious loans totaling over $500,000. Bender stated some of these loans are personal loans, and not secured and was not repaid.

1957

The Bakery and Confectionery Workers Local 19 in Cleveland found itself expelled by the national AFL-CIO under extreme suspensions of multiple corruption charges. This included Harvey Friedman and his team of tuff and rugged business agents.

1959

By April, it was learned that the Bakers Union Local 19 invested in a secure pension fund for the over 2,300 members. This secure retirement was listed to be $24,000 per year for their President, Harvey Freidman. However, the traditional pension for a single member was set at only $6,000 per year.

1935 HARVEY FRIEDMAN ON THE LEFT WITH ED MURPHY

(Courtesy of Cleveland State University Memory Project)

John DeConcini is the Executive Vice-President with the rival American Bakery and the Confectionery Union. He has charged that Freidman continues to operate with his "hand-picked council" to assist him behind the scenes. Harvey Friedman has recently hired his son Harold to become a union employee where he is paid a salary of $250 a week and a yearly bonus of $5,000. DeConcini claims Friedman used his union stewards to do landscaping at his home at 4510 Groveland Road in Cleveland Heights. Also, the stewards and business agents were compelled to contribute $15 to $25 each into a fund to help defray costs of installing a water sprinkler system in his yard, at the expense of $2,200. Friedman continues to go on expensive vacations for months at a time, with union funds. Two union officers obtained a personal loan from the union funds, one was for $5,000, and the other was for $10,000, both at a meager 3% interest rate. Then the union dues were raised from $5 to $7 a month to help maintain the positive balance for the future years to come. To add insult to injury, the union members were all forced to buy what was being called "labor stock" for $35 per share to help offset the cost of the construction of a new office building on East 19th Street. Then when the union member leaves the union or retirer, he cannot keep the stock he has paid for and is responsible for returning the stock back to the union members with little or no compensation.

William Presser is a streetwise man who knows how to control a situation and change the future for his own benefit. It all started with his earlier marriage to Faye Friedman, sister of Harry. This brought about a type of fusion of complementary forces, Pressers Teamster Union and Friedman's unstoppable Bakers Union in Cleveland.

1960

The Bakery Workers Union Local 19 was on the front pages of the local papers once again. This time, four union officials earned a massive salary of $82,968, which relates to half of the total amount of the annual membership dues. President Harvey Friedman received $30,908 in salary and expenses (equal to $266,409 in today's money). His son Harold received a sum of $26,328. This information came directly from Stanley Sincavage of the ABCW, the American Bakery Confectionery Workers Local 219.

The Bakery Workers union was a part of the National AFL-CIO, which has recently joined forces with the local AFL-CIO. With the help of the National Labor Relations Board, a vote was called for on August 7. The membership must make a choice on which union the Cleveland bakers preferred to be with.

1961

Local 219 of the ABCW Union stays focused on the illegal actions against Bakery Local 19. Local 219 maintains that Local 19 does not have any bargaining rights with their union members. ABCW is accusing Local 19 of having tuff looking, bodybuilding business agents with coercing union members, and using brute force and intimidation to the smaller shop employees to sign new contracts with Local 19 instead of their other union Local 219.

1962

A brand-new day for the Bakers Union Local 19 in Cleveland. They have separated from the once-dominant AFL-CIO. Local 19 announced in late January that they have enough union members and votes to make a positive change for the betterment of their Bakery union. They intend to join forces with the mighty National Teamsters Union. The independent union meeting was set for Monday, January 22, at the Hotel Sheraton in downtown Cleveland. Expected to address the audience at the convention, is Teamster President James Hoffa.

It was no surprise to anyone in Cleveland when the Bakers Union Local 19 salaries for last year was released. The father and son team of Harvey and Harold Friedman both received $62,868 in wages or a 41% share of the union membership dues for the year.

1966

By November, the Bakers Union Local 19 will become a part of a new organization. Harold Friedman, now 43-years old, was elected as the president of the new local. The goal of this new union is to organize where there is no other union present. William Presser, the current President of the Teamsters Joint Council 41, has promised they will be no raiding of the plants. Jackie Presser was named as the secretary-treasurer of the new local.

1968

The controversy and corruption scandal inside the multiple union organizations continued. Jackie Presser has found himself working with the Bakers Union Local 19. Harvey Freidman is the Local President, and Allen Friedman is the new Teamsters Joint Council Local 41, Secretary and Treasurer. Later both the Bakers Local 19 and the Teamsters Local 507 each created a secret severance fund account within one week of one another. This fund was designated for specific unknown officers.

69

By the end of 1971, the combined unions in Cleveland had a surplus of over $100,000 in their severance fund for individual beneficiaries. In 1972 the $100,000 severance funds were added to the total compensation to only three men. Jackie Presser from the Teamsters Local 507, Harold Friedman, and his brother Allen.

By November, the 1972 salaries were released to the citizens across the country. Cleveland William Presser had received a total of $143,921 in wages and expenses from five union positions and an additional $50,000 for a discontinued severance from the Teamsters Local 507. Jackie Presser earned a total of over $192,700 from six different union positions. Harold Friedman, who is the father-in-law of Jackie, received a total of $174,970 for his job in Local 19 and Teamsters Local 41. Harvey Freidman received only $48,900 as President on Local 19.

Other notable salaries for the year included Louis "Babe" Triscaro, who earned $58,332 for his three union positions. John Felice Sr. received a total of $45,864. His son, John Jr, received a total of $48,345 for his many union positions. Then, Anthony Liberatore, who served as a Business Representative for the Labors International Union Local 860, earned $29,711. John Nardi Teamsters Joint Council 41 and Business agent for Local 507 received a total of $58,167. John's Brother Nick served as Secretary-Treasurer of Teamsters Maintenance Local 416 earned $24,455.

(**Note**, in 1972 the average family income across the country was a mere $14,450 a year)

1976

To add controversy to the Presser's and Freidman's yearly earnings, additional facts have come to light in regards to William Pressers. In a surprise move, it was revealed by the local newspapers that last year, he purchased an expensive birthday gift for his devoted wife, Faye. The modest contribution was a brand-new Rolls Royce; valued to cost $65,000 (in today's money it would be worth $290,133.) As unbelievable as it sounds, William Presser was making about $145,000 a year from his seven union positions that year. Son Jackie made $222,000 from his five union jobs as Harold Freidman said to have earned $340,000 last year for his role as the President of the Teamsters Local 507 and the Bakers Local 19. These three men represent the highest-paid union officials in the country.

1978

From the *Cleveland, Plain Dealer*, it was now September as Jackie Presser sat down with a reporter and discussed his position as the International Teamsters Vice-president. Both Jackie and his father William are both perceived to be the most potent Teamster official in Ohio, and possibly the Midwest.

During the extensive interview, Presser discussed the depth of bitterness and frustration with some newspaper reporters and the government. During a question and answer section, Presser was asked if a union leader can be overpaid. His reply was, "No, not at all, I don't think that has any bearing on anything. In this country, a man is entitled to make as much money as he can possibly make honestly."

How much did you make last year, was the next question?

"I made $222,000 last year," the proud Presser said.

If that is true, Mr. Presser, while did your wife Carmen mentioned in your current divorce case that you make $350,000 per year?

Presser answered, "What business is it of yours or anyone else on how much money I make?"

At the close of the interview, Presser stated, "I'm not a gangster, I'm not a hoodlum, and I'm not a crook."

70
POLITICIANS, THE MAFIA AND THE UNION

The following is the original preliminary report on the status of organized crime influence in the labor unions in the United States. At least four international unions are dominated by people who either have strong ties to or are vested members of the organized crime syndicate. A majority of the locals in most major cities of the United States are a part of the International Brotherhood of Teamsters (IBT), Hotel and Restaurant Employees Union (HRE), Laborers International Union of North America (Laborers), and International Longshoreman's Association (ILA). Many executives have stopped the practice of requesting help from any of the law enforcement authorities. So, what do they do? They pay the high price required to obtain labor peace.

Teamster Central States Pension Fund. No attempt was ever made to analyze the organized crime influence in the fund. The fund has been the subject of several confused, political investigations in the past years by the Department of Labor and the Internal Revenue Service. There is a ridiculous amount of incredible information, which was uncovered by those two agencies.

The Hotel and Restaurant Employees Union represents the International Brotherhood of Teamsters. In the Teamsters, corruption and organized crime influence are a straightforward result of the extensive infiltration of the local unions. The HRE, on the other hand, was infiltrated starting from the top. This occurred as a consequence of the power wielded by the Chicago area locals and the joint executive board led by Joey Aiuppa.

Jackie Presser, resigned when the DOJ began an investigation of the International Union. Jack Lubin, Vice President, is convicted arsonist. He is currently a subject of a Strike Force investigation involving a massive fraud on the Northern Ohio Bank.

UNION INFLUENCE

The International Longshoreman's Association has a long history of organized crime influence since the 1950s.

INTERNATIONAL TEAMSTERS

The International Brotherhood of Teamsters has long been dominated and captivated by several organized crime families. One factor appears quite evident by the growth of the Teamsters over the past decades. Although there have been numerous prosecutions of high-ranking Teamsters officials, including Roy Williams, William and Jackie Presser, Allen Dorfman, and Jimmy Hoffa. The domination of the union by organized crime has gone unchecked.

Part of the problem of dealing with organized crime is the infiltration of the Teamsters. Although the files of the Justice Department have ample examples of specific transactions involving Teamster officials. An overall review of the organized crime influence inside the union, mainly because of a lack of confidential informants and their particular intelligence.

Teamster Joint Council 41 IBT Cleveland - William Presser was the President, and Jackie Presser was the Vice President. John J. Felice, Jr., was their recording secretary. Also, an employee of Joint Council 41 before his death was John Nardi.

Locals, 73, 293, and 796 IBT Cleveland - All three of these Teamster Locals were controlled by John J. Felice, Jr. In Locals 73 and 293, he was the Secretary-Treasurer, while his father was President. In Local 796, he was also the Secretary-Treasurer with Jackie Presser being the President.

Local 416 - IBT Cleveland - This local has long been a haven for members of the Cleveland LCN. John Nardi was the president of the Italian American Brotherhood Club in Little Italy. A former official President, Pat Catalano from Local 416, was murdered back in 1965. His new Cadillac was found in Stark County.

71

PART VII

THE POWERFUL NARCOTIC BUSINESS

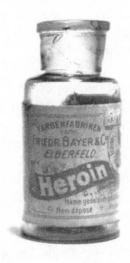

"Wine is at the head of all medicines; where wine is lacking, drugs are necessary."

Quoted in Burton Stevenson

The anti-drug faction of the old-time Sicilian Mafia firmly believed; their organization did not need or want narcotics trade in their families and would not allow any person to deal with drugs. Even in the movie, the "Godfather," the incredible profits, which drugs brought into the family was not worth the unwanted risks and pressure from law enforcement, the political, and the media attention it would bring. However, Sonny found it intoxicating as it distorted his judgment.

You cannot really speak about organized crime, whether it is in Cleveland or anywhere else around the world. You must always include drugs and narcotics of all kinds. The narcotic business is nothing like any other type of crime. It continues to get stronger and stronger with more and more people dying of an overdose than ever before.

The term **narcotic** is Greek in nature and referred initially medically to any compound with any sleep-inducing properties. When used in a legal context in the U.S., a *narcotic* drug is one that is prohibited or one that is used in violation of strict and current governmental regulation.

The **Federal Bureau of Narcotics** (or **FBN**) was an agency of the US Department of the Treasury, established on June 14, 1930, consolidating the agencies of the Federal Narcotics Control Board and the Narcotic Division. These older, outdated bureaus assigned to the Harrison Narcotics Tax Act of 1914. This act was to provide for the registration and to impose an individual tax on all persons who produce, import, manufacture, deal in, dispense, sell, distribute, or give away the drug of choice- opium.

The modern-day DEA or Drug Enforcement Agency was created in 1968, and submitted to Congress for their approval on, February 7, 1968. It came into force on April 8, 1968. In 1971 the whole DEA was composed of a meager 1,500 agents and had a budget of some $43 million.

In 1953 Detective Lieutenant Howard Hutchings, head of the police narcotics squad, stated, the junkies in Cleveland were moaning. The price of heroin has jumped up over the last six months and now costs an estimated $50 more an ounce for the bulk powder. They were paying only $20.

By 1954, a reliable source informed the Cleveland Police that an estimated narcotics racket generates $8,300,000 and affects well over 2,000 people who are known users, distributors, or salesmen. The narcotics squad currently consists of a meager twenty-five officers.

72

RECOMMENDATIONS BY THE DOJ

The following is a condensed list of actual recommendations.

1. Information concerning Labor Racketeering was not analyzed by the Department of Justice. There is no unit to monitors Labor Racketeering. It should be a function of the Organized Crime and Racketeering Section to receive copies of all investigative reports, and surveys concerning labor racketeering.

2. There are two agencies, which have jurisdiction over Labor Racketeering, yet they have no systematic approach to collecting information and analyzing it. Sadly, at this time, most of the Department of Labor's information submitted was ten years old.

3. New methods must be explored and developed for investigating labor racketeering cases. Investigation of these matters requires a thorough knowledge of the industry involved and must include the collective bargaining agreements, the trade skills, and the history of the unions involved.

4. New methods of intelligent legal action must be expanded!. Civil remedies under the RICO statute and other laws should be studied at great lengths, and then instituted? If such action could be taken to tie up their financial assets.

In Cleveland, the drug and narcotics trafficking increased tenfold after the unexpected death in 1976 of the John Scalish. At this time, the men who had worked alongside Scalish took a measurable advantage of his death and the alarming situation as a war started, which would become the demise of the Cleveland family.

Some of the many men who looked to the profits of the narcotics included James Licavoli and Angelo Lonardo. Others included Carmen Zagaria, Kevin McTaggart, Joe Gallo, Tommy Sinito, and Russell Pappalardo; brothers Fredrick and Hartmut Graewe, with many more opportunities to engulf the city with plenty of drugs to feed the needy men and women of Ohio.

KEVIN MCTAGGART

(Courtesy of Cleveland Memory Project)

During the late 1970s and 1980s, the new technology of pagers gave the dealers an edge. The salesman is not just in one rural neighborhood, or another, they now may live right next door to your home, school, and job and work on getting your children or even you fixed on drugs. Heroin, Opioids, and other narcotics are still killing many men, women, and children each and every day. Somehow, this terrible and overwhelming crisis must be stopped for the betterment of our future generations.

73

PART VIII

THE CLEVELAND MAFIA;

AFTER JOHN SCALISH

THE DEMISE AND MAYHEM CONTINUE!

The ambitious feud between James Licavoli and John Nardi for the control of the Cleveland underworld stated just days after the unexpected death of John Scalish.

Both men felt they were strong enough, tuff enough, and had enough political and criminal contacts. Most importantly, they actively believed they deserved the right to lead the Cleveland family.

In the aftermath of Greene's murder, the FBI intercepted some conversations through its Title III hidden-microphone surveillance at Licavoli's Little Italy home. Licavoli's right-hand man John Calandra and an unidentified male were complaining about Nardi, Frank Embrescia, and Frank Brancato and how they allowed Greene to become so powerful.

At this point in the trial James Licavoli, Angelo Lonardo, and Thomas Sinito had been acquitted of the murder along with charges of arson and engaging in organized crime. The jury convicted Ronald Carabbia and Pasquale Cisternino of aggravated murder, for which they could receive the death penalty.

Charles Carabbia, the older brother of Ronald, said, "It is a shame, we had good defense lawyers and witnesses of great character from Youngstown, which informed the jury where Ronnie was that day." The jury chose to take the words of Ray Ferritto and Louie Aratari that my brother was in the back seat of the getaway car."

One comment by an assistant prosecutor, Camren Marino, stated, "I simply do not understand it, what the jury has done is convicted the soldiers and let the two generals free."

James Willis, attorney for Licavoli, stated, "Organized Crime is a myth that exists only in the minds of the FBI and local police officials."

A sixth man indicted was Alfred Calabrese. The charges against him were dismissed by Judge James Carroll, only after the prosecution rested its case. The judge ruled the state did not prove its case against him.

Despite his shady ventures, another powerful man immersed, Anthony Liberatore craved respectability and often insisted, at lectures he gave on penal reform, that he had paid his debt to society and was now a useful citizen. Back in 1975, Cleveland Mayor Ralph Perk appointed Liberatore to the board of the newly created Regional Sewer District. (Liberatore was only one of the many organized crime figures who would surface at City Hall during the Ralph Perk administration.)

However, Liberatore's outward respectability was a cover to take over the mob leadership. Liberatore maneuvered to strengthen his influence in the unions and high underworld circles with the help of Tommy Lanci. Lanci, 35, operated a travel agency (specializing in gambling junkets to Atlantic City and Las Vegas) and a part-time salesman at Diamond's Men's stores. Lanci and Liberatore were inseparable, rarely making the slightest move without consulting each other. Their role in the Greene murder, however, would not surface until long after those initially arrested in the plot were jailed and awaiting trial. It was only when ex-convicts Louis (Little Tony) Aratari and Ronald (Vic Guiles) Guilliani were arrested that the spellbinding story that linked Lanci and Liberatore to Greene's demise.

Aratari, a Canton resident who looks and talks like the "Happy Days" Fonz, has served nine years for armed robbery. Aratari claimed that Liberatore wanted to help Licavoli with his problem. This would help him solidly with the mob. Aratari, then brought in his friend Vic Guiles, to help. Liberatore offered him $5,000 for the job and put them in touch with John Calandra. According to Aratari, Calandra introduced the two accomplices to Ray Ferritto, Carabbia, and Cisternino at a Greene murder planning session.

Also, a day before Greene's dental appointment at Brainard Place in Lyndhurst, Aratari said, Lanci, sent him to Kenneth Ciarcia, a salesman at Crossroads Lincoln-Mercury in Independence, to pick up a safe car for the job.

Lanci and Ciarcia both claimed they were not involved. Aratari maintained that Lanci, Ciarcia, and even Liberatore knew that he and Guiles were to serve as a backup team for Ferritto and Carabbia, with clear instructions to shoot Greene if bombing him was not feasible. They showed up at Brainard Place with a .357 magnum and 30-06 scoped rifle.

74

JOHN "PEANUTS" TRONOLONE

Other men who had a significant impact and helped to bring down
the Cleveland Mafia.

John Tronolone was born on December 12, 1910, in Buffalo, New
York. As a young man, he found a job passing out peanuts to the
children who would come into his father's laundry. The nickname
"Peanuts" stuck with him as did the knowledge of working with
people as it served him well when it came to working as a dealer in
the *Jungle Inn* casino and as a loan shark.

At fifteen, he was arrested for gambling, and by 21, he had
four arrests under his belt for gambling, and a first-degree burglary
charge, he served only nine months and his only stretch in prison.

By the age of 32, Tronolone was working with Joe (the wolf) DiCarlo in Buffalo. DiCarlo and Buffalo's "Boss" Maggadino were in the middle of a feud, so with the help of Al Polizzi from the Cleveland family, and to keep the peace, both DiCarlo and Tronolone went to work in the Youngstown area. It did not take long before the two men became enemies. Tronolone felt DiCarlo was holding back much of the profits for himself. Tronolone decided to move to Miami in the late 1940s. Miami was an "*Open Territory*" since almost 24 mob families had a member of their family working the sunshine state and raising profits for the hometown boys.

It only took a few years, and by 1949, Tronolone was arrested for running a gambling house. He paid the meager $500 fine and was free.

The story goes that by the 1960s, Tronolone made friends with New York's crime boss Anthony Salerno and sponsored a sports betting operation throughout most of South Florida. Tronolone continued to work his games and sports betting activity without fanfare for many years.

In 1975, he was convicted of operating a bookmaking joint that netted him an estimated income of over $1 million. He was sentenced to two years in jail and a minor penalty of $2,000.

In 1981, Tronolone and 14 others were indicted on federal racketeering charges, including 29 counts of conspiracy, murder, gambling, and labor racketeering.

John took over the role of Cleveland "Boss" in 1983 when he was 73- years old. Some mob guys thought he was only selected because there was no one else to fill the position. He kept a low profile living a comfortable life in Miami, Florida. His income continued to come from loan sharking and bookmaking on the beautiful Florida beaches. He organized mini-vacations called Junkets to Las Vegas for the older retired citizens like himself.

With Lonardo and Licavoli in prison, Cleveland was left without an influential figurehead to keep the Cleveland family alive. Many of the mob guys in Cleveland, felt he was a just crazy old man. During his reign as "Boss," John did not live or even visit Cleveland. The once proud and vigorous crime family was in ruins and considered to be deplorable and a joke among the other families across the country.

Tronolone was known as a violent and reckless, yet reliable man who did not attend high school. He did not have a keen business mind. At this time, in Cleveland, there were only two "Made Members" of the Cleveland Crime Family, Russell Pappalardo, and Joe Iacobucci. Sadly both had a reputation for being a soldier or worker and not made of "Boss" material.

By the late 1980s, Tronolone had a severe problem. He became involved with a dealer of stolen diamonds named Jack Roper. Roper allegedly smuggled them into American from Europe, they were said to be flawless and colorless and worth over $1.7 million.

The incredible story goes, Roper, was an undercover police officer and was to hand over to Tronolone $15,000 in diamonds to pay off gambling debt of one of his men. Both men agreed on a place to meet. As Roper pulled up, he got out of his car and walked over to Tronolone car, dropped the diamonds in, which were in a clear plastic bag onto the passenger's seat. Without any warning, several men came up to the vehicle and pulled Tronolone out, handcuffed him, and told him he was under arrest. Roper was actually Lt. Dave Green, a Boward County Deputy.

The lazy old man, the so-called "Boss" of the Cleveland Family, did not have any underlings he trusted to do this minor job for him. He was now facing serious jail time for receiving stolen property. Cleveland once again became the laughing stock of the Mafia across the country.

Tronolone died on May 29, 1991, just before he was to start his nine-year prison term.

RUSSELL PAPPALARDO

JOSEPH IACOBUCCI

Iacobacci started off as a bold and trusted member of a Collinwood burglary crew and became a made member of the Cleveland family in 1976. His previous rap sheet consists of narcotics and gambling convictions. Joe managed to avoid much of the trials and conviction of the late '70s and '80s following the war with and murder of Danny Greene.

Despite a brief federal prison stint in the late 1990s, when he was sentenced to thirty months for defrauding New Jersey banks out of an estimated 3 Million dollars, Iacobacci steadily rebuilt the Cleveland Mob, reportedly with the help of the Chicago Outfit. Since 1990, when no known Cleveland Mafia members were on the streets, there are believed to be 10 to 15 made members today, with many more associates.

In addition to its Chicago links, the Cleveland Mob has documented activities in Rochester, NY, Warren/Youngstown OH, Pittsburgh PA, and, of course, in Greater Cleveland, generating up to $30 million in illegal profits annually.

In 2005, Iacobacci reportedly left the Cleveland underworld and retired to Pittsburgh, Pennsylvania.

Russell Pappalardo is the alleged current leader of the Cleveland mob.

75

ANTHONY LIBERATORE

(Courtesy of the Cleveland Police Museum)

Born in 1919 to Chester and Catherine, who came to America seeking a better life than what they lived in Naples, Italy. Anthony found his true-calling in crime at the early age of 10, when he was caught stealing a spool of fishing wire from a local hardware store along with .34 cents from a local newsboy, who was only trying to sell a few papers on a corner street.

By 1937 Anthony was married with a young child and stole a Lincoln all within a few months. Two police officers identified Liberatore and his friend, Carl Ferritto. When the police finally caught up with the young criminals, a gun battle began. When the gunfire stopped, both police officers were dead. Liberatore and Ferritto were soon arrested, and their trial ended with being guilty in the murder of two police officers. Ferritto was sentenced to be executed in 1938 for being the man who had fired the fatal shots. Liberatore was given a lighter sentence of life in prison.

In 1957, Liberatore was released by Lt. Governor John Brown, who was placed as an acting Governor for eleven days. While in prison, Liberatore's first new friend was James Licavoli.

Liberatore admitted he learned a lot while in jail and once a free man, he made many influential friends over the next eight years.

By 1965 and out of prison, Anthony was elected as the Business Manager of Local 860, of the Laborers International Union of North America. Liberatore even teamed up with Frank Brancato and Danny Greene in the formation of the Cleveland Trade Solid Waste Guild.

In 1972, Governor John Gilligan finally succumbed to the presser, or possibly from a financial gift from influential businessmen, and issued Liberatore a full pardon from the 1938 killing of two police officers.

Then in 1975, Mayor Ralph Perk appointed Liberatore to the board of the Cleveland Regional Sewer District. Mayor Perk either did not know or was concerned that Liberatore was under investigation by the Cleveland Police.

In the early summer of 1976, after the premature death of John Scalish, Liberatore made a critical decision to bribe an FBI clerk. Liberatore was asking for information and other secret documents so he could make a play to become the new "Boss" in Cleveland. First on Liberatore agenda was looking to find the names of the secret FBI informants in Cleveland, then information on rival union officers, and even some mobsters in Cleveland. The constant investigative power of the FBI went to work and built a strong case against Liberatore, and by 1982, he was convicted of bribery.

As the FBI brought on the corruption charges against Liberatore. Somehow, and with a substantial bribe, Liberatore convinced a local FBI secretary, Geraldine Rabinowitz, to obtain the confidential information he was looking for. As a nine-year veteran of the FBI, she worked in the bank and robbery division and was seen to be trustworthy. It seems Rabinowitz's husband Jeff, was a close friend of Kenneth Ciarcia, who was a friend to Tony Liberatore and other prominent union officials.

In April of 1977, she took a secret thirty-page report on James Licavoli. She made copies of the file and gave it to Ciarcia at one of their meetings. Two months later, Liberatore wanted more information as she copied and delivered another record for him on an unnamed individual. The next time he spoke with Rabinowitz, Liberatore wanted information on people he believed were FBI confidential informants.

To earn more money, Geraldine went to a secured room once again, where this information was stored. At this time, the names were coded for safety and security. Most, if not all, of the documents filed, are referred to as CI (Confidential Informant) # 1234 and never by their real name. Not knowing this, and so nervous at times she wanted to scream, it made her task to find the actual name of the people, even more challenging. She worked diligently to match up the names in their secret filing system. By the end of the day, she obtained and copied the information of the fourteen people for Liberatore. Liberatore paid her a small sum of $1,000 for her extensive work.

Liberatore reviewed the list and proceeded to made up a fake list of his own to give to Licavoli as an offering of good faith and to show his loyalty to the old man, knowing very well that it was a false list and included some of his own enemies.

It took a few months, but the FBI finally caught up to the theft of information and quickly reacted to the dangerous situation. They doctored up their own complete list of indexed names to avoid another breach of sensitive information. In August, Geraldine went to the well again for another round of secrets in the FBI files. This time Liberatore wanted information on an alarming fifty-two people. It took Rabinowitz several weeks to gather the lengthy list. Unknowingly she passed on the tainted list to Ciarcia to give to Liberatore. Rabinowitz enjoyed the money coming into her family and continued to help supply the information. Then one month later, she collected more critical information. This time, the updated file was on Jack White. Earlier, Liberatore promised her a big payday for all of the work she did. Liberatore was to give her $15,000 for her help. However, he failed to live up to his agreement. Nervous, frustrated, and worried about her financial situation, Liberatore now stated he would loan them the $15,000 to buy a home of their dream.

After the confessions of two mob associates, Louis Aratari and Vic Guiles, the Rabinowitz were now faced with severe federal charges and many years in prison.

At one time, Liberatore and Danny Greene were friends and business partners. However, to win favor with the mob, mainly Licavoli, Liberatore took out his own contract to kill the "Irishman." Soon after Greene's death, Liberatore left town and disappeared and made the famous FBI, "Most wanted list."

During the same year, Liberatore was convicted along with Licavoli and four others on federal racketeering charges in connection with Greene's murder.

By 1990, Liberatore was facing federal labor racketeering charges and money laundering and soon returned to a Michigan prison.

By 1993, at the age of 72 and after his conviction and imprisoned in the Lake County Jail, his attorney Elmer Giuliani stated, "I found him delusional, paranoid and frantic and very confused. Liberatore has been suffering from fatal Alzheimer's disease.

Anthony Liberatore, known by the police and FBI as a tough, ruthless and powerful Mafia Leader, who spent time in jail for the murder of two police officers and a rival gangster, Danny Greene, died at the age of 77 in July 1998 after spending his last 10 years in prison.

76

THE MEN BEHIND THE MURDER OF

DANNY GREENE.

ANTHONY DELSANTER

Anthony "Dope" Delsanter; was a made-man and acting as the Cleveland connection for the productive gambling activities in the Youngstown and Mahoning County areas. "Dope" had a previous conviction of burglary, larceny, and robbery. Rumors around Youngstown was that "Dope" was the man who had killed *Jungle Inn* owner Mike Farah for James Licavoli.

Delsanter was considered being the leading man, acting on behalf of Licavoli to set up Greene's murder with Ferritto, Fratianno, Cisternino, and others.

ALLIE CALABRESE, AN UNKNOWN MAN AND CARMEN MILANO

Alfred "Allie" Calabrese; "Allie" had three earlier convictions for breaking and entering along with an armed bank robbery. Cleveland Police suspected Allie as being one of the men who attacked Nardi with a shotgun in an attempt to kill him. In retaliation for the attempt on Nardi, Nardi or Greene had authorized the use of a bomb on Allie's car. The car was parked in his neighbor Frank Pircio driveway at 1010 Evangeline Rd. Pircio shared a driveway with Allie and got into the Lincoln to move it when the explosion accord.

Calabrese was arrested in his home for taking part in Greene's murder only a few days after the incident. He was then released for lack of evidence against him at the trial. He died of natural causes while in prison in 1999.

JOHN CALANDRA

(Courtesy of the Cleveland Police Museum)

John Calandra was a retired owner of a Collinwood Tool and Die shop and heavily involved with Jack White and his own lucrative loan sharking empire. The FBI firmly believes he was the vital link between the men who kill Greene. Calandra was a good listener and overheard several conversations Jack White had with others mobsters, wondering if John knew how to keep his mouth shut. Calandra then confided to Ray Ferritto that Licavoli was obsessed with finding out who killed his cousin Leo Moceri.

Ronald "The Crab" Carabbia: was born in 1929, and one of the three brothers, who enjoyed a life of crime. Ron helped Delsanter with controlling Youngstown, and when he went away for murder, the Pittsburgh family took advantage of the situation and worked on muscling in on the old Cleveland territory.

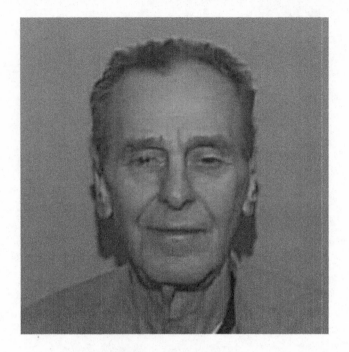

RONALD CARABBIA

(Courtesy of Cleveland State University Archives Division)

Ron was involved in most, if not all, of the planning meetings on how and when to hit Greene. Carabbia was the man who drove the Chevy Nova and parked it next to Greene's. He then got into the getaway car driven by Ray Ferritto. Ron was convicted of his part in Danny Greene's murder.

By 1980, rumors around the city said, brothers Charles and Ron Carabbia both worked with Joey Naples from time to time and were involved with Congressman James Traficant.

The Cleveland boys wanted to control Traficant and offered him a sum of $100,000 to help fund his political campaign for Sheriff in 1980. Cleveland gladly placed the money in the hands of Prato and Naples, then passed it along to Carrabba to deliver it to Traficant. For some unknown reason, the money was never given to anyone, and no one seemed to know what actually happened to it. This disturbing incident created bad blood and the constant tension between Cleveland and the Pittsburgh families. By the middle of 1982, Charles Carabbia's lifeless body was found inside a parked car on the east side of town. The mob believed he kept the money earmarked for Traficant.

As the Youngstown underboss, Carabbia once called the Cleveland Mob, "The gang that couldn't shoot straight." because of their many hasty and bungled attempts to kill Greene.

JAMES TRAFICANT

(Courtesy of Cleveland State Univesity Memory Project)

Pasquale "Butchy" Cisternino; arrest recorded showed he had three convictions of theft and burglary charges. One robbery took place in February of 1964 in West Palm Beach, Florida, with Frank Velotta and Jimmy Colavecchio. Cisternino became close with mob enforcer Eugene Ciasullo as they worked alongside one another in a loan sharking business. Ciasullo was viewed as the collection officers, where few men argued with him when they were late with their payment.

413

PASQUALE "BUTCHY" CISTERNINO

(Courtesy of Cleveland State University Archives Division)

Cleveland Police suspects "Butchy" as being one of the men who attacked Nardi with a shotgun and a rifle in an attempt to kill him.

He was convicted of Danny Greene's murder after only a seventy-nine-day trail.

77

EUGENE CIASULLO

On August 17, 1962, Ciasullo 31 and James Zimmerman, 40, were arrested in Chicago. The police believe that both men flew there to collect money owed to the Cleveland Mob. FBI agents arrested both men when they came off the plane at O'Hare airport. Both men were carrying a handgun and were charged with a Federal crime of taking a firearm across state lines. Ciasullo had minor police record up to this time with an attempted robbery charge in 1959 in South Euclid.

In June 1975, Ciasullo and Denny Donahue were arrested on three counts of aggravated arson in connection with a massive fire at the May-Green Shopping Center located on Mayfield Road in South Euclid. Three stores were severely damaged in the light, and police believe it was a sign for someone to pay up a debt that is owed to the Mob. Bond for Ciasullo was set at $30,000, and Donahue was set at $20,000.

On July 22, 1976, Ciasullo was seriously injured when a bomb, which was hidden in a plastic flower pot, exploded on his front porch in Richmond Heights at one in the morning. A second bomb soon exploded near his garage that destroyed most of his two 1976 vehicles. Ciasullo was taken to Richmond Heights Hospital on Chardon Road, where he had emergency surgery to remove shrapnel from his intestines. Surgeons found a vast number of nuts and bolts in his abdomen from the bomb as he stayed in the hospital for three weeks to recover.

Both homes on either side of his suffered extensive damage and the police believe his home sustained at least $15,000 in damages. By the grace of God, neither his wife or children were injured. Ciasullo told the police that he had just gotten home from working late at the Heights Auto Clinic on Lee Road when the bomb exploded.

Cleveland Police firmly believed that someone in Danny Greene crew was responsible for the bombing. Greene was confident Ciasullo was responsible for at least one of the attempts on his life.

During the ATF investigation into the bombing, they found a detailed map of four locations. Special Agent Yockey related how they firmly believed the attack is in connection with the trash hauling industry since the map indicating two other possible victims.

Soon after being released from the hospital, Ciasullo decided to move to Florida and leave the life of crime that almost cost the lives of his beloved family and himself.

Eugene Ciasullo quietly passed away in 2017.

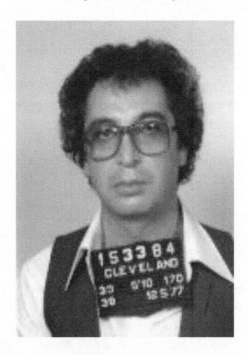

THOMAS SINITO
(Courtesy of Cleveland State University Archives Division)

Thomas J. Sinito was born on September 18, 1938. By 1975, he was a lieutenant under the watchful eye of Angelo Lonardo and worked as a bartender for "Big Ange" at the Highlander Restaurant. Sinito later found himself working in the vending machine business selling and placing washers and dryers into apartment complexes around the city. During Sinito short career, he was charged with racketeering, loan sharking, tax evasion, and an enemy of the Irishman, Danny Greene.

As the Cleveland family waged its war against Danny Greene, newly elected Mayor Dennis J. Kucinich fought hard to sever the Mafia's old ties to local government.

In 1977, Kucinich mandated that some city contracts had been under total mob control since the late 1940s. When Kucinich announced in both daily papers, the *Plain Deal*er and the *Cleveland Press*, that he planned to review all city held contracts

417

and open them to the lowest outside bids. This brave move infuriated the Cleveland family. Kucinich felt every mob-held company having any type of city contract was to be investigated thoroughly, and criminal charges brought against the racketeers. This meant being convicted on federal racketeering charges under the RICO Act, with its stiff penalties.

For these reasons, James Licavoli, on the advice of Lonardo, orders a hit on Kucinich in 1978. In the face of some opposition by lower-level associates, Sinito stubbornly defended Licavoli's harsh decision, and it was then decided to seek and use the services of an outsider professional hitman. Over a few weeks, several bizarre plans were discussed. One was to kill Kucinich as he left his favorite place to eat, Tony's Diner on West 117th and Lorain Avenue. The idea was for the hit-man to perch on an outside steel fire escape across the street with a sniper rifle. A second plan was to kill Kucinich as he marched down Euclid Avenue in the 1979 Columbus Day Parade. But the hit didn't happen because an ulcer inside Kucinich's stomach burst before the event. The assassination plot was considered for three long years but never came to fruition.

The lack of evidence never brought about even an arrest for Sinito. After Greene's death, Sinito became involved with drugs with Carmen Zagaria and his lucrative drug business after first getting the approval of Licavoli, and Lonardo.

78

JOEY GALLO

(Courtesy of Cleveland State University Memory Project)

From his small business in Orange, Joseph Gallo ascended to the top of the Cleveland Mafia family. It was on Dec. 16, 1980, as he began breaking one of the organization's most important rules of the Mob. Sitting in his office, 45-year-old Gallo was talking to someone outside the family about his plans to revitalize the mob. The Feds had a tight ear to every word the two men said.

The FBI tapes included Joey Gallo speaking with Joe Triscaro, (Babes brother.) Triscaro was upset and complained about how Lonardo rejected him to be president of the Teamster Local.

During the trial, Gallo explained how he was discussing only the problems in the trucking unions, and not dealing with any criminal activities. However, investigators said Gallo's comments showed he knew that without an orderly passing of power, the family would lose influence among national Mafia leaders.

The candid tapes were played in Federal court, as Gallo spoke freely with Triscaro, on how "Angelo's a beautiful guy - really the kind of guy we needed in this town a long time ago." Gallo went on to say, "He's probably one of the most respected guys in the whole United States," speaking of Lonardo. "So now we got to fill that big void,"

U.S. District Judge John Manos sentenced Gallo in April 1983 to life in prison without parole, plus more than 100 years, for helping to run the ring that controlled much of Cleveland's drug trade. Besides Gallo, three others were convicted of significant changes in the scheme:

Joseph Griffin, the FBI agent in charge in Cleveland, stated, "Gallo and Sinito decided on the most profitable of all illegal activities, to rebuild the family. This robust information was given to him by another informer Carmen Zagaria, who was a drug dealer at the time and turned state evidence discussing their 15 million dollars a year drug business.

1989

Keith Ritson's dream was to become a fierce fighter in the ring and seemed to look forward to is destiny with death. In his youth, he tried his hands at boxing, where he found enjoyment, excitement, and pleasure in beating others up. Ritson hammed his way to the Golden Gloves heavyweight championship in Cleveland.

Soon Riston's federal drug-dealing trial begins, but he first needed to make peace with a man he respected, yet feared, Carmen Zagaria. Zagaria was what the street guys called the "Warlord." He controlled the west side of Cleveland in an assortment of criminal activities. Zagaria was a man built to be feared, as he boasted of having upwards of seventy men working under him in a selection of robberies, arsonists, loan sharks, gamblers, murders, and of course, drug dealers.

KEITH RITSON

(Courtesy of Cleveland Police Musume)

Once, the FBI raided Zagaria home on the west side of town near Cleveland Hopkins Airport. The house was protected by a tall dog-eared fence and the meanest dog he could find named Al Capone II. Inside his home, the FBI uncovered over $1 Million in uncut diamonds hidden in a rear safe of one of the bedrooms along with six mink coats and an assortment of guns and rifles.

Somehow Ritson was in debt to Zagaria for some big money. Zagaria feared Ritson would turn on him and drop a dime to the Feds. He deliberated about sending another much-feared enforcer to take care of Ritson, German-born, Hermit "Hans" Graewe. Graeme was used enforcing Zagaria will on his enemies. The business dealings of Zagaria led to his teaming up with the low-powered Cleveland Mafia in 1978.

As the story is told and fearing that he was near death, Ritson met Zagaria at his Jungle Pet and Tropical Fish store located on West 94th Street and Lorain. Zagaria, a short-tempered powerful man, made his next move. Ritson planned to pledge his loyalty and to try and save his life. Zagaria feared that Ritson was lying to him and was an FBI informer. It was unknown to Ritson that a man stood close by. Suddenly a man jammed a gun into his throat and shot Ritson twice. Zagaria then grabbed the gun and shot Ritson again, for his own satisfaction. Ritson's death was unveiled a year later to the FBI by yet another informant.

Ritson's body has never been found.

Zagaria, who had turned informant in the 1980s, helped convict local Mafia leaders "Big Ange" Lonardo, Sinito, Gallo, and other mob associates.

79

THE SUPERTHEIF

THE STORY OF PHIL CHRISTOPHER

Phil was born in 1943, in the community of Collinwood, Ohio, on Alhambra Street. His family consisted of his mother, Irene, and father Joseph and a younger brother.

In 1955 at the age of twelve, Phil began having an earache and bloody noses, which turned into rheumatic fever. In his teens, Phil worked around the neighborhood, learning how to steal and make some money for himself and his family. Another way was he often borrow a truck then filled it with tires, groceries as he sold some and gave away most away. At the age of 16, Phil planned his first real score involving a safe in a local drug store with his friends, Eugene Ciasullo and Allie Calabrese. Phil and his friends each received $1,600 for a few hours of work. Phil was now hooked on robbery as a way to earn a pleasant and peaceful living.

It was in 1962 when Phil graduated from Collinwood High School, and later that year, he went to work downtown for Local 17, the Iron Workers Union. (Where he continues to work to this day.) When construction slowed down, Phil became a self-taught burglar, and gained a solid reputation, and doing small jobs around the area. He was working with some of the best guys from Cleveland and Pittsburgh, who all seemed to have a connection with the mob.

Now living in California during the 1960s, Phil did several jobs with a few friends. Men like Frank Velotta, Julies Petro, from the Collinwood area, and Bob Walsh, who was an ex-cop from Cleveland. At times he would join up with Ray Ferritto, from Erie, PA, and Ronnie Carrabba.

Living in Cleveland, from 1968 until 1972, Phil, along with a friend Charlie Broeckel and some other guys were hitting up drug and jewelry stores, along with supermarkets and a few post offices in Ohio, PA, Florida, New York. Also, in 1968, a local Cleveland pimp was murdered. His name was Andrew "Arnie" Prunella. It would not be until 1982, that Phil Christopher, and the brothers Owen and Martin Kilbane were indicted for his murder.

Later in 1983, Phil had his case separated from the brothers, and plea bargain to a lesser charge of manslaughter.

Phil's big pay would finally come in February 1972. He was in Cleveland when he received a call from a fellow burglar who he trusted, Amil. Amil was excited and told Phil that he found two outstanding scores in California. The bank job was the United California Bank, located in Laguna Niguel. The men were planning on hitting up the safe-deposit boxes of the wealthy citizens living in Orange County. By March Charlie Broeckel, Amil Dinsio and his brother James, and Amil's brother-in-law Billy, and Phil left for sunny California. Amil explained to his nephew Harry to get a "Joe Blow" car with a false bottom that could be used for their tools and, of course, the money they earned.

After arriving in California, the boys and Phil went to check out the location of the bank. United California Bank was located just off the Pacific Coast Highway inside a strip mall. During the day, the men cased the bank. First was the traffic and foot routine in the area and if there were any police patrols. The second was if a business or building was in view of the bank, where someone could notice them working. The third was if any other possible issues could cause them to be seen by the police or bystander. The men soon saw the bank was open 7 days a week, a potential problem, and a trailer parked about 150 yards from the bank.

After checking the surrounding area of the bank, they decided on a date. In one day, they would be ready for the most significant score of their lives and in the country up to this time.

At 10 PM, the next evening, the gang left their condo and walked for a short distance, then they began to run toward the shopping center the bank was in. A drug store was next to the bank and a supermarket on the other side. Phil, Amil, and James worked their way around the building then up to the roof. The team proceeded to cut a square hole in the roof so Phil, James, and Amil could drop down safely. Before the men climb to the roof, Phil climbed a telephone pole and checked the phone lines for the one dedicated to the alarm system but was unable to find one. He repeatedly tried, with the same results. Amil did not believe him, soon Amil found the same results. The guys could not think that a bank like this could not have an alarm system? They decided to pack it up for the night and try another night after they found where the damn alarm wires were hidden.

After they returned to the condo, the guys started to relax and discuss the problem facing them. After a while, Phil realized the problem. The bank still used an outdated closed-circuit phone line. It was an old way a security company wired their systems. Phil explained to the guys, all they had to do was to short circuit the line. The decision was made the next evening they would hit the bank.

When they arrived at the shopping center, the guys were surprised to notice a light shining onto the roof of the bank, that was not on the night before. They selected one light to be killed. Phil and Amil worked their way to the light pole, opened up the box at the base, and cut one of the wires; the light was now off. James and Amil then went up the pole to reach the alarm bell. The bell would alert the police and the nearby residents in the area to a break-in. The box was an old Diebold unit with a dead switch, just in case the wrong bolt was taken off first, the alarm would sound. Phil told the guys which one to remove to silence the signal. The box was now open enough for the guys to fill the alarm bell with a can of styrofoam spray that would silence the sound.

At the same time, Charlie was watching the trailer as the guys were once again on the roof and making their way down the hole and inside the bank. They diligently worked on the vault roof for some time. They were now ready and blew a hole into the vault, with dynamite. With this completed, the guys came up to the roof for a quick break and fresh air as the smoke cleared from the drill.

Charlie then came up the ladder on the backside of the building and met them on the roof. After a short period, the guys went back down to the vault. First thing, Phil and Amil worked on the safe-deposit boxes with sledgehammers. James and Charlie worked on the smaller safes. The first ten boxes contained an assortment of expensive jewelry, cash, and a significant amount of bearer bonds, which could be cashed quickly. Then, James and Charlie found about fifty-five thousand bonds in the small safes and joined Phil and Amil.

Keeping watch outside was Billy, who got on his walkie-talkie and announced to the guys that a car just pulled up in front of the bank, the men quickly froze in their tracks. The team of burglars was safe inside the vault. The man in the car got out and went into the bank. They thought the man was the night cleaner. After about forty-five minutes in the bank, the guy left. An hour before daylight, the bank robbers were finished as they held heavy bags full to the top with money, stocks, and bearer bonds. The men made their way one at a time to the roof and down the ladder and meet up with Billy, who had the car ready to be filled. One by one, the bags of loot were thrown into the deep truck. The guys made their way back to the condo on foot, just as the bright dawn light rose in the eastern sky.

Smiling, laughing, relaxing, and breathing freely for the first time all evening, the guys opened up the large bags and separated the bearer bonds. To their amazement, it totaled an astounding 20 million dollar. They had planned on splitting the heist equally. Their escape plan seemed sensible, James earlier had purchased a speedboat in California, and he intended to trailer it back to Ohio with the loot hidden inside.

The next morning after the bank employees found the debris and vandalism, the call was made to the police and FBI. When the FBI entered the vault, they quickly discovered that almost all of the five hundred safe deposit boxes had been opened up. After days of researching and examine the tools, they found left inside the safe. They took this essential piece of evidence and started looking for any similar robberies across the country. Soon an eye-opening pattern developed. Several of the FBI files showed multiple burglaries in Florida, Missouri, in Cleveland. It also showed that suspects were from the Youngstown area. The suspects included James and Amil Dinsio and Phil Christopher. The three were now the prime suspects in the most significant bank heist in recent history.

A few months later, Phil, James, Amil, Billy, and Charlie, along with a Cleveland hood named Joey Gallo, were looking once again for a heist. The decision was made as they robbed a Lordstown Bank near the Chevy Plant located in Youngstown, Ohio. (Sadly, the plant closed down in March of 2019.) The gang was surprised when they cleared five hundred thousand dollars in cash. With both scores, the guys were in heaven with their riches beyond their wildest dreams.

By June 1972, the FBI had its hands full. The alarming Watergate scandal was in full swing as five men were arrested in one of the biggest scandals of our lifetime. Back home in Ohio, the FBI was investigating the Lordstown robbery, which had the same MO as the California Heist. The gang would soon be in jail, as the diligent FBI investigators worked day and night and found the $1.5 Million in bonds. Phil was looking to be behind bars for the next 20 years. Amil received twenty years for both bank jobs. James, Billy, and Harry received a much lighter sentence. Somehow, Charlie Broeckel missed being sentence because of his loose tongue. Phil was now labeled, "The Mission Impossible Bank Burglar."

For the next 30 years, Phil was in and out of state and federal prisons as he did several more robberies and burglaries along the way, to just pay the bills. He spent his time in several prisons as the government sent him to different jails, to keep him moving around. When Phil was lucky enough to be out on parole, he always noticed undercover cops watching, even when he checked in with his PO.

Phil's last stint in prison was at the federal correction facility at Elkton, Ohio.

Phil was released in 2009 as he spent well over 32 years in jail, about half of his life.

One retired Police Chief said, "If there were a burglary Hall of Fame, Phil would have easily been in it."

The United California Bank Heist remains the most prominent bank heist in history with an estimated score reaching an astonishing 30 million dollars.

FRANK MONASTRA AND PHIL CHRISTOPHER IN 2016

(Courtesy of the author's collection)

80

PART VIII

THE CALIFORNIA MAFIA AND THEIR CONNECTION WITH THE CLEVELAND FAMILY

Jack Dragna took control of the LA family in 1931. Dragna realized he needed to act quickly and made peace with the National Syndicate, which included Cleveland's, Frank Milano. With prohibition ending in 1933, Dragna operated a massive loan sharking and illegal gambling operation throughout the state. Along with very close support from John Roselli, who would be linked to the conspiracy theory that the "Mob" helped to kill JFK.

According to the Jewish gangster Mickey Cohen, Dragna was mighty, and very well respected by the average criminal on the West Coast. However, he did not control Los Angeles the way the East Coast bosses preferred to do business. It is well known that the two men fought like cats and dogs to reign as king of LA.

While other Mafia families in the country were prospering in the 1950s, the L.A. family was beginning its drastic and humiliating decline.

Then on May 28, 1951, the *"Two Tony's,"* as they were called, made their biggest mistake of their life. The men planned and robbed significant sports betting operation at the Syndicate-controlled Flamingo Hotel in Las Vegas, Nevada. The two men escaped with only $3,500 in cash. Neglecting to wear a mask during the robbery, Brancato {no relation to Cleveland's Frank Brancato} was identified and placed on the FBI Ten most wanted list on June 27, 1951. Two days later, with his lawyer present, and instead of facing the man he stole from, Tony Brancato surrendered to federal agents in San Francesco. After posting a $10,000 bail, Brancato was immediately re-arrested before leaving the building on an earlier warrant charging him as a fugitive from justice. However, Brancato was now out of money and was unable to post bail.

Under the strict orders from his east coast Mob family, Dragna handled the murder of the Two Tony's. Without hesitation, Dragna gave the order to James Fratianno to handle the problem with the Two Tony's.

On August 6, 1951, Angelo Polizzi, along with James "The Weasel" Fratianno, Charles Battaglia, Nick Licata, and Cleveland's Leo "The Lips" Moceri were mentioned to have participated in the double murder of the Two Tony's. Anthony Brancato and Anthony Trombino were found shot to death in the front seat of their car near Hollywood Boulevard. It is alleged that Nick Licata set up an excellent alibi for the men, and no one was brought to trial for the double murder. The Two Tony's were arrested 46 times on charges ranging from robbery and rape to aggravated assault.

Over the years, Nick Licata secured strong alliances with other Mafia families in the Midwest, Clevelandas he maintained active contacts with his connections in Las Vegas.

Nick Licata held a party at his famous Social Club, and a waitress came forward and testified under oath that Fratianno and his friends were at the club the entire evening of August 6[th,] 1951, Fratianno, Licata, Charles "Charley Bats" Battaglia, Angelo Polizzi, and Leo Moceri were all arrested for the violent murder, but not one man was ever charged with the crime.

It was not until over 25 years later when James Fratianno became an informant and a government witness and disclosed the truth of the Two Tony's murder plot.

For some unknown reason earlier in 1952, Dragna had promoted Jimmy Fratianno to Caporegime (captain) over Nick Licata. To keep the peace in his family and to pacify Licata, who was the more logical candidate, Licata was allowed to work directly under Dragna without having to report to Fratianno for anything. With this freedom to operate, Licata made excellent connections with other Mafia families in Detroit, Cleveland, Dallas, Kansas City, and New Orleans.

THE MURDER SCENE OF THE TWO TONY'S

(Courtesy of the Authors collection)

81

PETER MILANO, AND THE CLEVELAND CONNECTION

PETER MILANO

(Courtesy of Cleveland State Memory Project)

Peter was born in Cleveland, Ohio on December 22, 1925, and died of natural causes on April 21, 2012, at the age of 82. Officially, he became the "Boss" of the Los Angeles crime family after Dominic Brooklier's death in 1984. Peter remained the "boss" until his death. Milano was credited with revitalizing the old and dilapidated crime family by bringing in new younger members as he expanded the Los Angeles crime families' influence into Las Vegas.

Peter's father, Anthony Milano, moved his family to the safety of Beverly Hills, California, by the early 1940s; when Pete was only a teenager. After graduating from high school, Peter Milano, with the help of his father, worked his way to become a member of Mickey Cohen's crime syndicate and was involved in its many illegal gambling operations.

Twice in Milano's early life, he and his young wife Constance had been attached to the do or die death situation, brought to their doorstep from God. It was in 1949, a few days after their elaborate wedding when Peter was only 29, and Constance was 22, as both sat setting upstairs of Anthony Milano's home where they had been living, looking at their selection of wedding gifts. The young couple and his parents had just left their home to enjoy a pleasant and enjoyable dinner at a local restaurant they enjoyed. To the surprise of the whole neighborhood, Anthony's s house caught on fire and burned down. By the grace of God and a dinner reservation, the family found themselves saved from certain death.

The second time a terrible experience came was almost twenty years later, on January 26, 1969. However, both would not be as lucky. After a massive rainstorm struck the area with over six inches of rain, which destroyed many parts of southern California. Now, living in the beautiful mountainside community of the Santa Monica Mountain range. Soon a powerful landfall with excessive mud falls raged an incredible path striking the rear of Peters home at 6:50 in the morning while the couple laid asleep in their bedroom. Peter told the police he tried to get out of the room to find his wife, but the massive amount of rain and mud consistently held him back as he tried desperately to search for his wife, Constance. By the time he found her weak, lifeless body, she was either unconscious or worse dead. By the time an ambulance arrived at the home, Mrs. Peter John Milano was pronounced dead.

After switching allegiance to the Los Angeles Crime Family, Peter Milano became a made-man in 1970; and soon after, this is when he was promoted to Caporegime (Captain) in the family. His father, Anthony, while being one of the leading criminal powers in

Cleveland, and held incredible influence in most of the major cities across the country. In addition, he had financial interests on the West Coast with the L.A family.

During the 1970s, the notorious Chicago Outfit sent Michael Rizzitello to Las Vegas to pressure a casino owner into giving the Outfit $1,000,000. However, the FBI received this critical information in time to intervene in the incident. Soon after this event, Dominic Brooklier had Rizzietllo setup to kill Jimmy Fratianno. This was a compelling and challenging turning point in Fratianno's life of crime. After he successfully lived through the attempt to terminate him, he decided to turn states evidence and testified against his fellow mobster buddy's breaking the solemn oath of "Omerta."

1973

While visiting his father and relatives in Cleveland over the holidays, Peter Milano found himself arrested by the Cleveland Narcotics Police on January 11. It seems he was involved in an elaborate narcotics ring. Peter was arrested inside a sophisticated drug factory in the Westside of town. After receiving a CI tip, the narcotics agents waited for over two-half hours for Milano to arrive at the building when they quickly took him into custody on a secret indictment for the possession of "speed," to sell it. Police confiscated 17 high-powered weapons hidden under a few blankets in his trunk, along with over $10,000 in different packages of "speed" and bundles of marijuana. The police claimed that the single building helped Milano earn at least $2,000 a week.

Some of the men known to have worked closely with the younger Milano brothers were Mike Rizzittelo. The story has been told by many that Rizzitello, became a made-man in the back of a car with three men, who consisted of Consigliere Frank Bompensiero, acting boss Jimmy Fratianno, and young Louis Dragna.

Rizzitello proved himself a good earner, and quickly moved up in the family and promoted to a Capo position by acting boss Fratianno a year later in 1977.

1974

On January 16, over 1 Million dollars in pure heroin had been seized in the beautiful island of Hawaii, after an exhausting six-month investigation. The story goes, an informant's information led to the arrest of three men in California for the extensive drug operation. The Federal Warrants charged them with conspiracy to transport drugs. One man was James Testa from Los Alamitos, Peter Milano from Northridge, and Raymond DeRosa of Tarzana. The Federal authorities stated the arrests culminated from an extensive investigation starting in Southeast Asia, which lead them to Hawaii and then to the mainland.

At this same time, Milano and six others were now being charged from the last Novembers arrest while running a rigged gambling operation in Los Angeles, which allegedly brought in up to $250,000 a month. The trial for the seven men was delayed when the critical informant and witness, a former Mafia associate John Dubeck, was shot and killed in Las Vegas. This unexpected event scared other witnesses from coming forward and testifying against the men.

In March, the Las Vegas Police were investigating the murder of John Dubeck, who was scheduled to give evidence against a successful slot machine operation and was slated to provide critical testimony about increased mob activities inside the Westward Ho Casino. Local police claim it was "definitely a rub out" of the casino manager, John Dubeck 31, and his wife Frances, now 27. Their murder occurred as "the couple was walking down a dark hallway when several feet ahead of them appeared a group of men. Without any hesitation, over fifteen shots rang out, hitting them. Several of the shots hit John in the upper body while Frances watched in horror, she promptly turned to run away when a bullet hit her square in the face. Both died near one another, without any witnesses.

According to the prosecutor, Dubeck was going to testify about how the casinos rig their games to gain additional income from their unexpecting guests. Dubeck estimated the profits to be close to $250,000 a month. The leading man the police were investigating for the double murders was Peter Milano. Milano has been linked with Nick Licata, the current "Boss" of the Los Angles Mafia.

By the end of March, Federal Judge Jesse Curtis has granted a request by the Federal Government to postpone the hearing against Peter Milano and six others until August 6th. The reason for the delay was to allow the government more time to investigate John Dubeck and his wife's murder. They believe this could be relevant and could interfere with their current case.

The seven men were intensely investigated for eighteen months by the Justice Department, the FBI, and the local police. Their focus included 54 men accused of being linked to or part of the active mafia organization in the area. The charges against the men under the newer RICO Act were for conspiracy, extortion, and interstate transportation of stolen currency. Addition charge includes interfering with domestic drug shipments, dealing with the threats of violence, loan sharking, prostitution, and assorted shakedowns of bookies and demanding protection money from businesses.

The government's primary interest is Peter Milano, who is a "top" man in the LA crime family. Others included Sam Sciortino and James Regace (aka Dominic Brooklier the Underboss to Licata.) Both men are a former member of Nick Licata's army of Mafia figures. Then there was Aaron Smehoff, aka Allen Smiley, who has been arrested for murder, robberies and once worked alongside Bugsy Siegel. Now we add in, Sam Farkus, a significant bookmaker in the LA area who worked with Mickey Cohen.

A few days later, the bail had been set for the men arrested. Milano's original bond was set at $50,000. However, it was lower to $25,000. The six other men received a $20,000 bail.

The US. district attorney's office, along with the attorneys for Milano, and his men sat inside the courtroom of Judge Jesse Curtis. A primary witness against Milano, Robert Diamenti, who was once a partner in the law firm of Martin Cataway. Diamenti was being questioned by prosecutor Attorney James Twitty. On the witness stand, Diamenti suddenly became very confused, nervous, and hesitant as he tried to answer the multiple questions asked of him. Twitty asked for a short recess. Back on the stand, Diamenti seemed to be in a fog and suddenly changed his earlier testimony. His first testimony dealt with a specific meeting, which took place in July 1971 with some of the defendants. The prosecution was upset as their case against the gangsters would now fall apart without his strong testimony. Twitty needed to ensure his witness fully understood the questions, and what was being asked of him, the court was soon adjourned for the day.

Inside the federal courtroom on August 17, and without the jury present, Judge Curtis, once again, was faced with another fantastic show in the federal gambling charges against Milano. Another federal prosecution witness named John Deems has apparently lost his exceptional memory in regards to Milano, and the illegal criminal activates in contradiction to his previous sworn statement and testimony back in November. Deems explained to Judge Curtis how he became scared when Federal Attorney Twitty said to him, "The judge will bury you in the courtroom" by charging you with perjury. Deems continued and told the judge that Twitty said, "You will go to jail and will be known as a fink."

Furious over these dangerous statements, Judge Curtis question Deems continued, and told the judge, " that a week ago Twitty gave him a serve warning, and said, "that he believes there is a lot of things going on in this trial. I am not saying what it is, and that he is going to make sure that I'm going to jail if I don't come out and repeat my earlier compelling testimony in court."

Deems is a blackjack dealer in Las Vegas and told the judge that these activities happened over three years ago. I do not remember, and I really do not know who ran the whole operation. "Everyone is trying to put me on the spot" if I can just fill in the spaces for them. If not, they will put me in jail or kill me.

The prosecution worked diligently to prove to the jury that Peter Milano is a "kingpin" in the illegal Las Vegas-style gambling operations in the San Fernando Valley. While the defense worked just as hard to portray Milano as just an everyday Bails Bondsmen from Van Nuys California.

It was now Saturday, August 30, and inside Federal Court, Peter Milano and four of his associates were found guilty after a three-day deliberation. The men were guilty of operating an extensive gambling operation "similar to a Las Vegas-style games" in San Fernando Valley. The men are looking to receive a ten-year prison sentence and a $30,000 fine each.

By the end of the trial, Milano found himself sentenced to four years in prison. Months later, in another matter, Milano and 11 other men were indicted on charges of conspiracy, racketeering, and extortion against bookmakers, loan sharks, and pornographers. Milano served only four years for both of these indictments.

It seems the Federal Grand Jury returned indictments for twelve men known to be aligned with organized crime figures. The Justice Departments were working to "Put the Mafia out of business."

82

1975

It is now April, and the trial on drug trafficking charges from last year found Milano and eleven others has taken another twist. Only five men soon found that they have had the charges against them dropped for lack of evidence. This now leaves just Peter Milano and six others, which include his friends, Sam Sciortino, James Regace, Frank Stellino, James Testa, Ray DeRosa, and Eugene Tyson.

This long-awaited trial began in U.S. District Court in front of Judge Robert Firth. The jury of nine men and three women were informed that they would be sequestered during the duration of the trial, which was expected to last from six to eight weeks. Milano is still waiting to serve his 4-year prison sentence from his trial last year.

In an opening day twist, the Attorney for James Testa told the court and Judge Firth that his client would not be in court today. Defense Attorney Joe Reichmann explained how Testa was not able to walk and was rushed to Long Beach Memorial Hospital. Infuriated Judge Firth has now ordered to have the doctor treating Testa to his court. Dr. DeBenedetti testified that Testa has a history of back problems and is currently having intense back spasms and will be in the hospital for several days to a week.

In a gutsy move, Judge Firth ordered, "James Testa to be brought into his courtroom even if he is in a hospital bed and gets here by ambulance.!" Testa showed up the next day in the bed, as the trial looks to finally start after a long ten-day delay.

A surprise decision was announced on the third day. The alleged mafia figures have now entered surprise guilty pleas to one count of racketeering and conspiracy charges against them. Peter Milano accepted the plea deal from the government on the condition that he will only be sentenced to five years in prison. The other men had separate agreements; Sam Sciortino agreed to 18-months in jail. Ray DeRosa and Ray Tyson agreed to a five-year term, Dominic Brooklier had only a 2-year sentence. Judge Firth and the prosecutor decided to waive the parole period. It seems that if the men went through the full trial and were found guilty of the charges, they would all be looking at 20-years in jail and a $25,000 fine each.

Milano, DeRosa, and Tyson's exclusive agreement included a guilty plea to the narcotics charges in regards to the Hawaii arrest.

The government Prosecutor Robert Crane; characterized Brooklier as the "boss," Milano, as the "field colonel" and DeRosa as a "field captain" and Tyson as just a soldier.

In June, according to the FBI and Alfred Kin, announced that back in February 1973, Peter Milano, Sam Sciortino, and Joe Lamandri, all known members of the California Mafia, were introduced at a gala event in Palm Springs to Teamsters Union President Frank Fitzsimmons. The FBI believes that the men then discussed a tentative agreement, which would allow the Mafia to sponsor a pre-paid health plan for the Teamsters union members, through a California Physician.

1976

Peter Milano; was detained in a fraudulent mail-billing scheme, and convicted. He was sentenced to three additional years in prison. Peter Milano's father, Anthony "The Old Man," Milano had died in Cleveland, Ohio.

1984

This was when Peter Milano became the boss, as he worked diligently to rejuvenate the depleted California family by inducting new members such as Stephen "Steve the Whale" Cino, singer Charles "Bobby Milano" Caci, Luigi "Louie" Gelfuso Jr. and shylock brothers Lawrence and Anthony Fiato into the family.

Another well-liked mobster, who turned informant, was Kenny Gallo. Gallo was credited with "helping" Pete Milano revamp the L.A. family." With a beefed-up family, the L.A. family became the principal loan shark operators on the West Coast. The family's influence stretched all the way to Las Vegas, where they had long-standing ties.

Earlier in the late 1970s, Jimmy Caci; moved to Southern California, with Peter Milano. Until his death, Caci remained active as a loan shark in Palm Springs and in Las Vegas. Caci kept close ties to the Buffalo crime family, where he started. Caci owned his own construction company in Erie, PA, and was the owner of a restaurant and nightclub in New York and California.

At this point in time, Peter made his brother Carmen Milano his underboss. Milano's reign was heavily involved in narcotics, pornography, and gambling, as well as loan sharking.

In late October, Peter Milano, Chris Petti, and Jimmy Caci were arrested with some twenty other Los Angeles mobsters for attempting to take over a $1 million a week illegal bookmaking operation in the Southern California area, buy muscling themselves in.

1987

It was now May, as Peter Milano found himself being on trial once again; this time, he was being charged with trying to market $1 million in stolen bonds. It seems Angelo Lonardo, the ex-underboss in Cleveland and the "Godfather to Peter will be testifying in court. For the third straight time.

"*The Orange County Register*" on May 23, written by Adam Dawson, found fifteen men had been indicted in an LA Mafia Investigation.

The fifteen men, one of which is local Mafia Boss Peter Milano and some of his La Costa Nostra friends, were arrested in Los Angles on a secret indictment for racketeering, extortion, loan sharking and for cocaine trafficking and plotting two murders. According to LA FBI chief Richard Bretzing, this eighteen-count indictment firmly believes this will give the Los Angeles County area a devastating and crippling blow to the mafia. Arrested with Milano, was his brother Carmen Milano, Luigi Gelfuso, Vincent Dominic and Jimmy Caci. Milano and his men were charged with overseeing and distributing the 25 kilograms of Cocaine.

The men are also accused of collecting a "Street Tax or Tribute" from local businesses.

FBI claims these arrests will cripple or at least weaken the LA Crime family, which is one of the 24 known active La Costa Nostra crime families in the United States. LA is believed to only have 30 known members and is considered to be weak.

The FBI stated they were able to place hidden microphones in Milano's business, "The Rome Vending Machine Company," for over six days without Milano's knowledge.

Carmen Milano is suspected to be the "Underboss" to his brother and is a disbarred attorney from Cleveland, Ohio. He moved to LA in 1984. Carmen claims he is a consultant to a lawyer in San Fernando Valley.

The federal government had once remarked that the LA crime family was nicknamed the "Mickey Mouse style Mafia" compared to the other larger and stronger families in New York.

It seems the Federal Government has two confidential informants under their belt. For more than two years; Craig and Larry Fiato were privy to the mob secrets and the planning of murders, drug deals, loan sharking and extortion.

Unknown to Craig and Larry Fiato, the FBI listened to excessive secret wire tapes in their home and phone without their knowledge in 1983. Fiato stated, "I would rather be in jail for 100-years rather than have those tapes heard in court. I'm no angel, and defiantly no saint. I might as well put a gun to my head. If they convict me, I'd be better off dead."

If convicted on all counts, the men will be facing a maximum prison sentence from 40 years each. However, for Peter Milano, he could be facing up to an astonishing 410 years in jail.

It was now close to the end of May, as Peter Milano was facing yet another attack from the Federal Government. This time it dealt with his top man, Michael Rizzitello (a capo in Milano's crime family), along with six other associates. It was on a six-count charge of dealing and selling over 1 million dollars in stolen bonds. Allegedly, a former New York La Cosa Nostra mobster who moved to Los Angeles brought the bonds with him.

Local FBI chief official Richard Bretzing disclosed that with the current arrests of Peter Milano along with his underboss brother, Carmen. The two men and over twenty-two of Milano's top men in his organization could be looking to be prosecuted. The "Top" Mafia families from New York and Chicago would not stand still and allow the area to go cold. Rival gangs in the area will undoubtedly try to take over the criminal activates, but the primary concern at this time is the mafia's reaction to this critical gap and lack of control in the mafia structure and monitoring of a significant area of Los Angles and the state of California.

1988

By March, in yet another power play to lower Milano's jail time, a plea bargain agreement with the government has failed. US Attorney Robert Donner has disqualified the possible deal made by Milano's attorney Donald Marks, which would give Peter Milano only a six-year prison sentence for his role in the excessive crimes. Donner stated the proposed plea agreement was too lenient.

LA Prosecutor James Henderson stated, "that a Cleveland Mob figure "Big Angelo Lonardo" will testify after the state's key witness, Larry Fiato, tells his story of Milano's extensive involvement. Lonardo began to co-operate after he was sentenced to 103 years in prison back in 1983 on 74 counts of racketeering and drug dealing and narcotics distribution, and was linked to six murders. The next day Peter Milano pleaded guilty to the charges against him. Prosecutor James Henderson announced he has overruled the earlier objection and agreed to the terms of the original agreement of six years for Milano, as Carmen will receive only a six-month sentence. Almost every member of the family pleaded guilty to receive lesser penalties, and the FBI considered the Mafia finished in Los Angeles.

83

CARMEN "FLIPPER" MILANO

Carmen was born on July 27, 1929, and died on January 3, 2006. He was disbarred as an attorney who once worked in Cleveland and Los Angles.

Living most of his life in Beverly Hills as a teenager and graduating from high school, he went to Loyola Marymount University in Los Angles and then went to Loyola Law School. By 1955, Carmen was engaged to Geraldine Giesler and had passed the California Bar exam. After moving back to Cleveland during the 1970s, Carmen was on a paid retainer for legal service for Teamsters Local 410 and 436 in Cleveland. Both unions were supposedly ruled by his father. Somehow over a few years in Los Angles, Carmen found himself under the eye of Michael Rizzitello.

Carmen J. Milano was an active defense attorney in Cleveland for many years. Until September 1976, when he and an assortment of other lawyers and doctors numbering 47 in all were indicted for making false claims against the Worker Compensation Department of Ohio. After more investigation by the state obtained reliable documentation and testimony. The people involved in the scheme were now raised to sixty-two as more indictments were expected.

Carmen was charged with four counts of fraud and grand theft. Some doctors, chiropractors, and lawyers in Cleveland were charged with anywhere from one to six counts of fraud and up to 37 counts of grand theft.

After the investigation, an assortment of dummy corporations where found. Milano is accused along with others of carefully creating a short-lived firm, which produced a healthy financial bottom line. State officials have indictments involving more than 1 million dollars in false claims. This, of course, depends upon the insurance companies or workers' compensation department of business who challenge the allegations of claims filed by their employees. Three businesses alone were found to have requested over $158,000.

Three attorneys, Carmen Milano, Charles Cassaro, and Patricia Musarra, have all claimed they are innocent of the charges against them and were freed on bond. By the middle of October, the investigation has now raised the filing of false claims, to eighty-eight. With substantial evidence building up against him, Carmen Milano pleads guilty in court to 5-counts of defrauding the Ohio Department of Workers Compensation. The Assistant County Prosecutor Michael Corrigan is seeking to have Judge Lloyd Brown order Milano to give up his license to practice law when Milano is sentenced. Carmen Milano is facing a five-year prison term and a fine of $2,500 for each count of fraud. Corrigan has now raised the indictments to over 100 people.

At the arrangement in May, 47-year-old Carmen J Milano, a lawyer for over twenty-three years, found himself placed on two years of probation, forced to relinquish his license to practice law and ordered to repay $90,000 that he milked from the Workers Compensation department.

1984

Carmen Milano arrived in Los Angeles from Cleveland, Ohio, and quickly became active in organized crime once again. His legitimate businesses were in real estate properties and a vending machine company with his brother Peter.

1990

Carmen Milano now moved to Las Vegas, where he was controlling the Los Angles family's interest. By 1998, Milano was named as one of the people involved in a series of indictments that stemmed from a lengthy federal investigation of organized crime in Southern Nevada. Under intense cross-examination, Milano admitted to developing a fraudulent diamond scheme in the winter of 1996 with Herbert Blitzstein, a Chicago outfit associate. The crime of fraud was never carried out as the men were to have laundered over $50,000 from the federal food stamp program.

In 2001, Camren was sentenced to 21 months in prison by federal judge Phillip Martin.

By the year 2000, the Cleveland Mafia was declared inactive by the FBI and was even labeled extinct by some local law enforcement.

For the state of Ohio, many of the highly respected and dedicated men who risked their lives day in and day out in the dangerous world of organized crime stayed alive. In most cases, they lived a long and prosperous life, unlike many of the other high-profile mafia cities across America.

THE FOLLOWING LIST OF MEN FROM OHIO,

ALL DIED OF NATURAL CAUSES.

These bright, proud, and resilient men all loved their Italian, Sicilian as well as Jewish heritage and profoundly loved their loyal families. However, they choose a lifestyle that could have meant at any time they would lose their precious lives to a bomb, gun, or knife.

THESE BRAVE MEN WHO FOUGHT THEIR ENEMIES,

THE ODDS AND WON.

- Louis Rothkopf died in 1956

- Frank Milano died in 1958

- Thomas McGinty died in 1970

- John DeMarco died in October 1972

- Mickey McBride died in November 1972

- Frank Brancato died in December 1973

- Louise "Babe" Triscao died in August 1974

- John Scalish died in May 1976

- Anthony Delsanter died in 1977

- Anthony Milano died in August 1978

- Frank Embressica died in August 1979

- Alfred Polizzi died in May 1984

- James Licavoli died in November 1985

- Jackie Presser died in July 1988

- Morris Kleinman died in May 1989

- Moe Dalitz died in August 1989

- John Tronolone died in May 1991
- Milton (Maishe) Rockman died in October 1994
- Tommy Sinito died in December 1997
- Anthony Liberatore died in July 1998
- Raymond Ferritto died in May 2004
- Carmen Milano died in January 2006
- Angelo Lonardo died in April 2006
- Peter Milano died in April 2012

I would like to thank you for reading my book.

I hope you found "Gangland Cleveland Style" enjoyable as it was a thrill to research and to write. These fascinating men who had a lust for life all had one thing in common, that was to be wealthy and control an empire of their own design.

I hope you have had an opportunity to read my first two projects, "Brancato Mafia Street Boss," the story of my grandfather Frank Brancato and "King of Clubs," the story of the many illegal casinos operating in and around the city of Cleveland.

Please take a few minutes and feel free to contact me at Mafiastreetboss@att.net and follow me on Facebook at Brancato Mafia Street Boss

Sincerely, Frank Monastra

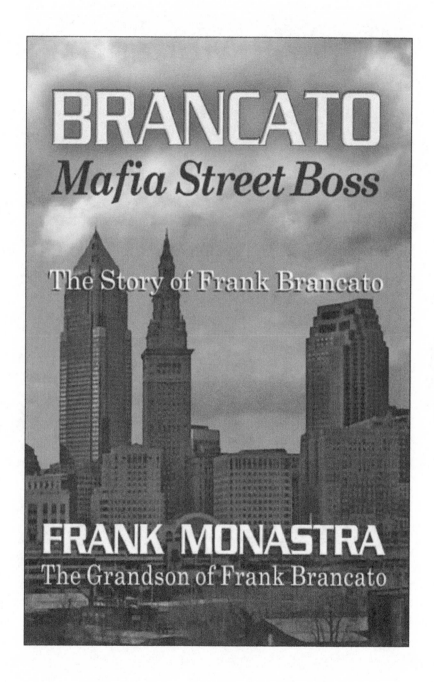

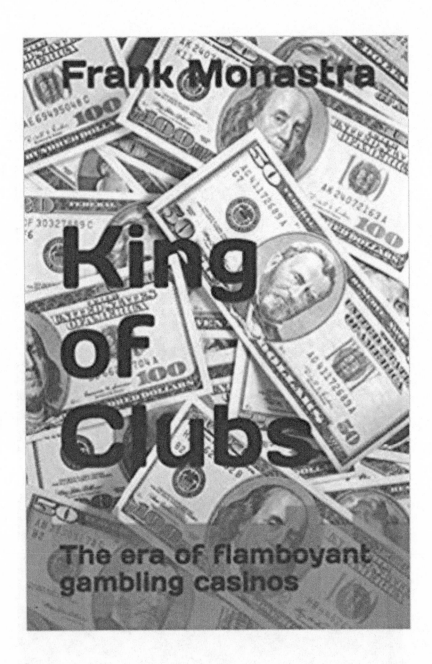

ACKNOWLEDGMENTS

FOR MORE DETAILED INFORMATION ABOUT THE PEOPLE MENTIONED IN THIS BOOK

- Rick Porrello's; *"The Rise and Fall of the Cleveland Mafia"* & *"To Kill the Irishman"* and *"SuperTheif"* The true story of Cleveland master burglar, Phillip Christopher

- Allan May *"Crime Town USA"* and the *"Sly-Fanner murder."*

- Ted Schwarz *"Shocking stories of the Cleveland Mob."*

- From Cleveland, Ohio Philosopher and Poet, Doug Rutti noted in Anthony Milano.

- *"Brancato Mafia Street Boss"* written by Frank Monastra

- *"Ferritto"* An Assassin Scorned, written by Susan Desantis-Ferritto

- *"Mafia Summit"* written by Gil Reavill

- *"The Silent Syndicate"* written by Hank Messick

- *The Mafia Encyclopedia*, written by Carl Sifakis

- *"Double Cross,"* The Sam Giacana story, written by Sam and Chuck Giacana

- The Cleveland Plain Dealer Historical newspaper division, over two hundred articles from the Cleveland Plain Dealer, Cleveland News, and the Cleveland Press

- The Cleveland State University, Michael Schwartz Library

- The Cleveland State University Memory Project

- The Cleveland Police Museum

- American News- Historical and Current website

- Cleveland State University, Special Collections Department

- Several exciting articles from Cleveland Magazine;

  August 1978, *"The Golden Era of the Mob"* written by Frank Kunznik

  August 1978, *"How Danny Greene Murder Exploded the Godfather Myth"* written by Edward P. Whelan

  October 1982, *"The Decline and Fall of the Cleveland Mob"* written by Edward P. Whelan

  December 1985, *A Mafia Family Legacy"* written by Stephen Sawicki

  August 1986, *"The Adventures of Jackie Presser and the FBI"* written by Edward P. Whelan and Kenneth D. Myers

  August 1989, *"Can the Mafia make a comeback"* written by James Neff

- The Encyclopedia of Cleveland History

- *"Mobbed up"* written by Jeff Neff the story of Moe Dalitz

- The Orange County Register and articles written by Adam Dawson

- American Mafia Website by Rick Porrello

- Research information from over 2,500 pages from the FOIA on several Cleveland Mobsters

- The National Archives

Made in the USA
Coppell, TX
12 June 2020